Acclaim for *Smart Trust*

"Trust is the essential ingredient for better teamwork. In this book, Covey and Link provide inspirational stories and practical tips on how to practice Smart Trust, which builds teamwork and high performance in life and in business. *Smart Trust* takes trust to a whole new level of understanding. It is a must-read for anyone looking to strengthen teamwork across functions and across entities, and even within your own family."

—Michael White, chairman, president, and CEO, DirecTV

"*Smart Trust* is an insightful and actionable guidebook for creating high-trust teams and cultures that spark innovation and growth. It teaches how to analyze both people and situations and to make 'smart' decisions by managing risk and optimizing possibilities. Those aspiring to influence people, enhance performance, and increase innovation will want to read this insightful book and master its principles."

—Clayton M. Christensen, professor, Harvard Business School, and author of *The Innovator's Dilemma*

"We have employed Smart Trust in our entire culture. My team is now a different team. It's the most exciting change in the culture I've seen in the twenty-eight years that I've been at PepsiCo, with most of those years at Frito-Lay. There's a buzz in this building. The team works as a team better than we've ever done before. Our recent profit growth was the best in the last ten years in the worst economic climate in ten years—I credit the principles in *Smart Trust* for our breakthrough performance. I feel optimism for our future as next-generation employees come up through the ranks mastering Smart Trust and learning to lead with trust from the start."

—Al Carey, president and CEO, Frito-Lay, North America

"Covey and Link hit the mark—again—with *Smart Trust*! As they illuminate convincingly in this beautifully written book, nothing is more important than building trust in relationships and in organizations. Trust is the glue that binds us together. Everywhere I go I see a remarkable loss of trust in leaders, and once lost, trust is *very* hard to regain. I feel this loss is tearing at the fabric of society, as so many people love to blame others for their misfortunes but fail to look in the mirror at themselves. They would do well to learn Smart Trust."

—Bill George, professor, Harvard Business School, and author of *True North*

"*Smart Trust* is a deep look into a subject that is truly foundational to our collective success. It provides both practical and philosophical wisdom about what it takes to grant and gain trust. Recommended with enthusiasm!"

—Dr. John Lechleiter, chairman, president and CEO, Eli Lilly and Company

"*Smart Trust* is without doubt one of the most powerful and seminal books of our age. It exposes and helps solve the most dangerous crisis apparent in almost all human institutions: how to trust in a low-trust world."

—Warren Bennis, professor, University of Southern California, and author of *Still Surprised: A Memoir of a Life in Leadership*

"Trust is a critical component for any organization looking to improve productivity and accelerate growth, and no one understands this as well as the Coveys. Their approach helps companies move faster, make better decisions, and deliver quality to customers; it can also help transform a corporate culture. That's why we've turned to Stephen M. R. Covey to help us train more than 100,000 AT&T managers, and why I recommend *Smart Trust* to anyone trying to succeed in today's fast-paced, global business environment."

—Randall Stephenson, chairman, president, and CEO, AT&T

"*Smart Trust* persuasively demonstrates that trust is the key to our new global reality. Growth in society can be traced to one individual trusting another. We have lost our way and are afraid to trust. This powerful book shows how to regain trust, prosper, and experience more energy and joy in the process. I highly recommend it."

—Muhammad Yunus, 2006 Nobel Peace Prize winner

"Trust is the most fundamental currency of business, and it has long been one of P&G's five core values. Without public trust in our company and our brands, and without internal trust in one another as colleagues and partners, we have no business. It's that simple. But with trust, we have unlimited opportunities to collaborate, to grow, and to fulfill our purpose as a company. The job of every leader at every level is to cultivate and protect trust, but this is especially challenging in a distrustful world. *Smart Trust* shows the way; it is both a mind-set and a toolbox for twenty-first-century leadership. I recommend it highly."

—Robert A. McDonald, chairman, president, and CEO, Procter & Gamble Company

"From all the people I've interviewed, I've learned that trust is everything. *Smart Trust* powerfully shows us how to increase it, which is more important than ever in this low-trust world. The best leaders I've ever met have the ability to create trust. *Smart Trust* is a great read! This is an important addition to your library."

—Larry King

"At a time when confidence in business, government, and other institutions is at an all-time low, leaders must be committed to building and maintaining trust. *Smart Trust* offers powerful examples of how visionary leaders in all fields have understood and addressed the challenges of sustaining trusting relationships—and realized the unique benefits they confer."

—James Quigley, CEO, Deloitte Touche Tohmatsu

"*Smart Trust* elegantly addresses the most important relationship issue at home and at work: Trust. It teaches you how to harmonize your head and your heart, resulting in sound judgment. This is a life skill that few have mastered and is the key to optimizing relationships for increasing success and fulfillment. Both Mars and Venus can learn tremendously from reading *Smart Trust*."

—John Gray, author of *Men Are from Mars, Women Are from Venus*

"When Lenovo acquired IBM PC, we quickly realized that our biggest challenges would not be in technology, supply chain, or even organizational structure. Our biggest challenge was in building trust among our teams, with our customers and partners, and with key influencers around the world. We partnered with Stephen M. R. Covey to help us build trust and turn this challenge into an advantage. His ideas worked then—and they are even more relevant and important today as we grow globally. Global businesses must view trust as a top strategic priority. A company can have an innovative spirit, great products, a strong strategy, and an efficient business model. But only by creating, embracing, and leveraging trust can a company truly thrive on the global landscape. *Smart Trust* delivers ideas that are thought provoking, tools that work, and a perspective that I think is essential for survival and success on the global stage."

— Yang Yuanqing, CEO, Lenovo

Also by Stephen M. R. Covey

The Speed of Trust: The One Thing That Changes Everything

SMART TRUST

Creating Prosperity, Energy,
and Joy in a Low-Trust World

Stephen M. R. Covey and Greg Link

with Rebecca R. Merrill

Free Press
New York   London   Toronto   Sydney   New Delhi

Free Press
A Division of Simon & Schuster, Inc.
1230 Avenue of the Americas
New York, NY 10020

First Free Press hardcover edition January 2012

FREE PRESS and colophon are trademarks of Simon & Schuster, Inc.

For information about special discounts for bulk purchases,
please contact Simon & Schuster Special Sales at
1-866-506-1949 or business@simonandschuster.com.

The Simon & Schuster Speakers Bureau can bring authors to your live event. For
more information or to book an event, contact the Simon & Schuster Speakers
Bureau at 1-866-248-3049 or visit our website at www.simonspeakers.com.

Designed by Carla Jayne Jones

Manufactured in the United States of America

10 9 8 7 6 5 4 3 2 1

Library of Congress Cataloging-in-Publication Data

Covey, Stephen M. R.
    Smart trust : creating prosperity, energy, and joy in a low-trust world / by Stephen M. R.
Covey and Greg Link ; with Rebecca R. Merrill.—1st Free Press hardcover ed.
        p.   cm.
    Includes bibliographical references and index.
1. Business ethics.   2. Trust.   3. Ethics.   4. Leadership—Moral and ethical
aspects.   5. Organizational behavior.   I. Link, Greg, 1950–   II. Merrill, Rebecca R.
III. Title.
    HF5387.C6767 2011
    174'.4—dc23   2011039458
ISBN 978-1-4516-5145-4
ISBN 978-1-4516-5147-8 (ebook)

To my magnificent parents, Sandra and Stephen R. Covey, for their love, devotion, faith, guidance, and trust in me. I am inspired by you both, and I love you dearly.

To Stephen's father, and my cherished friend and mentor, Dr. Stephen R. Covey, and my extraordinary wife, Annie Link, who have taught me everything I know about trust. Also to my children's children, on whom rests the challenge to live these principles, restore trust, and continue this renaissance for the benefit of future generations.

Acknowledgments

We are deeply grateful for and humbled by the generous support we have received from the many people who helped make this book project possible. We feel blessed and inspired by others' contributions and again feel that Albert Einstein said it best: "Every day I remind myself that my inner and outer life are based on the labors of other men, living and dead, and that I must exert myself in order to give in the same measure as I have received and am still receiving."

We are lifted daily by, and stand on the shoulders of, many wise "thought leaders"—both those who came before us and those who remain with us. We are thankful for them, and we cherish the privilege to be influenced by them.

Our special thanks goes to our dear friend Rebecca Merrill for her tireless efforts to translate our speaking and writing into a much more elegant and readable form. Her creative synergy and writing gifts improved our efforts immeasurably, and we have been privileged to work with such a remarkable person and talented writer.

Thanks also to:

- Gary Judd, our beloved business partner and friend, for his extraordinary contributions to our work. His tireless sacrifices and superb competence in continuing to lead and grow the business while we researched and wrote gave us the confidence and opportunity to take this book project on. His capacity to model and apply the principles of Smart Trust to all our stakeholders at a uniquely profound level consistently enhances and informs our work. We, as well as our customers and associates, are particularly favored by his remarkable ideas, practical application, and mentoring influence. Thanks also to Gary's wife, Julene, and their wonderful family.

- Barry Rellaford, our dear friend and business partner, for his remarkable ability to bring Smart Trust alive for workshop participants in a rare and entertaining way and to help us "walk our talk" by delivering the magic to our clients. He is a master mentor for colleagues and clients alike and selflessly shares his insights and presentation skills. As a former client CLO, he brings a unique perspective and makes an invaluable contribution. Thanks also to his wife, Lorilee, and their marvelous family, who selflessly support his many travels.

- Additional trusted members of the extended CoveyLink and Speed of Trust teams for their ongoing tireless support, sacrifices, and contributions. Special thanks to Tami Harmon and David Kasperson, who have been with us from the beginning and who have significantly impacted our work and lives. Thanks also to Dana Boshard, Donna Burnette, Dwight Hansen, John Harding, LeRoy Maughan, Harry Nelson, Dawn Newman, Candie Perkins, Leslie Rosewaren, Marshall Snedaker, and all of our presenting and sales partners over the years. And thanks to Jessica McKenzie and Han Stice for their research help and to Mary Wentz and her team for their work on transcription.

- Our Global License Partner, FranklinCovey, for its inspiring mission and instrumental partnership in bringing our work to clients around the world—especially to Bob Whitman, Sean Covey, Shawn Moon, Todd Davis, and Steve Young for trusting in our potential from the start and for "doing what they said they were going to do" in a fair and synergistic way (with special thanks to Sean for his vision of what was possible).

- The talented FranklinCovey Client Partner team, led by Josh Farrell, Mark Josie, Preston Luke, Brian Martini, Marianne Phillips, Elise Roma, Kevin Vaughan-Smith, and Paul Walker, and too many others to be named—all of whom create extraordinary value for clients—as well as to the FranklinCovey delivery team, including Kory Kogon, Michael Simpson, DeVerl Austin, Gary Jewkes, and scores of others who understand how to present and apply this work in helping our clients succeed. Thanks also to the internal FranklinCovey team: Steve Heath, Scott Sumsion, and Colleen Dom. And special thanks to our extraordinary FranklinCovey Licensee International partners all over the world. We are grateful to be partnered with you and look forward to being with you in your countries again.

- Stephen's siblings—Cynthia Haller, Maria Cole, Sean Covey, David Covey, Catherine Sagers, Colleen Brown, Jenny Pitt, and Josh Covey—and their supportive spouses—for their ideas, suggestions, and advice on improving the manuscript.

- David Covey and Stephan Mardyks, for their courageous and visionary leadership, domestically and internationally, and for their very early support of our work.

- Our publishers, Carolyn Reidy and Martha Levin, and our editor, Dominick Anfuso, for their assistance and for their continued confidence and belief in us, and to Leah Miller and the entire Simon & Schuster team for their ongoing efforts to position our work.

- Our many clients throughout the world, for providing an ongoing "living laboratory" to apply and validate our approach and for repeatedly proving the value of Smart Trust by implementing it to measurably increase their prosperity, energy and joy in the competitive marketplace.

- Friends and colleagues who reviewed various stages of the manuscript, including Mette Norgaard, Jean Crowther, and many others. Their feedback was instructive yet always affirming. We especially want to thank Roger Merrill, who not only reviewed the manuscript but also was deeply involved in generating insights and providing valuable synergy in helping us create it.

- Numerous thought leaders, some of whom are referenced throughout the book, for their influence on our thinking on the significance of trust.

Most importantly, we thank God for the blessings, inspiration, and support we have felt regarding this work from the beginning, and for inspiring the lifelong preparation that has enabled us to share it with the world. For us, He is the source of all the principles and possibilities that bring joy and meaning in our lives.

Stephen

In addition, I would like to deeply acknowledge my amazing wife, Jeri, for her love, goodness, and strength, and for being the best part of my life. I also acknowledge each of my dear children, Stephen, McKinlee, Christian, Britain, and Arden, as well as my dear daughter-in-law, Emily, and grandson, Stephen. Thank you all for your sacrifice and understanding in enabling me to finish this project!

Greg

And I would especially like to acknowledge my cherished wife, Annie. Her inspiration and proactive influence is the sole reason Dr. C and I finally got together. Her constant collaboration, brilliant mind, magical teaching skills, and sourcing sacrifices in shouldering our family (and literally every other responsibility of our complex life) not only informed this work but made it possible—for over thirty years. Annie, your light shimmers from every page of this book—I love you madly. Thanks also to my other sources of energy and joy—my loving kids (Jenny, Stephanie, Natalie, and Gavin), sons-in-law (Kevin Lavin and Richie Norton), and my beautiful grandkids—both on earth and in heaven.

Contents

Foreword

by Indra Nooyi

When I became CEO of PepsiCo five years ago, we needed to articulate how our company would manage itself over the long term. We encapsulated our thoughts in a simple phrase: "Performance with Purpose." While excellent operating performance had always been the lifeblood of PepsiCo, in order to make our work sustainable it was vital to add a real sense of purpose to our performance. We articulated three planks—human sustainability, environmental sustainability, and talent sustainability—that together laid out the roadmap for PepsiCo's future.

Following closely on that, we determined that, to the consumer, the idea of value is about a lot more than price. It is about a sustainable relationship, the knowledge that a transaction can be trusted, a brand can be trusted, a company can be trusted. A company has to define its mission and serve that mission over the long haul with multiple stakeholders. Doing so responsibly creates trust. But the significant loss of trust in today's volatile environment requires all companies—big and small—to think again about what we do to build and rebuild trust, and to think again about how to create, give, and add value. And most of all, it requires all companies to ensure that we embrace not just the commercial idea of value, but the ethical ideal of values, too. Again, in a word, *trust.*

These are our new realities. Stephen M. R. Covey and Greg Link have written a wonderful book, *Smart Trust,* that confronts these new realities head on—with practical solutions—and they do so in a way that is timely, relevant, and actionable.

This book is *timely.* Having emerged from the global financial crisis, organizations everywhere have now found themselves thrown into a far more corrosive and durable crisis—a crisis of trust. This corrosion is distressing for countries whose prosperity depends on the dynamic and creative spirit fostered in capitalism. And it is especially challenging for companies that rely on a daily exchange of trust with customers, consumers, investors, and other important stakeholders.

Second, this book is *relevant.* I believe all global businesses today find properly balancing the long term and short term to be a constant struggle. I think the right answer is the ideal balance of performance and purpose working well together. The company of the future will *do* better by *being* better. Companies operate under license from society and therefore have to give something back. When we do so, we earn trust. When we have that trust with our stakeholders all kinds of possibilities emerge that simply didn't exist previously.

We also have to take great care with the emotional bond that employees feel for our companies, because unless we have that emotional bond, companies cannot reach their real potential. At the heart of that emotional bond is trust.

Finally, this book is *actionable.* Leaders today need to lead with their hearts as well as their heads—the right side of the brain in concert with the left. That's one of the things *Smart Trust* does so well—it gives us practical actions we can take as leaders and organizations to consistently increase trust, balancing both risk and possibilities, character and competence. For example, one of the five actions of Smart Trust is to "declare your intent . . . and to assume positive intent in others." "Assuming positive intent in others" is perhaps the greatest lesson I've ever learned, and I learned it from my father. That simple step of assuming positive intent is an act of trust, and it significantly changes the dynamics of almost any relationship.

The way organizations have been doing business has many virtues but also too many vices. As a result, trust has been lost. We are at a crossroads. When it seems that our solid foundations have shifted, we must take a moment for reflection and a moment for re-creation. As *Smart Trust* illustrates, there are, today, numerous leaders and organizations that understand and live by this trust ethic. We at PepsiCo are striving to be one such organization. Like all companies with positive intent, the task we face is to make our convictions so clear and compelling that we *choose* to behave ethically.

We can indeed convert this crisis of trust into a great opportunity, what Stephen and Greg call a "renaissance of trust." When we do this well, we can minimize risk while maximizing possibilities. To do that, each one of us needs to start with our own behavior. And that's what *Smart Trust* is all about.

Indra Nooyi
Chairman & CEO, PepsiCo
Purchase, New York

Our Intent

Following one of our presentations on *The Speed of Trust,* a man made his way backstage to ask a question that was obviously troubling him deeply. "Are you really *serious* about this?" he asked incredulously. "Are there really more than just a few people out there who operate with the kind of trust you're talking about?" This man lived and worked in a country that was ripe with corruption, deception, and massive distrust. He was clearly feeling deeply torn. He sincerely wanted to believe what we'd said but was finding it almost impossible in the context of his environment.

To a greater or lesser extent, this same searching question comes to us from people around the world. They're surrounded by evidence that the world can't be trusted, yet we're telling them that trust works—that there are people and organizations that, even in the midst of a historic era of distrust, are experiencing the extraordinary benefits of high trust, both personally and professionally. And so they ask: Who are they? What are they doing? How are they doing it? And . . . is it really possible for me or my organization to do it, too?

These are the questions that have inspired this book. The short answer is "Yes—absolutely!" In the years since the publication of *The Speed of Trust*, we've had the opportunity to explore trust issues with a diverse range of highly successful leaders and organizations all over the world. In the process, we've gained compelling insights and discovered cutting-edge practical applications that are enabling people and organizations everywhere to exercise what we call "Smart Trust" to achieve extraordinary results.

Our intent in this book is to share these insights and applications with you—particularly the 5 actions these people and organizations have in common. In doing so, we will share some of the stories of these "outliers of success" and how the high-trust relationships and cultures they are creating result not only in the greater economic prosperity trust brings but—even more inspiring—in greater levels of energy and joy.

One of the most exciting dimensions of our work over the past many years has been to see firsthand the renaissance of trust that is gaining momentum and transforming lives and leadership around the globe—paradoxically, even in the midst of the "crisis" of trust that fills today's headlines. And it's been a refreshing validation to us to recognize the 5 actions these leaders and organizations share despite their incredible diversity.

We know there is risk in citing specific real-time examples. In the five years following the publication of Tom Peters's *In Search of Excellence*, some of the "excellent companies" he wrote about had already seen some "less-than-excellent" times. This led him to begin a follow-up book with the words "There are no excellent companies." Jim Collins experienced similar challenges with *Good to Great*. Recently Warren Buffett wrote to his managers at Berkshire Hathaway, "Somebody is doing something today at Berkshire that you and I would be unhappy about if we knew of it. That's inevitable: We now employ well over 200,000 people and the chances of that number getting through the day without any bad behavior occurring is nil." Because of these realities, we can confidently predict that some of the illustrations in this book will be turned upside down. But we are equally confident that this in no way negates the value of the insights to be gained and the possibilities realized by observing the results of what they're doing and experiencing *now*. In fact, it makes the very point that trust (or distrust) is a product of our behavior. With that in mind, we share a "snapshot" view of some present and past successes, along with our firm belief that in the coming years a great many more positive examples will become evident on every level of society as the ripple effect of this global renaissance of trust creates a rising tide that lifts all boats.

Our intent is also to give you a lens to see how trust issues impact every situation and how you can cut through traditional either/or thinking to extend what we call "Smart Trust," enabling you to operate with high trust in a low-trust world by minimizing risk and maximizing possibilities. In today's networked world, trust has become the new currency—the critical competency for individuals, teams, organizations, and even countries. It's our hope that this book will help you develop the judgment to recognize and extend Smart Trust deliberately so that you can enjoy greater prosperity, energy, and joy in all dimensions of life—to the ultimate end that together we might increase trust, and the benefits of trust, throughout the world.

PART I

The Paradox and the Promise

As we work with people and companies around the world, we come in constant contact with the pain and struggle many are dealing with as it relates to trust. One of the reasons the pain is so great is because somehow deep inside people innately know that the benefits of high-trust relationships, teams, and organizations are incomparably more productive and satisfying. They can sense that their lives would be a lot better, their jobs a lot more fulfilling, and their personal relationships a lot more joyful if they could only operate in an environment of high trust. And that makes the absence of trust all the more frustrating. Do any of the concerns they share sound familiar?

"With all the corruption, scandals, and ethics problems everywhere I turn, it seems like trusting people is a huge risk—maybe too much of a risk for me."

"Doing 'more with less' seems to bring out the worst in the people I work with. Tensions are higher than ever. How can we build trust in our organization when we are under such pressure to perform?"

"I wish I could trust my kids, but they've proven over and over that they can't be trusted. How can I get them to change?"

"I've seen so many people get burned. I have no idea anymore who I can trust."

"I know our department needs to collaborate with other departments, but how can I collaborate with people I don't trust?"

"We're part of an industry that's heavily regulated and subjected to all kinds of rules—all of which scream distrust. How can we build trust inside our organization in such a low-trust setting?"

"In deciding whether or not to trust someone, how do I know whether to go with my head or my heart?"

"Where's the excitement and fun I used to have in this job? Some days it feels like 'what's the use?'"

"My boss tells me he trusts me, but the way he micromanages and hovers over me shows just the opposite. Why can't he see that?"

"Our company leaders tell us we're supposed to be 'partners' on a global supply-chain team. But how can I trust and work with people I've never met face to face, especially people who come from a totally different culture and even speak a different language than I do?"

"How can I dare risk trusting people when the costs of being wrong are so great?"

"Trust might work in some situations, but it will never work in our country. Bribery, deceit, and politicking are just part of the way the game here is played."

"I'd like to believe trust works, but I've seen too many examples where it hasn't. Are there any leaders besides Warren Buffett who are succeeding with this? Are there any organizations? If so, who are they, and what are they doing?"

"How do I know who I can trust—and why?"

If any of these concerns sounds familiar, welcome to the club! But also know there's a solution, a third alternative to the blind trust that gets us burned and the distrust that cheats us out of prosperity, energy, and joy. Understanding that third alternative—Smart Trust—is what Part I of this book is about.

CHAPTER ONE

The Great Paradox

In 1974, a terrible famine swept through Bangladesh, a nation struggling in the aftermath of a devastating war for independence. Millions of starving people began to migrate from the remote villages of the north to the cities farther south in search of food.

In one such city, Chittagong, lived a thirty-four-year-old economics professor named Muhammad Yunus, who had recently returned from the United States, where he had gone as a Fulbright scholar to obtain his PhD in economics. As Yunus watched the growing influx of starving humanity, he began to feel a huge disconnect between what he was teaching his students at the University of Chittagong and what he was seeing on the streets: the skeletal bodies and vacant eyes of thousands of people literally starving to death. Heartsick and determined to find some way to help, he decided to begin with the poor people in the small neighboring village of Jobra.

As Yunus visited with these people, he discovered that most of the "poorest of the poor" were widowed, divorced, or abandoned women who were desperately trying to feed their children. Because they didn't have money to buy supplies, they were forced to borrow from "traders" and then sell their products back to them for a pittance. A woman with three children, for example, would borrow 5 taka (about 22 cents) to buy bamboo. After working from morning until night to weave the bamboo into a stool, she was forced to repay her loan by selling the stool to the traders for 5 taka and 50 poysha (about 24 cents). That left her a profit of only 2 cents a day, barely enough to keep her and her children alive.

Like many others in the villages of Bangladesh, this woman was stuck in a cycle that ensured that she and her children would remain in poverty for generations. As an economist, Yunus realized that the only way she could break out of the cycle would be to somehow get the five taka to buy her bamboo so that she could sell her stools for the full retail price in a free market. But there was no one who would loan her the capital at a reasonable rate. As he searched throughout the tiny village of Jobra, he found that there was a total of forty-two people—stool makers, mat weavers, rickshaw drivers, and so on—who were all dependent on the traders, and the combined amount they were borrowing was only 856 taka, or less than $27. "All this misery in all these families," he exclaimed, "all for the lack of twenty-seven dollars!"

In the end, Yunus loaned those forty-two people the money because no one else would, with the simple instructions to pay it back, without interest, when they could. He then he went to the local bank to talk with the manager about lending money to others in similar situations. "He fell from the sky!" Yunus said. "He said, 'You are crazy! It's impossible. How could we lend money to poor people? They are not creditworthy. Our rules don't permit it.'" The manager went on to say that 75 percent of the population of Bangladesh couldn't even read or write to fill out a loan application, and they had no collateral. There was no way those people would ever pay back a loan. The whole idea was too risky. So Yunus went up the line to the regional bank manager, and after explaining the situation, writing back and forth for six months, and finally pledging himself as the guarantor, he was able to secure a loan in the amount of $300 from the reluctant bank administration to distribute among the poor.

Thus began a new era in Yunus's life—and in the lives of the poor of Bangladesh and eventually throughout the world. Although Yunus had no intention of going into banking himself, he ended up doing so—despite the dire warnings of many in the industry. He studied how other banks set up their loan operations, and then he set up a bank, the Grameen ["rural" or "village"] Bank, that did the exact opposite. Whereas other banks tried to delay the borrowers' repayments as long as possible in order to increase the amount of the loan (making it hard for people to pay), Yunus instituted a daily payment program of very small amounts. He set up support groups and established incentives to encourage borrowers to help one another succeed. And at a time when the banks of Bagladesh effectively excluded women from ever being able to secure a loan, he set the goal that half of Grameen Bank borrowers would be women

In his book *Banker to the Poor,* he described a typical Grameen borrower in the early days as she walked from the bank with her loan—typically about $25—in hand.

> *All her life she has been told that she is no good, that she brings only misery to her family, and that they cannot afford to pay her dowry. Many times she hears her mother or her father tell her she should have been killed at birth, aborted, or starved. To her family she has been nothing but another mouth to feed, another dowry to pay. But today, for the first time in her life, an institution has trusted her with a great sum of money. She promises that she will never let down the institution or herself. She will struggle to make sure that every penny is paid back.*

Contrary to almost everyone's expectations, an amazing 98 percent of Grameen Bank borrowers do pay back their loans. (In comparison, the payback rate on a traditional small-business loan is 88 percent.) They include people such as Mufia, who was married at thirteen, verbally abused and half starved by her mother-in-law during her husband's long absences at sea, repeatedly beaten by her husband on his return, and finally divorced and left begging in the streets with three children to feed. With a loan from Grameen Bank, Mufia was able to sustain a business making bamboo products. With the profits, she was able to purchase clothes, cookware, and nutritious food for her children and to live with dignity. And people such as Amina, who, following the death of four of her six children and the prolonged illness and death of her husband, found herself destitute. Her in-laws tried to expel her from her home, her brother-in-law sold the tin roof over her head, and her mud home—unprotected with a missing roof—collapsed in the monsoon rains and killed her baby daughter. Through a Grameen loan, she was able to purchase bamboo to make baskets and sustain herself and her one remaining child.

With a growing desire to eliminate poverty on a larger basis, Yunus moved ahead step by step—learning, making mistakes, and adapting to meet the challenges. Slowly he began to change minds and enroll an increasing number of people in his vision—people in banking, government, and other related industries. Through Yunus's leadership, Grameen Bank continued to expand its reach and impact, and to date the organization has made more than $6 billion in loans to more than 8 million borrowers in Bangladesh, 97 percent of whom are women.

Grameen Bank affiliates operate on a similar basis in most countries around the world. Yunus's efforts have been so successful that he is widely considered the founder of the "microcredit" movement, which has turned into a global phenomenon. The United Nations declared 2005 the International Year of Microcredit, and in 2006 Muhammad Yunus and Grameen Bank were jointly awarded the Nobel Peace Prize for helping to lift tens of millions of people out of poverty. In 2009 the United States awarded Yunus the Presidential Medal of Freedom, the nation's highest civilian honor.

A Crisis of Trust

To us, the most intriguing aspect of the story of Muhammad Yunus is that it is, at its very core, a story of trust . . . of Smart Trust. It is the story of one man believing—trusting—that with intelligent measures in place, impoverished people with no collateral, no steady employment, and no verifiable credit history could actually be trusted. They could be trusted to use borrowed money wisely, and they could be trusted to pay back their loans. Yunus said:

> *If Grameen was to work, we knew we had to trust our clients. From day one, we knew that there would be no room for policing in our system. We never used courts to settle our repayments. We did not involve lawyers or any outsiders. Today, commercial banks assume that every borrower is going to run away with their money, so they tie their clients up in legal knots. Lawyers pore over their precious documents, making certain that no borrower will escape the reach of the bank. In contrast, Grameen assumes that every borrower is honest. There are no legal instruments between the lenders and the borrowers. We were convinced that the bank should be built on human trust, not on meaningless paper contracts. . . . We may be accused of being naive, but our experience with bad debt is less than 1 percent. And even when borrowers do default on a loan, we do not assume that they are malevolent. Instead, we assume that personal circumstances have prevented them from repaying the money.*

Even more inspiring is the fact that Yunus was able to accomplish all he did and to maintain a strong belief in trust in the face of the resistance of an entire industry—in fact, an entire culture—historically and pervasively *steeped* in cynicism and distrust. What's more, Yunus held tenaciously to his belief in trust in the midst of what has become a massive trust deficit, indeed a veritable global crisis of trust. And it is this crisis—with its exhaustive media coverage of rampant corruption, corporate fraud, high-profile misbehavior, and political scams—that has consumed our attention as we've read the headlines and watched the news over the past decade.

During or around the time Yunus was being awarded his Nobel Prize and Presidential Medal of Freedom, for example:

- Numerous global businesses—or their executives—including Parmalat, Enron, Tyco, and WorldCom—engaged in significant fraudulent activity, and more than two hundred public companies were ultimately forced to redo their financial statements following the passage of Sarbanes-Oxley legislation in the United States.

- In China, some two hundred airline pilots falsified their flying histories in order to avoid being connected with the parent company of China's worst plane crash in several years.

- Ramalinga Raju, the chairman of Satyam Computer Services, shocked the outsourcing industry by admitting that he had "inflated the amount of cash on the balance sheet of India's fourth largest IT company by nearly $1 billion, incurred a liability of $253 million on funds arranged by him personally, and overstated Satyam's September 2008 quarterly revenues by 76 percent and profits by 97 percent," earning for Satyam the title of "India's Enron."

- In the United States, five educators (a principal, an assistant principal, and three teachers) resigned in a scandal over test tampering after being investigated for unethically helping their fifth-grade students score higher on standardized tests, receiving performance bonuses for themselves in the process.

- Thousands of investors were devastated to discover that the U.S. stockbroker and investment adviser Bernie Madoff had defrauded them of more than $65 billion in the biggest Ponzi scheme in history.

- A British tabloid newspaper abruptly shut down after 168 years in print when the exposure of a massive phone hacking and police bribery scandal resulted in numerous resignations and arrests and mushrooming investigations.

In part as a result of the thousands of headlines and news clips that blazoned these and similar stories into the public awareness, there was, and still is, a literal crisis of trust in most of the world—in our societies, our institutions, our governments, our media, our health care services, our organizations, our relationships, and even our personal lives. In some cases, trust has never been lower than it is today. Consider the following from recent surveys measuring trust by Gallup, Edelman, and Harris Interactive:

- The U.S. finds itself becoming an increasingly lower-trust society as trust in government, business, media, and NGOs has dropped considerably compared to both prior years and to other industrialized nations.
- Trust in media in the U.S. reached the lowest point in 2010 since Gallup started measuring it in the early 1970s.
- Only 46 percent of informed respondents in the U.S. and 44 percent in the U.K. trust business to do what is right
- Only 40 percent of informed respondents in the U.S. and 33 percent in Germany trust government to do what is right.
- Only 33 percent of Americans had a great deal of trust in medical leadership in 2011, down from 73 percent in 1966.
- 53 percent of U.S. employees do not think their boss is honest, and 69 percent of Americans are dissatisfied with the ethical climate in which they find themselves in today's society.

The crisis of trust is not just in our institutions; it extends to our economic system and to much of global society. According to the Chicago Booth/Kellogg School Financial Trust Index of May 2011, only 20 percent of Americans have trust in our financial system—which is a mere one percentage point higher than the all-time low hit in the midst of the global financial crisis in 2009. The inability of government leaders in Washington, D.C., to collaborate on a deficit/debt solution that would inspire confidence resulted in a historic national credit downgrade in 2011, exacerbating the crisis of trust in government as well as in economic systems. Similarly, European Union leaders are facing growing distrust in their capacity to manage their expanding debt crisis.

> *2011 will be the year of distrust in government. From the sovereign debt crisis in Europe, to the government's response to the earthquake in Japan, from the high-speed rail crash in China, to the debt ceiling fight in Washington, people around the world are losing faith in their governments.*
>
> RICHARD EDELMAN
> PRESIDENT AND CEO, EDELMAN

Moreover, distrust has spilled into much of broader society. For example, sociologists measure societal trust within countries in response to the question "Generally speaking, would you say that most people can be trusted or that you need to be very careful in dealing with people?" In response, only 13 percent of Chileans and 24 percent of Turks believe other people can be trusted, which contrasts markedly with certain higher-trust societies, such as Denmark, Sweden, and Norway, where more than 80 percent of people believe that others can be trusted.

The headlines and the statistics leave no doubt that the world is in a crisis of trust. What is less clear is that this crisis is simultaneously having a profound impact on economic well-being and quality of life around the globe.

> *Trust is like the air we breathe—when it's present, nobody really notices; when it's absent, everybody notices.*
>
> WARREN BUFFETT

The Cost of the Crisis

So what is the cost of this crisis? And how can we quantify it? As the two of us have worked with people and organizations around the world over the past twenty years, we have found that trust always changes three profound outcomes in personal and professional lives and in society. Those three outcomes are prosperity, energy, and joy. Let's take a look at each one.

Trust Changes Prosperity

More and more it is becoming abundantly evident that in today's economy, the bottom line is directly connected to trust. Put another way, there is a "business case for trust"—and it's a compelling case. A company's reputation, its ability to partner and collaborate with others, its capacity to innovate, its effectiveness in engaging its people, its ability to attract and retain great people, the speed at which it can execute—all these dimensions of success, plus many more, are powerfully affected by trust.

In fact, trust has become the *new currency* of the global economy. It is the basis on which many people do business—or don't. For instance, the 2009 Edelman Trust Barometer showed that 77 percent of informed respondents said they refused to buy products or services from a company they distrusted, while 72 percent criticized a distrusted company to a friend or colleague. But when trust is high, the benefits are equally tangible, with 55 percent saying they are willing to pay a premium to buy products and services from a trusted company and 76 percent saying they recommend trusted brands to a colleague or friend. In fact, referral business is the ultimate example of trust as a currency, in that it represents a "transference of trust" that goes from a current customer to a new prospect and back to the seller. With today's social media, both criticisms and recommendations go much farther and faster than ever before. According to Brian Singh, the founder of the Canadian social media firm Zinc Research, "One day, a company might be better off asking not what its margins are but what its trust factor is."

Trust is what makes our markets work. It "makes the world go round." At its core, capitalism is based on three things: capital, liquidity, and trust. Though all three are vital, it is primarily the lack of trust that will cause the other two to be most deeply discounted. According to Dov Seidman, the founder of LRN, a global ethics and compliance management company:

> *The world's financial markets nearly collapsed last fall for one reason: lack of trust. Credit, the lifeblood of the global economy, all but stopped flowing. Even big banks refused to lend to each other because they didn't trust they would be repaid. We'd been taking trust for granted. Contracts back up our deals and transactions, but who would sign them without trust in their counterparties? Trust is essential to building enduring connections with em-*

DILBERT © 2009 Scott Adams. Used by permission of UNIVERSAL UCLICK. All rights reserved.

ployees, suppliers, customers, and the communities in which we do business. And it drives the risk-taking that leads to innovation and progress.

In speaking of competitive advantage, Seidman says:

> It's about who has the most trust in their relationships, and where most people want to work. This will be the soft currency of the 21st century.

The relationship between trust and prosperity in a country becomes obvious when we compare Transparency International's Corruption Perceptions Index,* a justifiable proxy for *trustworthiness,* with the gross domestic product per capita of the countries involved. Generally, the less corrupt (more trustworthy) a country is perceived to be, the more prosperous is that nation's economy. Conversely, the more corrupt (less trustworthy) a country is perceived to be, the less prosperous is that country's economy. As you can see in the graph below, the correlation between trustworthiness and prosperity is self-evident.

The reason there is such a direct connection between trust and prosperity is that trust always affects two key inputs to prosperity: speed and

---

*An annually published ranking of almost two hundred countries based on their perceived levels of corruption.

Trustworthiness and Prosperity of Nations
Corruption Perceptions Index with Gross Domestic Product (Per Person)

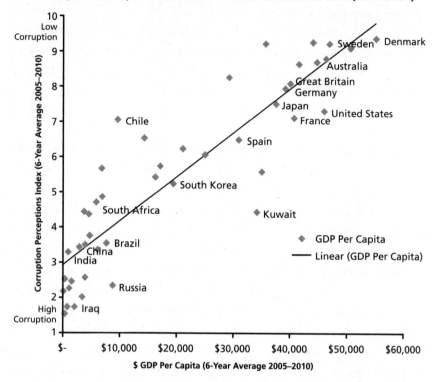

cost. When trust goes down in a relationship, on a team, in an organization, or in a country, speed goes down and cost goes up. Why? Because of the many steps that have to be taken to compensate for the lack of trust. This is a *tax*—a low-trust tax. Everything takes more time, and miscommunication, redundancy, and rework create costly delays.

⇧ Trust = ⇧ Speed ⇩ Cost

> It can be plausibly argued that much of the economic backwardness in the world can be explained by the lack of mutual confidence.
>
> KENNETH ARROW
> NOBEL PRIZE–WINNING ECONOMIST

This formula plays out in high-profile corporate examples such as Satyam, which lost 78 percent of its market capitalization the first day the company scandal was exposed. Or Enron, where the loss of trust was so great that it cost the life of the company—and created an environment of increased and burdensome accounting. Or the global financial services firm Lehman Brothers, which went bankrupt after losing the trust and confidence of its clients, partners, and even competitors, triggering a multitrillion-dollar ripple effect loss that ushered in a global financial crisis from which we've still not fully recovered. You can see it in the lives of individuals such as Bernie Madoff, who defrauded thousands and whose son tragically committed suicide on the two-year anniversary of his father's arrest. Or Tiger Woods, whose behavior stood in contrast to his carefully cultivated image as a company spokesperson, resulting in the loss of both his credibility as a spokesperson for many companies and tens of millions of dollars in endorsements. You can see it in the cost of fraud in industries and in the resulting excess of rules, regulations, policies, and procedures in most organizations today. In fact, you may even be able to see it in your own company or team—or in one you know.

On the other hand, when trust goes up in a relationship, on a team, in a company, or in a country, speed goes up and cost goes down. People are able to communicate faster, collaborate better, innovate more, and do business faster and more efficiently. We call this a high-trust dividend.

$$\Uparrow \text{Trust} = \Uparrow \text{Speed} \Downarrow \text{Cost}$$

These "economics of trust" play out time and again in the market. According to a Watson Wyatt study, high-trust organizations outperform low-trust organizations in total return to shareholders (stock price plus dividends) by 286 percent. A similar study analyzing *Fortune* magazine's 100 Best Companies to Work For, which acknowledges trust as two-thirds of the criteria, showed that those high-trust organizations outperformed the market over the thirteen years of the study (from 1998 to 2010) by 288 percent.

> *Our approach is based on the major findings of 20 years of research—that trust between managers and employees is the primary defining characteristic of the very best workplaces.*
> GREAT PLACE TO WORK INSTITUTE

Other research shows a similar phenomenon playing out among nations. In a landmark 2001 study of forty-one countries, economists Paul Zak and Stephen Knack identified a clear and direct correlation between the level of trust within a given country and the economic growth and investment in that country, concluding that "investment and growth improve with trust."

> *Because trust reduces the cost of transactions . . . high trust societies produce more output than low trust societies.*
> PAUL ZAK AND STEPHEN KNACK
> ECONOMISTS

High trust is a *performance multiplier*—a multiplier that translates directly into greater prosperity: increased revenues, profits, economic outcomes, and results. High trust creates a dividend that enhances and increases the productivity and profitability of interactions, thereby increasing prosperity. Low trust creates a tax—a wasted tax—that penalizes interactions and diminishes prosperity.

People's growing awareness of the relationship between trust and prosperity was starkly evident to the two of us when we had the opportunity to participate in the summer 2008 meeting of the World Economic Forum in Tianjin, China, the Forum's "summer Davos." This respected forum—which is "committed to improving the state of the world"—included 1,400 leaders from business and government as well as selected academics and journalists from more than ninety nations throughout the world. This particular meeting promised to be especially insightful because of the economic crisis at the time. Just two weeks earlier, Lehman

Brothers had collapsed, and the markets were in free fall. That very weekend the U.S. Congress and other governing bodies worldwide were meeting in emergency sessions to discuss options. People everywhere were in deep panic as the full extent of the interdependence of the world economy began to surface.

At the closing session of the forum, participants were divided into table groups of ten to twelve participants, and each group was asked to identify the number one challenge threatening global economic growth for the coming year. From the hundred or so tables, the top seven challenges were taken and presented to the group as a whole for keypad voting. Surprising to many who reviewed the results of this informal survey was the fact that—even in the midst of all that was happening on the economic scene, with markets literally unraveling before people's eyes—the global financial crisis was ranked as only the *second* biggest challenge facing the world's economy. What was ranked first? "Loss of trust" and "loss of confidence." This group of informed decision makers and thought leaders recognized that all other conditions in society—including the global financial crisis—were being exacerbated by a crisis of trust and confidence.

We believe the participants of the World Economic Forum got it right, and in fact, we had seen their very conclusion affirmed that same weekend as we participated in a televised debate about the world financial crisis on CNBC Asia. The participants of that debate agreed that the economic crisis was, at its roots, a crisis of trust. They recognized that governments could put more capital into the system. They could try to improve liquidity in attempts to get money flowing. But without trust, banks were not going to loan money to other banks or to consumers because they didn't think they were going to get their money back, so money didn't flow. It had become clear that not only was prosperity a huge benefit of high trust, it was also a casualty of low trust.

Trust Changes Energy

The second outcome dramatically impacted by trust is *energy*. By energy, we mean not only physical and emotional energy but also engagement, creativity, and health and well-being. To get an idea of the extent of the impact, just think about someone with whom you have a low-trust relationship. Which of the words below would you say best describe what it's like to work or interact with that person?

Stressful	Fun
Complicated	Easy
Exhausting	Exciting
Difficult	Invigorating
Unpleasant	Productive
Frustrating	Energizing
Deadening	Enjoyable
Nonproductive	Straightforward
Unfulfilling	Stimulating
Painful	Beneficial
Risky	Safe
Scary	Freeing
Dangerous	Liberating

Now look at the list again and think of someone with whom you have a high-trust relationship. Which of the words best describe what it's like to work or interact with that person? As you consider the contrast, what impact do you think trust—or the lack of it—may be having on the energy you feel in your personal life or family life, or in your team or organization? How do you think it might be affecting your ability or the ability of your organization to partner and collaborate with others?

When we do this exercise with work teams, participants are struck by the sharp contrast between the extraordinary energy generated in high-trust teams and the exhaustive tension in low-trust teams. This phenomenon creates a tremendous ripple effect—in either direction—that changes the overall spirit of energy and momentum in the organization at large, particularly in two critical dimensions: engagement and innovation.

Engagement. Nowhere does trust change energy in organizations more than in employee engagement.* Although there are numerous drivers of engagement, the two biggest drivers are: (1) the relationship of trust employees have with their supervisor, and (2) the trust they have for the organization at large. A 2008 Dublin City University Business School study shows that trust and engagement create a virtuous, upward, mutually reinforcing cycle—in other words, as trust goes up in an organization, so does engagement; and as engagement goes up, so does trust.

Doug Conant, CEO of Campbell Soup Company, described the connection of trust to energy and performance in these words:

> *We have what we call our Campbell Leadership Model and we drive off of that. It basically says you have to inspire trust, and once you earn people's trust, you have permission to do some amazing things. Trust gives you the permission to give people direction, get everyone aligned, and give them the energy to go get the job done. Trust enables you to execute with excellence and produce extraordinary results. As you execute with excellence and deliver on your commitments, trust becomes easier to inspire, creating a flywheel of performance.*

Innovation. Trust also increases energy in the form of positive synergy (where 1 + 1 = 3 or more) and creativity, which drive innovation. When you get down to it, where does innovation come from? It comes from the collision of differences in the right environment. As the psychologist Carl Jung put it, "The greater the contrast, the greater the potential. Great energy only comes from a correspondingly great tension between opposites."

But without trust, differences won't necessarily create positive synergy; in fact, the more common outcome is negative synergy (where 1 + 1 = 1½ or less). Bottom line, when people trust each other, differences are strengths; when they don't trust each other, differences are divisive.

---

*To view a short video and download a white paper on the impact of trust on employee engagement, go to SmartTrustBook.com.

As the research shows, innovation flourishes in a high-trust environment but withers in a low-trust environment. A U.K. study contrasting the top 20 percent of the Times Top 1000 companies with the bottom 20 percent in terms of innovation and performance found that trust was "the number one differentiator." According to the report, "Trust between people which enabled them to share ideas freely was the single most significant factor in differentiating successful innovators."

> [T]he existence of trust frees the human spirit to be creative, generous, and authentic instead of protective, cynical, and false.
>
> TOM HAYES
> AUTHOR OF *JUMP POINT*

Innovation expert Robert Porter Lynch describes the innovation process and the role of trust as follows:

> *All innovation comes from people who think differently—that is, one perspective meets another, and something new can be born. . . . But two differing perspectives don't automatically create something new, and all too often the differences become destructive: like Republicans vs. Democrats, old vs. new, my way or the highway. So the art becomes: how can you increase the creative aspect of interactions between opposites? And the answer is trust. When this tension exists in a trusting environment, people's creative juices are aligned, and they become jointly innovative, thus trust is an alignment of human energy. This aligned energy is also referred to as synergy—something that is so often elusive in organizations and relationships.*

> No low trust society will ever produce sustained innovation.
>
> THOMAS FRIEDMAN
> PULITZER PRIZE–WINNING JOURNALIST

In addition to engagement and innovation, trust changes energy in the dimension of health and well-being. Though there are many societal measures, one widely accepted indicator is life expectancy. A growing body of data suggests that there is a correlation between longevity and trust. Simply put, people who trust tend to live longer; people who distrust tend to die sooner. For example, a study of 97,000 women over an eight-year period showed that those who were more cynical and extremely distrustful of people had a 16 percent higher risk of death than their counterparts. In his classic book *Bowling Alone*, Robert Putnam notes that trusting people not only live longer but also are healthier. When we look at data showing the well-being of nations compared to the trust levels within those nations, the result suggests a clear relationship between the two.

> [A] nation's well-being, as well as its ability to compete, is conditioned by a single, pervasive cultural characteristic: the level of trust inherent in the society.
>
> FRANCIS FUKUYAMA
> STANFORD FELLOW

Trust Changes Joy

By joy, we simply mean happiness, fun, satisfaction, and what psychologist Dr. Martin Seligman calls "flourishing." For many people around the world, happiness is the most important goal in life.

As we work with teams and organizations worldwide, people don't necessarily use the word "joy" in describing high-trust relationships at work, but you can see it—or the lack of it—in their faces. When people talk about low-trust relationships, you see tension, sorrow, pain, and sometimes even fear. When they talk about high-trust relationships, everything changes—eyes light up, smiles appear, people become animated, and conversation focuses on the positive outcomes that bring happiness.

> More than any other element, fun is the secret of Virgin's
> success.
>
> RICHARD BRANSON
> CEO, VIRGIN COMPANIES

Increasingly, happiness is also a pursuit of nations. This is reflected in the recent shift from an exclusive focus on gross domestic product—which measures only economic output—to a more holistic focus that seeks to include evaluation of happiness and well-being. In effect, this is a nation's version of a balanced scorecard.

Attempts to measure this social dimension include instruments based on "gross national happiness," a term coined by the king of Bhutan in the 1970s, and tools such as the Better Life Index and the United Nations Human Development Index. According to a BBC survey in the United Kingdom, 81 percent of the population think the government should focus on making citizens happier rather than wealthier.

> The happiness of society is the end [goal] of government.
>
> JOHN ADAMS
> SECOND PRESIDENT OF THE UNITED STATES

According to Canadian economist John Helliwell, the number one factor linked to happiness—even more than income and good health—is relationships of trust. In *The Happiness Advantage*, Shawn Achor pointed out that "social relationships are the best guarantee of heightened well-being and lowered stress, both an antidote for depression and a prescription for high performance." He described the Harvard Study of Adult Development, which tracked the lives of 268 men from entering college in the late 1930s to the present day. The results showed that "there was one—and only one—characteristic that distinguished the happiest 10 percent from everybody else: the strength of their social relationships."

At the core of strong and enduring relationships is trust, while the very definition of a bad relationship is "little or no trust." Based on their research, Paul J. Zak and Ahlam Fakhar conclude that "While increasing incomes are only weakly associated with increased happiness, the neuroscientific evidence suggests that there are bidirectional feedbacks between happiness and trust."

> The only relationships in this world that have ever been worthwhile and enduring have been those in which one person could trust another.
>
> SAMUEL SMILES
> SCOTTISH AUTHOR AND REFORMER

Interestingly, the happiest nation on Earth, Denmark, is also the highest-trust nation. Take a look at the relationship between the happiness and trust levels within countries in the graph below:

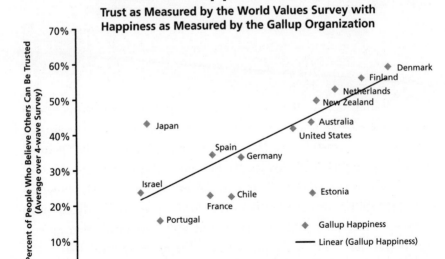

Trust and Happiness of Nations
Trust as Measured by the World Values Survey with Happiness as Measured by the Gallup Organization

Trust also has a profound impact on joy in teams and organizations in terms of employee satisfaction and the ability of companies to attract and retain talent. Remarkably, a 2008 study by John Helliwell and Haifang Huang showed that a 10 percent increase in trust inside an organization has the same effect on employee satisfaction as a 36 percent increase in pay!

Bottom line, in the same way that trust *quantitatively* changes prosperity, it *qualitatively* changes energy and joy. The formulas are simple, predictable, and clear:

$$\Downarrow \text{Trust} = \Downarrow \text{Prosperity} \Downarrow \text{Energy} \Downarrow \text{Joy}$$

$$\Uparrow \text{Trust} = \Uparrow \text{Prosperity} \Uparrow \text{Energy} \Uparrow \text{Joy}$$

> *The advantage to mankind of being able to trust one another, penetrates into every crevice and cranny of human life: the economical is perhaps the smallest part of it, yet even this is incalculable.*
>
> JOHN STUART MILL
> BRITISH PHILOSOPHER AND ECONOMIST

Trust Is a Principle of Power

Clearly, trust is directly linked to the degree of prosperity, energy, and joy we experience in our personal and professional lives. The reason is that trust is a fundamental and timeless principle of quality of life—not only for us in our personal relationships but also for teams, organizations, societies, industries, and even nations. Trust is an enabling and empowering catalyst that is woven through every part of a strong, civilized society. But most of us are not even aware of it, or our dependence on it, until we lose it.

The greatest destruction caused by terrorist attacks—perhaps even more than the immediate damage inflicted—is the destruction of trust. Suddenly we become fearful of doing the everyday things we would normally do without thought or worry. A few years ago, when the Washington, D.C., area became the target of sniper terrorist attacks for a period of several months, entire neighborhoods all but closed down to the bare essentials required to sustain life. Fear and distrust had become so great that people altogether avoided "optional" activities, such as high school football games and cultural events.

> *The more open societies are exposed to indiscriminate terrorism, the more trust is removed, and the more open societies will erect walls and dig moats instead.*
>
> THOMAS FRIEDMAN
> PULITZER PRIZE–WINNING JOURNALIST

To get an idea of how fundamental trust is, just try to imagine a world without trust. Imagine what it would be like to drive your car if you had no trust in the character or competence of other drivers on the road . . . or to get onto a plane where you had no trust in the competence of the pilot or the safety of the maintenance procedures . . . or to admit yourself into a hospital for surgery if you had no trust that the doctor and medical staff were properly certified and trained . . . or to get married if you had no trust that your partner loved and cared about you. One reason why violations of trust are so damaging is because trust is such a vital principle, and, consciously or not, we count on trust to make our world meaningful and our relationships worthwhile.

In the Midst of the Crisis: A Renaissance of Trust

The good news, and the Great Paradox about which we're writing in this book, is the fact that in such a low-trust world, there are "outliers"—people, leaders, companies, industries, and even countries that, like Muhammad Yunus, are helping to create a literal renaissance of trust—and that they are enjoying and spreading the benefits of prosperity, energy, and joy throughout the world. We call this a renaissance because it's not some new fad or technique; it is a game-changing rebirth or rediscovery of a timeless principle that has brought rich dividends to people consistently throughout time, similar to the way in which the Renaissance, beginning in fourteenth-century Europe, elevated all of society and humankind.

Consider the Maghribi traders of the tenth-century Middle East. In the midst of the chaotic social and political climate in Baghdad at the time, a number of traders emigrated to the Maghrib, an area on the African continent between the Atlas Mountains on the south and the Mediterranean Sea on the north. Motivated by the rich business opportunities throughout the Mediterranean region—and not wanting to see those opportunities imperiled by the political chaos—they set up a system of trade that could exist independently of government intervention. That system was based on trust. In *Jump Point,* Tom Hayes observed:

> *The incentives for participation in the trading were great and the inducements to remain in the trading alliance abundantly clear. Remarkably, the system, even across many miles and cultures, operated basically on a handshake [which itself was an expression of trust that showed that the hand held no dagger]. Given the cost and time of going to court over business disputes—not to mention the often corrupt and uneven disposition of justice from the Fatimidi judges—the Maghribi created their own stateless form of justice that worked very well. The key to ensuring performance and compliance: cheats and deadbeats were immediately humiliated and ostracized. In today's parlance, they were voted off the island. The fear of public reprisal and shunning proved to be an extraordinary self-enforcing mechanism.*

By exercising trust and using social sanctions rather than legal recourse, the Maghribi traders were able to participate successfully in Mediterranean trade for several centuries.

Even in the midst of today's crisis of trust, we have modern Maghribi traders, many, in fact, who give evidence to the reality that trust is simply a better—a more prosperous, more energetic, more joyful—way to live and to lead. One example is Azim Premji, chairman of Wipro, one of the largest IT services companies in India. To give you an idea of the trust-building values on which Premji operates, one morning he sent a communication to all the managers at Wipro that he was flying down to Bangladore to meet with them that evening. He said he didn't want to take up much of their time, but he felt the matter was important and he needed to speak with them directly. In the meeting, he explained that a general manager would be leaving the company because he had inflated a travel bill. The manager had made a significant contribution to the organization and the amount of the indiscretion was not large, but it was a question of principle. Premji said he had come down to personally explain the situation because he didn't want any rumors surrounding the man's departure and he also wanted to make it clear that any attempts to belittle this individual would be met with a similar swift and appropriate response.

In another instance, some critical consignments for Wipro were being held for clearance at the Mumbai port at the same time a government budget presentation was being made. Many people believed that the presentation might result in an increase in the duty rates Wipro would have to pay, so the customs officials thought they would take advantage of the situation by offering to clear the consignments quickly in exchange for a small consideration. Due to the irregularity of the transaction, the issue had to go all the way up to the chairman. Premji said, "Go and plead with the customs officials unfailingly every day to speed up clearance of our imported consignments purely in the normal course. Do not part with a single rupee. If your efforts do not succeed, do not lose heart. If at the end we have to pay a much higher duty, never mind. We will pay. But make diligent efforts to clear our consignments only in the normal course."

Premji's trustworthy behavior has created trust. As a result, he has been recognized by *Time* magazine as one of the hundred most influential people in the world and by the *Financial Times* as one of twenty-five people worldwide who are "dramatically reshaping the way people live, work or think [and] have done most to bring about significant and lasting social, political or cultural changes."

Nobody can enjoy the fruits of success if you have to argue with your own conscience. . . . People may listen to what you say but they will believe what you do. Values are a matter of trust. They must be reflected in each one of your actions.

AZIM PREMJI
CHAIRMAN, WIPRO

Another modern Maghribi trader is Tony Hsieh (pronounced "Shay"), the CEO of Zappos, who began his career just out of college in 1996 by creating a company with his roommate called LinkExchange. Two years later, the two sold the company to Microsoft for $265 million. Why did they sell? According to Hsieh, it was because the company culture had gone downhill. "When it was just five or ten of us," he said, "we were all really excited, working around the clock, sleeping under our desks, had no idea what day of the week it was." But by the time the company roster reached a hundred, Hsieh "dreaded getting out of bed in the morning and was hitting that snooze button over and over again."

That's why, when Hsieh became an adviser and investor and eventually the CEO of Zappos, his top priority was creating a company culture that would incorporate not only prosperity but also energy and joy. In the process, he took the company from almost no sales to more than $1 billion in sales annually and put Zappos on *Fortune*'s list of 100 Best Companies to Work For. And the way he did that in the midst of what's been called the worst economic climate in decades was to trust his employees and his customers.

The Zappos culture literally epitomizes trust. In his book, *Delivering Happiness,* Hsieh says, "We don't have scripts [for their customer service call reps] because we trust our employees to use their best judgment when dealing with each and every customer." Unlike at most call centers, call times are not tracked, and reps are encouraged to take whatever time is needed to make a customer happy. Hsieh says, "Empower and trust your customer service reps. Trust that they want to provide great service . . . because they actually do. Escalations to a supervisor should be rare."

Zappos also trusts its customers, giving them the opportunity to order any shoes they want, try them on, and return what they don't want—with free shipping *both ways* and a 365-day return policy. In addition, the company consistently behaves in ways that inspire trust. In May 2010, for example, a pricing error resulted in all items available through 6pm.com, a Zappos sister site, being offered for a six-hour period at a maximum price $49.95. Because some of the items carried on that site normally sold for thousands of dollars, the six-hour sale resulted in an enormous loss to Zappos. Nevertheless, Zappos honored the advertised price.

> *While we're sure this was a great deal for customers, it was inadvertent, and we took a big loss (over $1.6 million—ouch) selling so many items so far under cost. However, it was our mistake. We will be honoring all purchases that took place on 6pm.com during our mess up. We apologize to anyone that was confused and/or frustrated during out* [sic] *little hiccup and thank you all for being such great customers. We hope you continue to Shop. Save. Smile. at 6pm.com.*

What's most impressive about Hsieh and Zappos is the results they've achieved in the midst of an economic downturn. And those are not just financial results, though they are clearly impressive. To Hsieh, the most important results Zappos has created have to do with energy and joy. In fact, delivering happiness to Zappos' people, customers, and partners is really what defines the company. The company's vision and purpose statement is clear and distinct: "Zappos is about delivering happiness to the world."

> An enormous pleasure in life is to be rightly trusted.
> CHARLIE MUNGER
> VICE CHAIRMAN, BERKSHIRE HATHAWAY

Wipro and Zappos are only two of literally thousands of teams and organizations that are creating the ripple effect of this modern renaissance of trust that is gaining momentum around the world.

Denmark-based LEGO trusts customers with tools to "do their own thing" in creating, designing, and assembling their own kits of LEGO bricks. LEGO's view is that the consumer owns the LEGO brand as much as the company does.*

Amazon creates customer trust by providing an online shopping experience second to none, including serving as broker or middleman to a variety of resellers—even undercutting its own pricing sometimes in order to provide every possible choice to consumers. Amazon founder Jeff Bezos says, "If you do build a great experience, customers tell each other about that. Word of mouth is very powerful."

Geisinger Health System increases trust with its patients by providing "surgery with a warranty"—a flat rate for heart bypass surgery that includes all preoperative, postoperative, and follow-up care for ninety days, resulting in significantly improved outcomes on nearly every measure.

Max Hamburgerrestauranger [Hamburger Restaurants] of Sweden publishes its total carbon emissions for all items on the menu, allowing customers to consider the impact on the environment in making their choices. Operating with this kind of transparency, as well as providing the best-tasting sandwiches, has created enormous loyalty, giving Max the highest customer satisfaction ratings in its industry nine years in a row.

In addition to creating trust with customers, thousands of teams and organizations are also working to create high-trust cultures. The India-based Tata Group has created such a culture for its 400,000 employees through its "Leadership with trust" maxim, which plays out in the company's purpose ("To improve the quality of life of the communities it serves"), its Code of Conduct, and its philanthropy.

In 2003 IBM inspired employee trust by engaging all 319,000 employees worldwide in a three-day intranet "values jam" to re-create the values they felt should govern the company. One of the three values they selected was "trust and personal responsibility in all relationships." Today they model that trust by openly embracing telecommuting and flexible

---

*To view a brief video on how LEGO extends trust, go to SmartTrustBook.com.

work arrangements as a better approach for the majority of its workforce, resulting in enhanced productivity and loyalty.

General Mills creates employee trust through its commitment to sustainability, including its relentless CSR initiatives and its commitment to "nourishing lives." As a result of this trust, GM CEO Ken Powell is perhaps the most popular boss in America, with a 100 percent approval rating from his own people in 2010.

The Dalton Company, a building services firm in Canada, creates employee trust with its "alternative approach to building," which starts by enhancing trust with its own people, moves out to its trade partners, and ultimately becomes a force in restoring trust within the construction industry as a whole.

Virginia Mason Medical Center in Seattle inspires employee trust through its "Physician's Compact," an agreement that transforms the often tenuous, adversarial relationship between hospitals and physicians into a high-trust relationship built on clear expectations and mutual accountability. The result is a high-trust culture that ultimately ripples out into the communities Virginia Mason serves.

Governments and societies are also taking part in this renaissance of trust. As part of a campaign to tackle endemic corruption, the attorney general's office of Indonesia led in setting up "honesty cafés" that put the responsibility on people to pay for their meals by putting the money into plastic cash boxes on their own. According to a *New York Times* article, "By shifting the responsibility of paying correctly to the patrons themselves, the cafes are meant to force people to think constantly about whether they are being honest and, presumably, make them feel guilty if they are not." As of this writing, the cafés are considered a success, with more than seven thousand in operation in twenty-three provinces. In Transparency International's inaugural Corruption Perceptions Index in 1995, Indonesia was ranked dead last out of all the nations surveyed. By 2010 that ranking had moved up to 110th out of 178 nations, and the honesty cafés were recognized as having contributed to the popularity of Susilo Yudhoyono, the nation's first popularly elected president, who championed the program as part of his massive anticorruption campaign.

Trust and the Rise of Social Responsibility

As part of this renaissance of trust, individuals and organizations are embracing the idea of corporate social responsibility, or the honoring of the triple bottom line: people, planet, and profit. The idea is that the fruits of high trust (prosperity, energy, and joy) are sustainable only when organizations and industries act in ways that benefit all *stakeholders,* not merely *shareholders.*

A standout advocate of this shift is PepsiCo CEO Indra Nooyi, under whose leadership PepsiCo seeks "to deliver sustainable growth by investing in a healthier future for people and our planet" in conjunction with its manifesto, "Performance with Purpose." Many other companies and even industries have also begun to shift from an exclusive profit focus to a more ecofriendly, people-friendly focus, with positive results in terms of prosperity, energy, and joy for all stakeholders. Those shifts represent a sea change and are critical to success as more and more people around the globe begin to realize that individuals and companies can't just operate their businesses and abuse the world with impunity. Increasingly, trust and the benefits of trust are being shifted to the people and organizations that consistently demonstrate social responsibility.

> A company is granted a license to operate from society and therefore owes society a duty of care. Pursuit of short-term performance is not enough. That performance needs to be allied to a purpose; otherwise, the performance disappears too . . . companies can do well, long term, only if the societies in which they operate also do well.
>
> INDRA NOOYI

The "stakeholder versus shareholder" focus has led to a number of other social responses. For example, in addition to his Nobel prize–winning work with microcredit, Muhammad Yunus created the world's first consciously designed multinational "social business"—a business designed to address social issues with no dividends being given to the investors and all profits being put back into the company to improve products and services and increase availability. The plan grew out of a luncheon meeting in October 2005 with Franck Riboud, the chairman and CEO of Groupe Danone in France (the maker of Dannon Yogurt in the United States as well as other products worldwide). Riboud had heard about Yunus's work and invited him to lunch to find out more about it and to get his ideas on how he might use his food company to help feed the poor. When Yunus proposed a joint venture between Grameen and Danone to provide healthy foods to improve the diet of the children in Bangladesh, Riboud stood, reached out to shake Yunus's hand, and said, "Let's do it." Thinking that he might have been misunderstood because Riboud's response was so quick, Yunus carefully reiterated what he had just said.

"I got it!" Riboud replied. "I shook hands with you because you told me that, in Grameen Bank, you rely on mutual trust between the bank and the borrowers, making loans on the basis of a handshake rather than legal papers. So I am following your system. We shook hands, and as far as I am concerned, the deal is final." Still thinking that Riboud might not understand what he was getting into, Yunus went on to explain that it would be a "social business"—a business that would sell products at prices that would make it self-sustaining but would pay no dividends to its investors, as the profits would be put back into the venture to "do more good for the world." Riboud quickly agreed and once again shook hands and said, "Let's do it!"

Grameen Danone built its first factory in Bogra, Bangladesh, in 2006 and has now established a distribution network of more than 1,600 shops. The company reached financial sustainability in 2010 and is achieving its social goals by creating hundreds of jobs and providing affordable, nutritious food to the undernourished children of Banagladesh. Grameen has since formed similar business joint ventures with BASF, Intel, Adidas, and others.

Bill Gates, a cofounder of Microsoft and of the Bill & Melinda Gates Foundation, the largest private foundation in the world, approaches the stakeholder issue from the perspective of "creative capitalism." In his address to the 2007 Harvard graduating class, Gates said:

We can make market forces work better for the poor if we can develop a
more creative capitalism—if we can stretch the reach of market forces so that

more people can make a profit, or at least make a living, serving people who are suffering from the worst inequities. We also can press governments around the world to spend taxpayer money in ways that better reflect the values of the people who pay the taxes.

If we can find approaches that meet the needs of the poor in ways that generate profits for business and votes for politicians, we will have found a sustainable way to reduce inequity in the world. This task is open-ended. It can never be finished. But a conscious effort to answer this challenge will change the world.

A number of thought leaders have written about this movement, including Columbia University's Jeffrey Sachs in his book *The End of Poverty* and the University of Michigan's C. K. Prahalad in *The Fortune at the Bottom of the Pyramid.* Prahalad frames the movement as not only a social movement but also one in which there is significant economic opportunity for those who venture to meet social needs. The subtitle of Prahalad's book, *Eradicating Poverty Through Profits,* reflects the convergence of social and economic benefits that make this a truly third-alternative, high-trust approach.

The point is that more and more, individuals and businesses are recognizing the importance of their responsibility to society and to planet Earth and are behaving in ways that reflect that understanding and inspire trust. And enterprises that do so are creating prosperity, energy, and joy for all stakeholders. This shift reminds the two of us of the "universal mission statement" we helped create during the 1980s at Covey Leadership Center, a statement of only twelve words: "To increase the economic well-being and quality of life of all stakeholders." That was our early attempt to shift from a shareholder-only focus to a broader focus on all stakeholders and to shift to well-being and quality of life (energy and joy) in addition to financial profit (prosperity).

> If you don't have the trust of the societies you serve, you don't have a long-term sustainable business model.
>
> ANDREW WITTY
> CEO, GLAXOSMITHKLINE

One Person Can Make a Difference

As you can tell by even the few illustrations we've shared in this chapter, the Great Paradox we're talking about is very real. Even in the midst of an enormous crisis of trust, we are truly witnessing a renaissance of trust. In the age of Bernie Madoff, we have Muhammad Yunus. In the age of Ken Lay and Jeff Skilling of Enron, we have Warren Buffett and Charlie Munger of Berkshire Hathaway. In the age of Ramalinga Raju of Satyam (India's Enron), we have Azim Premji of Wipro.

As we work with individuals, teams, and organizations around the world, we see time and again that those who choose to live and to lead based on trust are the ones who are enjoying the fullness of the benefits of prosperity, energy, and joy—as are the societies that have made that choice. Bottom line, one person can make a difference. One team can make a difference. One organization can make a difference. One country can make a difference. And in today's world, the high-trust actions of one can create a ripple effect that spreads the benefits of prosperity, energy, and joy to stakeholders around the globe.

QUESTIONS TO CONSIDER

- What evidence do you see of the renaissance of trust in the world?
- What is your current level of prosperity? Of energy? Of joy?
- In what ways might high-trust relationships enhance these dimensions in your personal life? On your team? In your organization? In your country?

CHAPTER TWO

Blind Trust or Distrust: Which Glasses Are You Wearing?

Do not expect the world to look bright, if you habitually wear gray-brown glasses.
CHARLES WILLIAM ELIOT
Longest-serving president of Harvard University

We see the world, not as it is, but as we are—or as we are conditioned to see it.
DR. STEPHEN R. COVEY

A t different times in our lives and in different situations, most of us tend to look at our personal relationships, our teams, our organizations, and our governments through one of two sets of glasses: "blind trust" (naiveté) or "distrust" (suspicion). At times, we may even go back and forth between the two. These glasses have been created by a number of factors, including the way our parents and grandparents may have seen the world (or our response to them and their perception), the experiences we've had in our personal and professional lives, the people we interact with, the things we read, the things we watch, and the things we listen to.

However, most of us don't even realize that we have these glasses on. We think we're seeing the world as it is, rather than as the lenses we wear make it appear. And we never take our glasses off and really look at them to see what kind of effect they're having in our lives—or what might be different if we were to put on different glasses.

In our workshops, we often share an experience Stephen had while vacationing in Montana.

Stephen:

One time, I hired a guide to take me fly-fishing. While we were fishing, he asked me, "What do you see?"

"I see a beautiful river."

"Do you see any fish?"

"No."

Then he told me to put on a pair of polarized sunglasses.

Suddenly everything looked dramatically different. I could see through the water, and I could see fish—a lot of fish. Suddenly I saw enormous possibilities that I had not seen before. The fish were there all along, but until I put on the glasses, they were hidden.*

*To view a brief video of Stephen illustrating this story, go to SmartTrust Book.com.

In chapter three, we'll look at a different set of glasses, which, in a way similar to polarized sunglasses, enable us to see tremendous possibilities that have been hidden from our view but have been there all along. In this chapter, however, we'd like to ask you to stop and take a good look at whatever glasses you might be wearing now, and ask yourself:

- What kind of glasses am I wearing?
- Where did I get them?
- Are they creating the results I want in my life?
- Are they enabling me to see the abundant possibilities that exist for creating prosperity, energy, and joy?

Only as we understand how we're seeing the world now—and the impact it's having on the quality of our lives—can we truly appreciate the difference a new pair of glasses can make.

The Glasses of Blind Trust

In the extreme, blind trust is a naive, gullible, blissful, Pollyanna-ish trust in almost everyone and everything. Wearing blind-trust glasses is easy for many of us at times because it doesn't really require much effort or thought. It's also easy because, as the University of Maryland's Eric Uslaner points out, "We may not be born trusting, but our inclinations to place faith in others start very early in life." Indeed, most children have a high propensity to trust.

> *No question children are more trusting, and therefore much more creative. Somewhere in adolescence, I suspect, that changes.*
>
> CHARLES GREEN
> FOUNDER, TRUSTED ADVISOR ASSOCIATES

Even as adults—even if we have had bad experiences with blind trust—deep inside, most of us really *want* to trust. We want to believe that somehow our political leaders will really do what they promised us they'd do . . . that our work peers really do have our best interests at heart . . . that some new investment opportunity really will produce a high return with little risk . . . that a spouse or partner really does have a reasonable explanation for what appears to be totally untrustworthy behavior . . . that the e-mail offering a sizable fortune in exchange for providing our checking account number to help someone get funds out of a foreign country really will end up with a life-changing deposit into our account.

Because we want those things so badly, we ignore the evidence. As the expression goes, "That which we want most urgently, we believe most easily." And the cost can be great. When we view the world through blind-trust glasses, we become ripe targets for scams, frauds, and "con" artists. Contrary to the assumption of some people that the "con" in "con artist" is short for "convict" (meaning criminal), it is actually short for "confidence"; in other words, a "con artist" or a "con man" is someone who works to earn your confidence and trust and then, having gained it, takes you for everything you're worth.

> If it seems too good to be true, it IS too good to be true.
>
> MARK TWAIN

Blind trust was one of the reasons Bernie Madoff was able to defraud investors out of billions of dollars, deprive thousands of people of their life savings, and wreck charities. After pleading guilty to fraud, Madoff said that the problem with officials at the Securities and Exchange Commission was that he'd had "too much credibility with them" and the SEC examiners had never asked for basic records to validate his operations. "It never entered the SEC's mind that it was a Ponzi scheme," he said. Additionally, Madoff's accountant did not meaningfully audit Madoff's business or confirm that securities even existed.

Many observers believe that the global financial crisis was precipitated by too much trust being given to the mortgage industry in the United States without sufficient oversight—in effect becoming blind trust that was ultimately abused, resulting in the housing bubble that triggered the problems initiating the crisis. Others point to what might appear to be the near-blind trust given to traders at some financial firms—traders such as Nick Leeson, who was trusted by Barings, the United Kingdom's oldest investment bank, to operate as both floor manager for trading *and* the head of settlement operations (positions normally held by two different employees for purposes of checks and balances). Leeson engaged in unauthorized speculative trading that literally brought Barings down.

Pyramid schemes, financial scams, fraud—all add up to an enormous cost, estimated to be as high $2.9 *trillion* a year globally, with 88 percent of enterprises having been hit by at least one type of fraud in the past year. Fraudulent activity becomes more apparent in difficult economic times, when perpetrators find it more difficult to hide behind their perpetual cycle of attracting and deceiving new victims. In the words of Warren Buffett, "It's only when the tide goes out that you learn who's been swimming naked." It is also during hard times when people desperately want to believe what they're hearing that they find themselves more likely to extend trust blindly.

There are times when blind trust might appear to work. In August 2010 *New York Post* articles told of an ad executive who was approached by a homeless man outside a SoHo restaurant, asking her for some change to get some Vitamin Water. She told him she didn't have any change, all she had was a credit card. So the man asked if he could borrow her card and get a couple of other things as well. She asked, "Can I trust you?" "I'm honest, yes," he replied. So she handed him her American Express card. People who saw the interaction thought what she did was insane and told her they doubted he would ever come back. But a little more than ten minutes later, he surprised them by returning with the card in hand. He had bought deodorant, body wash, a pack of cigarettes, and Vitamin Water, totaling about $25. Giving her the card, he said, "Thank you for trusting me."

That particular extension of blind trust turned out to be a good experience for both the giver and the receiver, and perhaps there are some lessons here that can be learned. However, the blind-trust approach is risky, and it typically does *not* represent the smartest way to operate in a low-trust world.

The Glasses of Distrust

Far more often than blind trust, we tend to put on glasses of distrust. We view the world through the lens of *suspicion*—and with what we feel is good reason. We're bombarded daily with headlines that repeat evidence of today's trust crisis from every possible angle. In addition, our own experience validates it.

Stephen:

I remember a time years ago when I was traveling with my parents. We visited a less developed country that was known to be corrupt. We hired a driver we thought we could trust to take us several places, and we left a number of watches and other gifts we had purchased in our bags locked in the trunk of his car while we did some sightseeing. When we returned, we checked inside our bags to make sure the boxes were all there. They were. But when we got back to the U.S. and opened the boxes, we discovered they were all empty!

Greg:

Several years ago my wife, Annie, and I invested a significant amount of money in salvage wood from old buildings. We never drilled down on the particulars of the investment because the man handling it was our neighbor, who assured us of the wisdom of the venture and repeatedly told us to trust him. Imagine our shock one evening when we saw the arrest of this neighbor on the local television news. We came to find out that he had sold the same inventory to several other investors as well as to us!

Experiences such as these affect us on a personal level. Even more, deeply wounding experiences—such as discovering someone has lied to you, finding out your spouse has cheated on you, going through a difficult divorce (either as a spouse or a child), having a "friend" talk about you behind your back, discovering drugs in your child's room, having your wallet stolen, finding out that your child has been mistreated at day care, or having a business partner continually break promises to you—can easily shift an innate propensity to trust into an acquired propensity to distrust.

Just as with blind trust, it's sometimes easy to put on the glasses of distrust. In fact, if we start out wearing blind-trust glasses but then get seriously burned, we often swing the pendulum to the other extreme and trade them in for thick glasses of distrust and suspicion. It seems like a natural response in a low-trust world. It's an approach that's easy to hide behind. It feels safer and less risky and that we're more in control. It can make us appear more careful, more intelligent. It seems more expedient in an urgency-addicted world where the focus is on short-term gains rather than long-term sustainability. Moving quickly to distrust and suspicion is the common response of society to almost any violation of trust because it is the easiest lever to pull and seems to provide the best legal and defensive cover. Two examples are the dramatically increased airport security after 9/11 and the Sarbanes-Oxley legislation following the Enron and WorldCom scandals in the early 2000s. Both have clearly served their purpose, but both have also come at a very high price.

Wearing distrust glasses is easy also because many of us are "scripted" to distrust. Even something as well-meaning as Stranger Danger—an important program designed to help young schoolchildren protect themselves against predators—can condition us at a very early age to become suspicious, wary adults, especially if we don't ever stop to reexamine our old scripts from a mature perspective.

A Few Examples of Stranger Danger Rules

- Never talk to strangers.
- Never accept candy or gifts from a stranger.

- Never go anywhere with a stranger.
- Never get near or into a stranger's car.
- Never let a caller at the door or on the telephone know that you are alone.
- Always try to walk with a friend or a grown-up.
- If a stranger grabs you, yell for help as loud as you can.

Though we've become very good at recognizing the cost of trusting too much, we're not nearly as good at recognizing the cost of not trusting enough. In fact, we seldom, if ever, even consider it, and most of us wouldn't know how to measure the cost if we did. Though we think we're being smart in taking precautions to protect ourselves against all the things that can happen in this low-trust world, the cost of this approach can be incredibly high, particularly in terms of prosperity, energy, and joy. Whenever there is distrust in a relationship, on a team, in an organization, or in a community, a wasted tax—sometimes a huge wasted tax—is being paid. You can see at least some of the seven common low-trust taxes in many organizations: redundancy, bureaucracy, politics, disengagement, turnover, churn, and fraud.

> The cost of trust may on occasion be devastating, but the high cost of distrust is virtually guaranteed.
>
> FERNANDO FLORES
> FORMER FINANCE MINISTER OF CHILE

Low-trust taxes result not only from the way we see but also from the way we *are seen*—in other words, not only in our not trusting but also in our being perceived as untrustworthy. Consider the economic cost to countries perceived as untrustworthy. Look back at the graph on page 15 that shows a direct correlation between the prosperity of various countries and their trustworthiness. As the Zak and Knack study cited earlier clearly showed, "investment and growth improve with trust."

Moreover, some companies from nations that are not perceived as trustworthy by citizens of other nations inherit a "country tax" as they attempt to do business on a global basis. A company or brand based in Russia, for example, is likely to inherit such a tax, resulting in increased cost and decreased speed in doing business. Conversely, companies based in nations perceived as trustworthy—such as Sweden—receive a "country dividend" that decreases cost and increases speed.

More specifically, think about the impact to the country of Haiti on the world stage when, in the aftermath of the disastrous earthquake in 2010, a former Haitian leader was interviewed and asked whether there were any institutions in Haiti that could be trusted with donations to help with the relief effort. He replied, in effect, that unfortunately there were no Haitian institutions that could be trusted and encouraged donations to go through outside international organizations rather than Haitian entities.

Much like countries that pay a metaphorical "country tax," industries that are not perceived as being trustworthy pay an "industry tax." For example, since the global financial crisis of 2008, the financial services industry has seen a precipitous drop in its perceived trustworthiness as measured by people's lack of trust in the industry to "do the right thing." As a result, to some degree almost all firms in that industry are struggling with increased cost and decreased speed of doing business. Though it is possible to break out of and transcend country and industry taxes, the effort is clearly an upstream swim.

Apart from inherited country or industry taxes, many companies incur huge taxes based on their own distrustful behavior. One example was shared by one of our workshop participants, who told us about a business that sold sunglasses. When the company changed hands, the new owner discovered that the biggest problem was a shrinkage of inventory, which was costing him about 2 percent of revenues and directly hitting the bottom line. Clearly, the shrinkage was coming from theft, so the new owner thought, "If we could just eliminate that shrinkage, we could dramatically increase our profit." He viewed the situation through the lens of distrust. "Somebody is cheating us. It's either the customers or our employees— maybe both. So we can't trust either of them." He put in place a control mechanism to address the problem. On the racks where the frames were displayed, he placed a tie-down on every frame so that the glasses could not be pulled off. That way, no one could walk out of the store with a frame that had not been paid for. The problem was that now customers could not even take the frames off the rack to try them on. So although the shrinkage was reduced from 2 percent to 0.2 percent, sales decreased by 50 percent! Without being able to try on the sunglasses and see how they looked in the mirror, people didn't buy them.

An insurance company we* were invited to work with in Europe had been burned in the past by a few customers who had filed fraudulent claims. In response, the company put into place a rigorous, even onerous, process of verification and validation so that whenever anyone filed a claim, the starting point with the customer was "We assume you are a crook and you are trying to cheat us unless you can prove otherwise." Since adopting this approach, it had not been defrauded, but its customers had been leaving en masse. They didn't like being treated with suspicion and distrust and were going to companies they felt trusted them.

The cost of distrust to companies not only affects relationships with customers, it also affects prosperity, energy, and joy within and between companies. There's a cost to excessive rules and regulations in terms of both administration and also creative energy. For example, although Sarbanes-Oxley has served its purpose to help improve accountability in U.S. companies and restore confidence to the markets, almost anyone involved in carrying it out will tell you that the amount of time, money, and energy spent to comply with the requirements is enormous. For the average company, the compliance cost is more than $2.3 million each year. The cost of Sarbanes-Oxley is hurting especially smaller firms, for which the burden is more than seven times that of large companies relative to their assets. Compliance regulations have become a prosthesis for trust—and a very slow-moving, energy-draining, and costly prosthesis at that!

---

*In stories throughout this book, "we" or "us" often refers to an experience had by one or the other of us, though in some instances we've had reason to specifically identify the author involved.

> *Our distrust is very expensive.*
>
> RALPH WALDO EMERSON

There's also a cost to organizations in terms of attracting and retaining talent. The vast majority of people, both managers and workers, want to be trusted, and they want to work in high-trust environments. When they're not trusted, they become disengaged (i.e., they "quit but stay"), or they leave—particularly the best performers. Employee turnover in a low-trust environment is substantially higher than in a high-trust culture. For example, compare the average turnover rate in the supermarket industry—47 percent—to the mere 3 percent in high-trust Wegmans. Or consider the fact that 25 of *Fortune's* 2011 100 Best Companies to Work For—for which trust is two-thirds of the criteria—had a turnover of 3 percent or less! The cost of turnover to a company can be enormous, ranging from 25 percent to 250 percent of pay.

There's also a cost in partnering and collaboration, both internally within a company and externally with other companies. According to a Gallup survey, the best partnerships are almost all characterized by mutual trust, while in poor partnerships, less than 3 percent strongly agree that they trust each other. In most situations mutual interest is not enough to override mutual distrust.

Without trust, we don't truly collaborate; we merely coordinate or, at best, cooperate. It's trust that turns mere coordination into true collaboration. It's trust that turns a group of people into a team.

> *Trust is the linchpin of a partnership. With trust, both people can concentrate on their separate responsibilities, confident the other person will come through. . . . Without trust, it's better to work alone. . . . No trust, no partnership.*
>
> RODD WAGNER AND GALE MULLER
> GALLUP EXECUTIVES AND AUTHORS

Just think of a typical team meeting in a low-trust culture. You go into a conference room, and you may see meeting rules posted on the wall. They sound like kindergarten rules: "Be nice." "Speak one at a time." "Take turns." A more realistic representation of the rules might be the Miranda rights: "You have the right to remain silent" (because you probably will). "Anything you say can and will be used against you" (because it probably will). It's interesting that even though the United States has a system in which a person is assumed "innocent until proven guilty," people who are picked up by the police are still called "suspects."

Most painfully, there's a cost to distrust in our personal lives. One of the richest experiences of being human is to enjoy open, caring relationships with others. When we view the world through the lenses of distrust, we alienate ourselves. We cut ourselves off from the fullness of the rich relationships we could be having with a spouse, partner, children, associates, and friends—even with ourselves.

> It is . . . happier to be sometimes cheated than not to trust.
>
> SAMUEL SMILES
> SCOTTISH AUTHOR AND REFORMER

Clearly, although there is risk in trusting too much, there is also a huge risk in not trusting enough. It puts a tax—often a huge one—on every interaction that could be generating prosperity, energy, and joy.

Which Glasses Are You Wearing?

You've likely been scripted, conditioned, and/or experienced into primarily one set of glasses or the other. Whichever glasses you wear tend to magnify the evidence that fits your paradigm and filter out the evidence that doesn't, and they significantly affect the degree of prosperity, energy, and joy in your life. Keep in mind that the differentiation is not all or nothing, black or white. You may be wearing a strong prescription or a mild one. You may switch back and forth. You may even be wearing bifocals, so to speak—looking at your professional relationships with distrust and your personal relationships with blind trust or vice versa. Or you may view your family with blind trust and people dating your daughter with distrust. The point is that whatever glasses you're wearing at any time are affecting the way you see the world—and as a result the quality of your life and your ability to enjoy relationships with others and work with them to accomplish meaningful goals.

So why don't you take a moment now and examine your glasses? Remember, they are just "glasses." You can choose to wear them, or you can choose to take them off. As we'll discuss in chapter three, you can even choose to put on a completely different pair.

Thinking about how you see people can help you understand more about whether you have a dominant paradigm that's affecting the results you're getting in your life. Consider the two sets of statements in this table that represent the extremes of blind trust and distrust. Do you identify with one more than the other? Do you tend to respond differently in different situations?

How Do You Tend to See Others?

Blind Trust	Distrust
I trust people too easily and believe whatever they say. As a result, I often get burned.	I am inherently suspicious of people and question whatever they tell me.
I never check up on people or what they tell me; I just always assume the best.	I always feel I have to investigate people's credibility and validate what they say.
I openly and freely share information about anything and everything.	I believe information is power. I hold it close to my chest and give it out only sparingly.

(continued on next page)

Blind Trust	Distrust
I accept everyone as trustworthy and feel comfortable with the thought of working openly with anyone.	People have to earn my trust before I am willing to work with them.
I trust people to do what they say they will do, and see no reason to question otherwise.	I tightly supervise my direct reports (or my children or others) and thoroughly and frequently check up on their work.

The reality is that there is a high cost to both blind trust and distrust. And whether you're looking at the world primarily through the lens of blind trust or distrust, neither approach is sustainable in the long term. Those who live with blind trust eventually get burned; those who live with distrust eventually experience financial, social, and emotional losses.

> *It's a vice to trust everyone, and equally a vice to trust no one.*
>
> SENECA
> FIRST-CENTURY B.C. ROMAN PHILOSOPHER

Smart Trust Glasses Will Change Your World

Bottom line, the way we see the problem *is* the problem. It's not either/or. It's not just blind trust vs. distrust. The solution is a *third alternative*—a whole new set of glasses, a truly different way of seeing and behaving, which we call "Smart Trust."

As we'll see in the following chapter, like the polarized sunglasses that revealed the enormous possibilities just beneath the surface of that river in Montana, Smart Trust glasses reveal a whole new world of possibilities for achieving prosperity, energy, and, joy. The good news is that you have the power to choose this third alternative. Even if you've been looking through the lens of blind trust or you've been scripted, disappointed, betrayed, or abused into viewing the world through the lens of distrust, you don't have to allow either paradigm to remain the dominant one through which you view the rest of your life.

In chapter one we asked you to imagine a world without trust—a world in which you could have absolutely no confidence in the trustworthiness of other drivers on the road, an airline pilot, a doctor, a partner, or a spouse. Now we ask you to imagine a high-trust world—a world in which you were free to interact and engage with others in highly productive, creative, and enjoyable ways, without blind-trust risk and also without debilitating suspicion or fear. Though you may not be able to change the whole world, you will be amazed at what happens when you change *your* world through the power of Smart Trust.

In the following chapter, we invite you to set aside whatever other glasses you may be wearing, put on a set of Smart Trust glasses, and see the amazing possibilities that lie just below the surface. And we invite you to consider your own potential for increasing prosperity, energy, and joy—in your personal life, on your team, in your organization, and in the world.

> To trust is to take a risk, and risks are to be taken wisely. But to trust is also to open new worlds.
>
> FERNANDO FLORES
> FORMER FINANCE MINISTER OF CHILE

QUESTIONS TO CONSIDER

- What experiences may have scripted you to view the world through either the lens of blind trust or the lens of distrust? What has been the result?
- What behavior have you observed in others that shows a tendency toward blind trust or distrust?

CHAPTER THREE

The Third Alternative: "Smart Trust"

Knowing a great deal is not the same as being smart; intelligence is not information alone but also judgment.
CARL SAGAN
Astronomer, writer, and scientist

To trust or not to trust: that is the question.

Stephen:

Recently I was invited to visit a group of students from a "Leader in Me" school, one of the hundreds of K–6 schools that are embracing leadership principles at an elementary school level throughout the world. I was excited to walk into the school to find about five hundred kids waiting for me. As I looked at their faces, I saw that they were bright and happy and radiated an amazing amount of energy and joy. After I spoke to them, they had the opportunity to ask some questions, and their questions were great: "How do you earn trust?" "How do you restore trust?" "How do you build trust with your friends?" I was really enjoying interacting with these amazing kids until one fifth-grade student asked, "How do you know if you can trust somebody?"

My immediate reaction was to say what I would have said in a business presentation or in most other settings: "Start with the premise that people can be trusted until they prove otherwise." But as I looked into the faces of these elementary school–aged kids, I thought, "Wait a minute! These are young kids. Many walk home from school every day. There are some bad people out there. Their parents and teachers have undoubtedly taught them about 'Stranger Danger,' or its equivalent, which would have been a wise thing to teach kids that age because the consequences of even one child being too trusting are so great."

Because I wasn't really prepared for that question in an elementary school environment, I don't think I responded with the best answer. I said, "You've got to be really smart about it. You can't trust everybody. You can trust most parents and teachers and most of your friends. But you've got to be careful. You've got to listen to that voice inside you and watch out for people who might mean you harm." Basically, I tried to reinforce what I thought their teachers and parents had probably taught them. Though I wanted to encourage them to lead out with trust, I clearly didn't want to lead them down a blind-trust path where even one of them might become physically vulnerable, so I took the more cautious approach.

As I thought about it afterward, I realized that although Stranger Danger may be a good thing to teach kids, it can become a huge problem if it becomes the basic way we look at all relationships throughout our lives—if we allow a protective response to the 5 percent who can't be trusted to drive the way we interact with the other 95 percent who can. Stranger Danger can script us, at a young age, to be suspicious and distrusting. If we don't ever recognize that scripting and we grow into adults who treat everyone with suspicion and distrust, we lose out on the collaboration, partnering, engagement, and speed of trust, as well as the deep relationships that are vital to a rich human experience. In addition, we lose out on the prosperity, energy, and joy that come from high trust in both our personal and professional lives.

S o how do we know who to trust? How can we operate with high trust in a low-trust world without getting burned? And how can we extend trust wisely to people when not everyone can be trusted? Before we share a framework for thinking about these questions, let's look at a few companies that seem to have figured it out.

When Meg Whitman joined eBay as CEO in 1998, she said the reason was because she was "blown away by the power of trust." The company was founded by the French-born Iranian-American entrepreneur Pierre Omidyar, and from the beginning, it quickly became wildly successful. Today the company has a market capitalization in excess of $35 billion, with 235 million registered users (buyers and sellers) engaging in more than 1 million transactions a day.

So how has eBay managed to become so successful, especially considering that "success" involves millions of transactions each year between people around the globe who don't even know each other? The company was built on Omidyar's high-trust belief that "most people are basically good." Whitman said:

> More than a decade later, I still believe that Pierre was right: the fundamental reason eBay worked was that people everywhere are basically good. We provided the tools and reinforced the values, but our users built eBay. Our community's willingness to trust eBay—and one another—was the foundation of eBay's success.

Does that mean that eBay operates on blind trust? Not at all. According to Whitman:

> Pierre's premise was not that all people are good; it was that most *people* are basically *good.* I agree that it is an optimistic statement, but let's be clear: we did not build eBay by sticking our heads in the sand. We did not ignore or deny that fraud, distasteful behavior, or unlawful activities occurred on eBay from time to time. Quite the contrary: we invested significantly in eBay's Trust & Safety division, which policed the site. We created software that looked for patterns that might be signs of trading in counterfeit goods,

illegal bidding, or even behavior that was simply inappropriate, such as one user stealing a digital photograph from another user's auction page. But from day one it was clear to us that such behavior involved only a tiny minority of people.

A fundamental element of eBay's approach is self-policing, much like that engaged in by the Maghribi traders in the tenth-century Middle East. eBay buyers and sellers do business in a highly transparent way, publishing onsite feedback on their trading partners after each interaction. This feedback creates a reputation for each trader, which affects his or her credibility in the eyes of other traders. A strong positive reputation increases a trader's ability to do business; a lesser reputation diminishes it. If a trader gains a sufficiently negative reputation, the company's software prohibits the person from trading on the site. In addition, eBay encourages the formation of communities of traders in different category areas to watch out for one another and to be on the lookout for counterfeit goods and rogue traders.

In *Jump Point,* Tom Hayes observed:

> *If we believed that we would or might be cheated, few of us would be eager to transact on eBay. But we do trust, not only eBay as the intermediary, but also the user community itself. The eBay community is self-policing and self-correcting of cheats and fakes. Sellers and buyers earn their reputations. And reputation is one's calling card and bond on eBay. Sure, a cheater may get away with it once, but the system will brand and marginalize that person quickly.*

The sociologist Peter Kollock said:

> *Many participants report that they are more willing to trade with someone with a high rating, or even that they will only trade with individuals with high ratings. In that sense, some traders are able to create a brand identity that increases their volume of sales or even the price at which they are able to sell items. . . . Even a few negative ratings can seriously damage a reputation, and so frequent traders are very careful about nurturing their rating by providing swift execution of honest trades.*

Surprisingly to the skeptics, out of the 2 million auctions that occurred during the first two years of eBay's operation, only twenty-seven were considered to involve possible fraud, and those were referred to the proper authorities for prosecution. Even today, as the number of transactions has skyrocketed (and along with it the number of fraudulent cases), eBay refuses to allow the extremely small percentage of people who abuse the trust to define the vast majority of users who respect it. Its business model focuses on the great many who can be trusted rather than on the relatively few who can't. And eBay goes to great lengths to weed out those few. The company's objective is not only to increase trust among buyers and sellers but, at a minimum, to increase trust in the system. In 2005, when Omidyar was asked what the most significant lesson learned from eBay was, he responded, "The remarkable fact that 135 million [now 235 million] people have learned they can trust a complete stranger."

Another company that has figured out how to navigate risk in a low-trust world is Netflix, the DVD rental and on-demand video-streaming company that has more than 20 million subscribers in the U.S. and Canada. Like eBay, Netflix is based on the idea that most people can be trusted. Subscribers pay a monthly fee in return for renting a certain number of DVDs at a time, which are sent to them in the mail. Though some DVDs are lost or stolen, by and large the Netflix community has proven to be honest, enabling the company to operate successfully on the business model of extending trust to customers. Netflix does not allow the small untrustworthy minority to derail the business. In fact, also like eBay, Netflix aggressively seeks to identify and eliminate that small minority through a robust, sophisticated system that monitors suspicious activity and identifies both untrustworthy customers (whose accounts are canceled) and postal delivery workers (against whom charges are filed). Though Netflix can't root out all the offenders, it's remarkable that a high-trust system that involves thousands of postal workers delivering millions of DVDs each week has as few problems as it does.

Another standout is L.L.Bean, a $2 billion online and catalog retailer specializing in clothing and outdoor recreation equipment. It is best known for its extraordinary customer service, having ranked number three in MSN's 2011 Customer Service Hall of Fame. The company's excellent customer service—which grows out of its remarkable customer service guarantee—inspires enormous loyalty and trust. The guarantee reads, "Our products are guaranteed to give 100% satisfaction in every way. Return anything purchased from us at any time if it proves otherwise. We do not want you to have anything from L.L.Bean that is not completely satisfactory."

What's particularly remarkable about this guarantee is the fact that the company puts the evaluation of customer satisfaction completely in the hands of the customer—and not for only thirty days or even a year. There is no time limit. The current chairman, L. L. Bean's grandson Leon Gorman, said this of the guarantee when he first introduced it in 1968: "If we expected customers to trust us in buying products through the mail, we had to trust them in deciding whether or not the products were satisfactory throughout their expected lifetimes."

Now, it's not hard to imagine how customers might abuse this policy and take advantage of L.L.Bean. And on extremely rare occasions, the company has had to draw a line and close an account. An L.L.Bean executive told us, "It is not blind trust on our part. We do occasionally and reluctantly have to suggest that a customer shop elsewhere. But remarkably, we have very little abuse. Our customers seem to appreciate and respect the integrity of our service guarantee, and they are loyal. They like being trusted. Particularly in the recent difficult economic times, customers look to a company where they can trust the value proposition and know that the company will stand behind it."

Now, as you think about eBay, Netflix, and L.L.Bean, notice that the trust being exercised by those companies is different in kind. It's not blind trust; it's not distrust. It's Smart Trust.

What Is Smart Trust?

Smart Trust is *judgment*. It's a competency and a process that enables us to operate with high trust in a low-trust world. It minimizes risk and maximizes possibilities. It optimizes two key factors: (1) a propensity to trust and (2) analysis. Simply put, Smart Trust is *how to* trust in a low-trust world.

1. A Propensity to Trust

The propensity to trust is the inclination, bias, or desire to trust people. As we observed in chapter two, young children typically have a higher propensity to trust. This propensity may be affected one way or the other by personal experience or conditioning. In our work, we see it powerfully affirmed—many times even restored—as people become more aware of high-trust individuals, teams, and organizations around the globe and the results of their high-trust interactions.

The propensity to trust is primarily a matter of the heart. Having a high propensity to trust—extending trust deliberately and intentionally—is a vital dimension of Smart Trust . . . as long as it's combined with equally high analysis. In our experience, those who have a low propensity to trust have usually had experiences that have decreased their willingness to extend trust.

The propensity to trust almost always provides the best starting point of Smart Trust; in other words, we lead out with trust first. We don't ignore analysis; we just suspend it. We approach situations with the belief that "most people are basically good," and the reason we do this is because it opens up a whole new world of possibilities.

Starting with a high propensity to trust doesn't necessarily mean that we will ultimately decide to extend trust to someone; in fact, we may not—especially after we've done the analysis. What it does mean is that *we open ourselves up to the possibilities.* When we lead out with distrust, we don't even see the possibilities. It's like looking at the river without the polarized sunglasses.

After one of our programs, an attorney approached us and said, "I can't believe what I've been doing! I've just realized that I've allowed distrust to be the lens through which I see my entire world. My profession has trained me to lead out with distrust as my starting point. This has worked at times at the office, but at other times it's cost me enormously—and it's absolutely killed me in my personal relationships. Because I've been scripted to be suspicious, I've missed a lot of possibilities to create happier and more energizing relationships. I've also missed opportunities to get better results."

For people such as Muhammad Yunus and companies such as eBay, Netflix, and L.L.Bean that begin with a high propensity to trust, the possibilities are limitless. They design their businesses based on the 95 percent who can be trusted rather than on the 5 percent who can't—and in turn they enjoy the reciprocal benefits of high trust. For many in the midst of this global renaissance of trust, reconnecting with their innate propensity to trust is a personal renaissance or reawakening.

2. Analysis

If we were to focus solely on our propensity to trust, we'd often be trusting blindly, and in a low-trust world, we'd constantly be getting burned. To exercise Smart Trust, we need to combine a high propensity to trust with equally high analysis. This is why, even with a strong propensity to trust, successful people and organizations set up provisions for the rogue 5 percent or so, depending on the situation or context. For example, the eBay system we mentioned earlier is built on a strong foundation of transparency and feedback procedures that encourage and empower traders to police the site on their own. But in addition, eBay has sophisticated measures in place to detect inappropriate behavior, fraud, or efforts to market counterfeit goods. And it tenaciously polices the system, weeding out untrustworthy traders. In other words, the system is clearly based on trust, but it's not blind trust. Though it leads out with a high propensity to trust, it combines it with equally high analysis. The same can be said of Netflix and L.L.Bean.

> Doveryai, no proveryai. (*Trust, but verify.*)
>
> RUSSIAN PROVERB

While the propensity to trust is primarily a matter of the heart, analysis is primarily a matter of the mind. Analysis refers to our ability to assess, evaluate, and consider implications and consequences, including risk. As with a high propensity to trust, strong analysis is a vital dimension of Smart Trust, but it, too, must be tempered. If it's not—if we start out with a low propensity to trust—most of us are so steeped in analysis that the analysis will color our judgment. We'll find all kinds of reasons to not trust our boss, our reports, our partners, our customers, our suppliers, our colleagues, or even our family. The point is that analysis is necessary but insufficient and, in most cases, shouldn't lead. Fortunately, in today's Web-based world, information technology and Internet transparency can enhance Smart Trust by making faster, more thorough real-time analysis possible.

Smart Trust analysis involves the assessment of 3 vital variables:

1. **Opportunity** (the situation—what you're trusting someone with)
2. **Risk** (the level of risk involved)
3. **Credibility** (the character and competence of the people involved)

Let's look at each in turn.

Vital Variable #1: Opportunity. Assessing an opportunity or situation is simply a matter of clearly identifying *what* you're trusting someone with. Are you trusting someone to telecommute? To close a deal? To manage a project? To be a partner in the supply chain? Netflix, for example, trusts its customers to receive and return DVDs. Grameen Bank trusts its borrowers to pay back their loans.

Vital Variable #2: Risk. Life is filled with risk. There's no way we can avoid it. To trust is to take a risk; not to trust is also to take a risk. The objective of Smart Trust is to manage risk wisely—to extend trust in a way that will maximize prosperity, energy, and joy. In order to do so, we need to be able to evaluate the degree of risk involved:

- What are the possible outcomes?
- What is the likelihood of the outcomes?
- What are the importance and visibility of the outcomes?

For contrast, let's compare the risk in two different situations. During one of our programs, the admiral of a nuclear submarine said, "On a nuclear sub there are procedures for everything. We even have a list of protocols to use the bathroom. Are you suggesting that this is distrustful and that we should get rid of our procedures on most of the things we do?" "Not at all," we replied, "because the risk on a nuclear submarine is so great. The protocols show respect for that risk and can actually build trust."

At another program, a bank employee from a foreign country shared an experience he'd had when his young daughter asked, "What's it like in America?" The father had replied, "You can be walking on a street and come to a vending machine where they sell newspapers. They have a whole stack of papers in there, and when you put in two quarters, it unlocks the door, and you just take one paper and then lock the door again. And there's no one to check that you don't take more than one." "Wow!" said the daughter. She could hardly believe it was possible that people would extend that amount of trust. (Incidentally, those vending machines are nicknamed "honor boxes.")

These two examples frame the risk issue in the extremes: "Is this situation about nuclear subs, or is it about newspapers?" In other words, what is the degree of risk?

> *Civility has two parts: generosity when it is costly, and trust, even when there is risk.*
>
> STEPHEN CARTER
> HISTORIAN AND LAW PROFESSOR, YALE UNIVERSITY

In the Stranger Danger program we mentioned earlier, significant caution is justified because the risk is so great. For even one child to be abducted or abused is one too many. In that situation, Smart Trust involves putting a number of protective measures into place. As we've noted, however, it also needs to involve helping children gain a maturing awareness that most people are basically good so that distrust does not become the governing paradigm of their young or adult lives.

In his microcredit program, Muhammad Yunus felt that the risk was small, even though his borrowers had no collateral. Although banks and financial advisers disagreed, he believed that most poor people would repay their loans, which belief was justified by the 98 percent payback rate. Nevertheless, he set up support groups for borrowers not only to encourage and help one another but also to create a self-policing system that would ensure the responsible behavior of the group members since all their reputations would be bound together.

Some modern companies have been created with the express purpose of helping people mitigate the risk of doing business in today's global electronic world. One example is VeriSign, a company that makes it easy for customers to do business quickly by verifying the legitimacy and security of Internet sites. Case studies show that the presence of the VeriSign Trust Seal on a company's website increases online transactions by 10 to 34 percent. Another example is PayPal, which keeps credit card and bank account numbers on a secure site for its 87 million customers worldwide and enables them to make quick and easy payments for online purchases without the risk of sharing financial information with many Web merchants. PayPal also provides a benefit for merchants, who have the security of knowing that their customers' payments are good.

> We are witnessing the growth of the trust industry.
>
> JEFF JARVIS
> JOURNALIST AND AUTHOR

Vital Variable #3: Credibility. Credibility is the character and competence of the person or people involved. Perhaps you've heard the apocryphal story of the little boy whose mother asked him to take lunch to his father, who was digging down inside a deep, dark hole. As the boy approached the edge of the hole, his father called to him and told him to toss the lunch to him, which the boy did. Then his father said, "Hey, there's plenty of food here for two. Why don't you jump down and join me? We'll have lunch together." The bright sun shining in the boy's eyes kept him from seeing down into the hole, so he said, "But I can't see you." The father replied, "But I can see you. Go ahead and jump. I'll catch you." What would you have done if you had been that boy? In the story, the boy jumps into the dark, his father catches him in his strong arms, and they have an enjoyable lunch together.

Obviously, the father had great credibility with his son. The boy knew he could trust him. But what if the person at the bottom of the hole had been someone else instead? What if he'd been another worker whom the boy barely knew or even a stranger whom he didn't know at all? How willing would the boy have been to make that jump?

Extending trust is an act of faith—sometimes a leap of faith. In making that leap, it nevertheless pays to exercise due diligence in ascertaining the credibility of the people or organization involved. If the credibility is low and the risk of extending trust in a particular situation is high, you may decide that the smart thing to do is to simply not extend trust. Or you may choose to extend trust cautiously, believing that the very act of taking the risk and extending trust will help the person or organization increase in trustworthiness.

> *The chief lesson I have learned in a long life is that the only way to make a man trustworthy is to trust him; and the surest way to make him untrustworthy is to distrust him and show your distrust.*
>
> HENRY L. STIMSON
> FORMER U.S. SECRETARY OF STATE

In any event, considering the credibility of the other party is part of good analysis. For example, consider what you might do if you were offered an opportunity to partner with someone such as Jon Huntsman, Sr., the founder of Huntsman Corporation. If you were to research Huntsman's credibility, you might find that at one time he was involved in negotiations with Charles Miller Smith, the president and CEO of Imperial Chemical Industries, one of the largest companies in the United Kingdom. Huntsman described the potential merger as the largest deal of his life, a deal that would double the size of Huntsman Corp. The negotiations were especially difficult because the transaction was complicated and there was intense pressure on both sides. Toward the end of the negotiations, Smith became emotionally distracted. His wife was suffering from terminal cancer, and she died before the negotiations were complete. Having earned his reputation as a tough negotiator, Huntsman knew he probably could have pulled another $200 million out of the deal, but it would have been at the expense of Smith's emotional well-being. So he chose instead to let the details of the last 20 percent of the deal stand as they were. "The agreement as it stood was good enough," he said. "Each side came out a winner, and I made a lifelong friend."

You might also discover that at another time, Huntsman partnered with Mitsubishi to open a plant in Thailand. After a time, a Mitsubishi executive called Huntsman to tell him that every company in Thailand had to pay government officials annual kickbacks in order to do business there, and that Huntsman's share of the kickbacks for their partnership that year would come to $250,000. Huntsman discovered that, without his knowledge, Mitsubishi had been paying his annual share as a cost of doing business, but it had now decided that Huntsman needed to carry its share of the load. Huntsman wrote in his book, *Winners Never Cheat:*

> *I said we had no intention of paying even five cents toward what was nothing more than extortion. . . . The next day, I informed Mitsubishi we were selling our interest. After failing to talk me out of it, Mitsubishi paid us a discounted price for our interest in HMT. We lost about $3 million short term. Long haul, it was a blessing in disguise. When the Asian economic crisis came several years down the road, the entire industry went down the drain. . . . [A]fter our refusal to pay "fees" in Thailand became known, we never had a problem over bribes again in that part of the world. The word got out: Huntsman just says no. And so do many other companies.*

I have never had anyone refuse to deal with me for lack of trust.

JON HUNTSMAN, SR.
FOUNDER, HUNTSMAN CORPORATION

You would be able to uncover many stories that attest to Huntsman's credibility. Other factors being equal, his proven track record of ethical, caring, trustworthy behavior would likely have a significant positive impact on your decision to extend trust to him in a business relationship.

Credibility involves both *character* (integrity and intent) and *competence* (capabilities and track record of results). Just as you likely wouldn't want to do business with someone who, though very skilled, was a known liar and cheat, neither would you want to do business with someone who was honest but incompetent. Credibility also involves the relevance of the person's competence to the job to be done. Though you might trust an associate to take over your job while you're on vacation, you might not trust that same person to cut your hair or operate on your daughter's knee.

When we know someone is credible, we can have far greater confidence that we can trust that person. The same is true for organizations. The problem comes when we don't do due diligence to ensure that someone is credible or when we assume that because they were once credible, they remain so. This is what happened when the Securities and Exchange Commission failed to thoroughly investigate Bernie Madoff, thus failing to discover a multibillion-dollar swindle.

> Do not trust all men, but trust men of worth; the former course is silly, the latter a mark of prudence.
>
> DEMOCRITUS
> FIFTH-CENTURY B.C. GREEK PHILOSOPHER

The Smart Trust Matrix

If we chart the two elements of Smart Trust—propensity to trust and analysis of situation, risk, and credibility—on a matrix, we can see that a high propensity to trust combined with low analysis results in gullibility, or *Blind Trust* (Zone 1). A high propensity to trust combined with high analysis results in good judgment, or *Smart Trust* (Zone 2). A low propensity to trust combined with low analysis results in uncertainty and indecision, or *No Trust* (Zone 3). A low propensity to trust combined with high analysis results in suspicion, or *Distrust* (Zone 4).

As you look at this matrix, think about how it feels to be in each of these zones. Though we may feel blissful for a time in Zone 1 (Blind Trust), we're usually not happy there for long. We're gullible. Sooner or later, we get burned. We inevitably pay for our failure to engage our minds as well as our hearts. In Zone 3 (No Trust), we engage neither mind nor heart. As a result, we feel indecisive and insecure, thinking we can't trust anybody—including ourselves. This is particularly frustrating in teams and organizations when bureaucratic indecision grinds momentum to a halt. In Zone 4 (Distrust), we only engage our minds. As a result, we become so suspicious and guarded we don't trust anybody *except* ourselves, and we miss out on the benefits of rich personal relationships with others. Zone 2 (Smart Trust) is the only place that combines heart and mind—the innate propensity to trust with the analysis to manage risk wisely. It is the only zone that gives us the judgment we need to discern when to trust, when not to trust, and how to extend trust in a way that minimizes what can go wrong and maximizes all that can go right.

Having identified the essential elements of Smart Trust, we also need to say this: more than a science, Smart Trust is an art. It's an act of judgment. We're reminded of the movie *Dead Poets Society* in which Robin Williams plays the fictional character of John Keating, an unorthodox English teacher at the Welton Academy boys' prep school. In one scene, Keating has a student read from the introduction to the boys' poetry textbook, written by "J. Evans Pritchard, PhD." The page gives a dry mathematical formula for rating the quality of poetry. Keating then tells the boys:

> *Now, I want you to rip out that page. Go on, rip out the entire page. You heard me, rip it out. . . . [D]on't just tear out that page, tear out the entire introduction. I want it gone, history. Leave nothing of it. . . . Begone, J. Evans Pritchard, Ph.D. . . . It's not the Bible, you're not going to go to hell for this. Go on, make a clean tear, I want nothing left of it. . . . This is a battle, a war. And the casualties could be your hearts and souls.*

As the boys first react with astonishment and nervousness and then hesitatingly begin to rip out the pages, Keating continues:

> *We don't read and write poetry because it's cute. We read and write poetry because we are members of the human race. And the human race is filled with passion. And medicine, law, business, engineering, these are noble pursuits and necessary to sustain life. But poetry, beauty, romance, love, these are what we stay alive for.*

We share this scene to say that although we've given you a formula that contains the critical elements of Smart Trust, as with poetry, what we're dealing with is art, not science. Smart Trust requires judgment—informed judgment. It's not a "one-size-fits-all" proposition, nor is there typically only one "right" answer. In addition to the elements themselves, the interaction between the two elevates even instinct and intuition into the realm of good judgment.

Because judgment is developed through experience, we sometimes make mistakes. And we *will* make mistakes in trusting people. But the more we can recognize and exercise our propensity to trust and our ability to analyze situation, risk, and credibility effectively and the more we can create the empowering synergy between them, the more successful we will be in creating high-trust relationships and opportunities and increasing prosperity, energy, and joy.*

> Good judgment comes from experience and experience comes from bad judgment.
>
> RITA MAE BROWN

The Other Side of the Coin

The Smart Trust matrix can be of enormous help to us in making decisions about extending trust to others. But there is another, equally important dimension of Smart Trust—*being* credible or worthy of trust so that others will feel confident in extending trust to you. We might refer to this as the other side of the Smart Trust coin. But there's one big difference: though you may or may not decide to extend trust to someone based on your propensity to trust and your analysis of opportunity, risk, and credibility, there is *never* a situation in which Smart Trust involves *not* being trustworthy yourself. Your own credibility is a critical constant.

Consider the example of Jon Huntsman, Sr., whom we mentioned earlier. Because of his credibility, an infinite number of possibilities to create prosperity, energy, and joy are open to him that would not be open

---

*To take a brief survey to assess your current level of Smart Trust and receive a complimentary, personalized analysis, go to SmartTrustBook.com.

to someone less trustworthy. Also consider Warren Buffett, the chairman and CEO of Berkshire Hathaway, recognized by many as the most successful investor of all time. Buffett regularly sends memos to his seventy-seven reports (whom he calls his "All-Stars") that reinforce his absolute and unyielding commitment to trustworthiness and engages them in helping to maintain it. He has said:

> *We can afford to lose money—even a lot of money. We cannot afford to lose reputation—even a shred of reputation. Let's be sure that everything we do in business can be reported on the front page of a national newspaper in an article written by an unfriendly but intelligent reporter. In many areas, including acquisitions, Berkshire's results have benefitted from its reputation, and we don't want to do anything that in any way can tarnish it. Berkshire is ranked by* Fortune *as the second-most admired company in the world. It took us 43 years to get there, but we could lose it in 43 minutes.*

As we mentioned in "Our Intent" at the beginning of the book, Buffett also said:

> *Somebody is doing something today at Berkshire that you and I would be unhappy about if we knew of it. That's inevitable: We now employ well over 200,000 people and the chances of that number getting through the day without any bad behavior occurring is nil.*

Then he went on to say:

> *But we can have a huge effect in minimizing such activities by jumping on anything immediately when there is the slightest odor of impropriety. Your attitude on such matters, expressed by behavior as well as words, will be the most important factor in how the culture of your business develops. Culture, more than rule books, determines how an organization behaves.*

A case in point occurred in 2011, when it became apparent that a senior executive in Berkshire Hathaway had behaved in a way that severely violated Buffett's trust. Some used the man's rogue behavior to argue that Buffett's trusting style doesn't work anymore. But consider the outcomes:

the executive resigned from the firm with no severance compensation (but denies that his stock trades violated the law or Berkshire's policy); Buffett turned all the information over to the Securities and Exchange Commission, and he reinforced to his managers that untrustworthy behavior would not pay off nor be tolerated at Berkshire Hathaway. What Buffett wisely *didn't* do was to treat his other seventy-six direct reports as if they couldn't be trusted because of the one who had abused the trust. As a result, despite the blow, Berkshire Hathaway continues to enjoy the benefits of its high-trust culture.

Buffett's personal credibility inspires trust. And the way he extends trust to his managers inspires their loyalty and diligence in helping to ensure that Berkshire Hathaway remains trustworthy. Cathy Baron Tamraz, one of the seventy-seven All-Stars and the CEO of Business Wire, which she sold to Buffett in 2006, had this to say: "Warren makes us feel like we can do no wrong. . . . We're not going to sleep at night because we're going to get it right every single day. It's extraordinary." As a result of his approach, Buffett has become the third richest person in the world, and he is spreading prosperity, energy, and joy to millions through his decision to donate 99 percent of his $47 billion fortune to charities that improve living conditions for people worldwide, principally through the Bill & Melinda Gates Foundation.

In today's low-trust world, it's sometimes easy to justify untrustworthy behavior. "It doesn't matter. Everyone does it." But everyone doesn't do it. In fact, in Buffett's 2006 memo to his All-Stars, he said:

> *The five most dangerous words in business may be "Everybody else is doing it." A lot of banks and insurance companies have suffered earnings disasters after relying on that rationale.*
>
> *Even worse have been the consequences from using that phrase to justify the morality of proposed actions. More than 100 companies so far have been drawn into the stock option backdating scandal and the number is sure to go higher. My guess is that a great many of the people involved would not have behaved in the manner they did except for the fact that they felt others were doing so as well. The same goes for all of the accounting gimmicks to manipulate earnings—and deceive investors—that has taken place in recent years.*

You would have been happy to have as an executor of your will or as your son-in-law most of the people who engaged in these ill-conceived activities. But somewhere along the line they picked up the notion—perhaps suggested to them by their auditor or consultant—that a number of well-respected managers were engaging in such practices and therefore it must be OK to do so. It's a seductive argument.

But it couldn't be more wrong. In fact, every time you hear the phrase "Everybody else is doing it" it should raise a huge red flag. Why would somebody offer such a rationale for an act if there were a good reason available? Clearly the advocate harbors at least a small doubt about the act if he utilizes this verbal crutch.

Behaving in untrustworthy ways is never part of Smart Trust. It isn't smart. Although some people and organizations may get away with being untrustworthy for a while (and we can all point to some), the approach is not sustainable. At some point there will be a comeuppance. Bernie Madoff's came many years after the fact—but it did come. Untrustworthy behavior simply will not—over time—create *sustainable* prosperity, energy, and joy.

Smart Trust in Action

Now, with your Smart Trust glasses more firmly in place, you might want to recall the examples we shared earlier of eBay, Netflix, Berkshire Hathaway, and L.L.Bean and think about the way those successful companies have blended their propensity to trust with analysis to come up with a winning Smart Trust approach. You might also want to think about the Maghribi traders of the tenth-century Middle East or Muhammad Yunus.

Also, remember the insurance company in Europe we mentioned that was burned by its experience with a fraudulent claim. At one time the company leadership adopted the attitude of assuming that all their customers were crooks unless they could prove otherwise, and that attitude drove many customers away. But the story didn't end there. The leaders decided to change their approach. They put out a public announcement that said to their customers, "We trust you. If you submit a claim, we are going to honor it." At the same time, they communicated that they wanted to work only with honest customers, so they dropped some. In addition, they had done an analysis and discovered that the bureaucratic process was actually costing them more to administer than it would have cost them to reimburse the bad claims. What happened as they implemented their new approach was that trust and speed went up dramatically. Claims that had been taking weeks or months to process were now being processed in days or even hours, and the customers loved it. Their loyalty to the company increased, as did the number of referrals. And, surprisingly to all, the total number of claims went down substantially. Because they felt trusted, people quit filing petty claims.

A terrific illustration of Smart Trust in the social sector is in the field of community policing. Back in the early 1990s, the National Police of Colombia used to ride in their patrol cars through neighborhoods whose members were engaged in drugs and violent crime. In those neighborhoods, children and teenagers were forced to steal and sell the drugs, being threatened if they didn't cooperate and paid with drugs if they did. The police were not trusted. There was no thought of cooperation from the local residents to address the situation. But when Antanas Mockus was elected mayor of Bogotá in 1994, he decided to make some important changes. He shifted the paradigm from a low propensity to trust to a high one. That one change affected his analysis of the situation and the risk of involving people in the community. The decision was made to train police officers in social skills, organize them into teams of two, and assign the teams to specific neighborhoods for several years at a time. The officers began to ride on bicycles instead of in patrol cars. They visited local residents and stopped to chat with them on street corners. They organized neighborhood security workshops and helped schools provide preventive education for children on security issues. They set up community-based crime-monitoring committees to run alarm systems and share information with the police. According to one report:

> *The effort has borne extraordinary fruits. . . . Today [September 2010], Bogotá has the lowest homicide rate of any major city in the country.*
>
> *Public perceptions of law enforcement have also been turned upside down. In a 1983 survey, 73 percent of Colombians interviewed said they had a negative image of the police. But in 2002, a survey conducted by the Javeriana University found that 85 percent of Bogotá residents said they had a positive view of community policing. In addition, 86.3 percent said the community policing program had addressed their needs and complaints, 99 percent said community police were friendly toward the public, and 86.5 percent said the police's performance had improved.*

By extending Smart Trust, those police officers inspired community members to trust them. They reduced the risk of involvement for citizens who wanted to improve their community. And in addition to the visible evidence of trust and lower crime, they began to see kids who would normally have been involved in drugs start to make better choices.

In Vancouver, British Columbia, the Royal Canadian Mounted Police, Richmond Detachment, tried a different Smart Trust approach. It decided to partner with local businesses to provide "positive tickets" to youths they caught doing something right. These tickets not only expressed trust in the young people, they also took them into the local stores to redeem the tickets for an ice cream cone, a slice of pizza, or a movie theater show so that they got to know the local businesspeople and interacted with them in positive ways. Police issued three positive tickets for every one traditional (negative) ticket. The impact of this approach was measurable. Police officers' morale increased significantly, and trust developed not only with the youths but also in the broader community. Court referrals and juvenile arrests in Vancouver dropped by nearly 50 percent over a three-year period. Recidivism dropped to 5 percent, meaning that 95 percent of the youth sent through the newly created Restorative Justice Program never reoffended or came into negative contact with police again. And the cost of processing offenders was reduced by 90 percent. The leader of the initiative, Ward Clapham, has now worked with more than fifty-three countries to implement positive ticketing. According to Clapham, "It's not about how many tickets are redeemed. The ticket is the gateway to the relationship. And it is all about the relationship."

> When you build relationships, you build trust . . . and when you have trust, anything can happen.
>
> WAYNE YEE
> ADVISOR YOUTH SERVICES,
> CITY OF RICHMOND, BRITISH COLUMBIA

The Reciprocity of Trust

As you can see from these examples, big dividends come from the ability to wisely extend trust and to be trusted. Perhaps the most exciting is the upward virtuous cycle that is created because of the reciprocal nature of trust. When we trust people, they tend to trust us back. When we withhold trust or project distrust, they tend to reciprocate with distrust. In many organizations the main reason employees don't trust management is because management doesn't trust employees. Employee distrust, therefore, is a reciprocation of management distrust. And the same phenomenon frequently occurs between organizations and customers, partners in a supply chain, even parents and children.

In fact, time and again, studies have demonstrated the reciprocity of trust in a wide variety of situations, including trust between complete strangers. One such study was performed by Paul Zak and his associates. The purpose of the experiment was to study the relationship between the hormone oxytocin, which facilitates positive social behaviors, and trust and trustworthiness.

If you had participated in this experiment, you would have been given $10 for participating when you arrived, assigned a partner (whom you did not know, did not meet, and could not communicate with during the experiment), and randomly assigned a role as "Decision Maker 1" or "Decision Maker 2." You would have been told that the amount of money you would take home would depend on the choices made by you and your unseen partner and that all interactions would take place through a computer interface in a lab.

Had you been chosen as Decision Maker 1, the software would have prompted you to send any part of your $10 (or none if you preferred) to your partner. You would both have been told that whatever you sent would triple in your partner's account. According to Zak, the amount you sent would have been a measure of your willingness to trust. After receiving your payment, your partner would have been prompted to send whatever amount he or she wanted (including $0) back to you. The amount your partner sent to you would have been an indication of his or her trustworthiness. Immediately after each decision, blood would have been drawn from both of you and your oxytocin levels measured, and after all the decisions were made, you would have been paid privately and sent home.

The most interesting dimension of the experiment was that it was conducted in two different scenarios. The first was just as we described. But in the second, the amount you sent to your partner would not have been your choice but determined by a random draw of a numbered ball (from 0 to 10) from an urn. The results of the experiment showed that if you had made the decision—if you had sent an *intentional* signal of trust—your partner would have had *twice* the oxytocin levels he or she would have had if the decision had been made by random draw, *even though the average monetary transfers in both situations would have been identical.* In other words, the consciously recognized act of extending trust induced measurable physiological benefit. It also resulted in measurable economic benefit. If you had sent the *intentional* trust signal, your partner would have returned around 53 percent of the amount he or she received. If the amount you sent had been determined by random draw, your partner would have returned only 18 percent to you.

Organizations and individuals who exercise Smart Trust understand the principle of reciprocity. Consider Google. The company extends trust to engineers by allowing them to spend 20 percent of their time (or the equivalent of one day a week) working on something that is company-related and interests them personally but is not necessarily part of their job description. The engineers reciprocate by using the time to fix something that is broken or develop something new, making an enormous difference in Google's innovation and ultimately its profitability. As Google Vice President Marissa Mayer has said, "We let engineers spend 20 percent of their time working on whatever they want, and we trust that they'll build interesting things." And the engineers reciprocate that trust, thus far having used their 20 percent time to create an enormous number of Google's products (at one point 50 percent), including Gmail, Google News, Google Sky, and Google Talk.

> When you're passionate about something and it's an idea you believe in, you're bound to work harder on it. Just about all the good ideas here at Google have bubbled up from 20 percent time or something like 20 percent time, where people have their own idea and run with it.
>
> ALEC PROUDFOOT
> ENGINEER, GOOGLE

Another organization that understands the reciprocity of trust is BestBuy.com—the group that decided to take advantage of its flexibility as an online retailer by trusting employees to work whenever and wherever they like as long as they get their jobs done well and on time. This extension of trust gives employees the freedom to work early in the morning or late at night, depending on whether they're naturally early birds or night owls. It enables them to go to the doctor, watch their child in a school play, or take a vacation without stress. Employees reciprocate by giving their employer their best. Within a short time after implementing the new approach, employee productivity increased by 35 percent. In a *60 Minutes* feature, Chap Achen, one of the company's managers, said, "The ironic thing about it is that it's that trust factor that actually makes them work harder for you." When asked about the workload, one employee replied, "I am a happier employee with the trust."

> The right people will feel far more pressure to perform well when they are trusted.
>
> HECTOR RUIZ
> CHAIRMAN AND CEO,
> ADVANCED NANOTECHNOLOGY SOLUTIONS

Nordstrom is another outlier. One of the world's most trusted retailers, Nordstrom is known for its exemplary customer service. But the trust the company builds with its customers comes about because company leaders first establish trust with their employees. The Nordstrom Handbook, which is given to all employees, is printed on a postcard and contains one simple rule in serving the customer: "Use good judgment in all situations." Employees reciprocate this extraordinary extension of trust back to the company, as no employee wants to violate or lose that kind of trust. But they also extend that trust to customers, who come back again and again. This has enabled Nordstrom to become one of the top retailers in the world and to be perennially on *Fortune*'s 100 Best Companies to Work For list.

Trust Is Contagious: The Virtuous Upward Cycle

In the end, reciprocity works both ways: When we extend trust, we generate trust; when we withhold trust, we generate distrust. Our actions lead either toward a virtuous upward cycle of prosperity, energy, and joy or toward a vicious downward cycle that eventually results in the destruction of those outcomes. Either we add to the renaissance of trust, or we contribute to the crisis of trust—in our personal lives, our families, our communities, our teams, our organizations, our nations, and the world. And every action and every interaction makes a difference. Indeed, trust is contagious—and so is distrust.

> *He who does not trust enough, will not be trusted. No trust given, none received.*
>
> LAO TZU
> AUTHOR OF *TAO TE CHING*

Perhaps you remember the character of Jean Valjean in Victor Hugo's classic novel *Les Misérables*. Valjean is imprisoned for nineteen years for stealing a loaf of bread during difficult economic times and making several attempts to escape. Upon his release, he is required to carry a yellow passport that brands him as a convict. Because of the passport, no innkeeper will give him shelter and no employer will pay him a full wage. He is finally taken in by the kindly Bishop Myriel, who feeds him and gives him a bed for the night. During the night, however, Valjean steals the bishop's silverware and silver plate and runs away. He is caught and brought back to the bishop, who surprises Valjean by telling him in front of the police that he forgot to take the silver candlesticks and admonishing him to remember his promise to use the silver to become an honest man.

Bewildered and then inspired by the bishop's trust, Valjean does become an honest man. He serves as mayor of and brings prosperity to the town of Montreuil-sur-Mer. He brings comfort to a dying woman and raises her daughter. He saves the life of the man the daughter loves. And ultimately he releases the cruel and manipulative police officer who had attempted to arrest him for years but fell into Valjean's hands as a prisoner of the French Revolution. As the story plays out, it becomes obvious that the bishop's one simple act of trust had a profound impact on the life of Jean Valjean and on the many people with whom he came in contact.

Bottom line, Smart Trust is the ability to extend trust wisely in a world that seems to be saying you can't trust anyone, and it leads to a virtuous upward cycle of prosperity, energy, and joy. With the thousands of examples we have seen around the globe, we can declare with confidence that even in the midst of today's crisis of trust, there truly is a simultaneous renaissance of trust, and Smart Trust is a supremely powerful generator, enabler and enhancer of these three critical outcomes.

We also affirm—as we will explain more fully in chapter eight—that it is a leader's job to go first. Whether you are a leader in your company, your team, your industry, your nation, your family, your classroom, your community, or even a personal relationship, you have the opportunity to proactively lead out in being trustworthy and in extending Smart Trust to others. And even if you've been burned or even if you've done things (or your predecessor has done things) that have lost trust for you or your organization in the past, the sooner you lead out in building or rebuilding trust, the sooner you can experience the tremendous benefits of trust in your life.

In Part II, we'll share the 5 specific actions leaders are taking to create Smart Trust interactions, relationships, and cultures. We encourage you to keep in mind, as we'll point out in Part III, that *one person can make a difference.* The rest of this book is designed to empower you—if you choose—to be one who will.

QUESTIONS TO CONSIDER

- Who do you trust? Who trusts you? Why?

PART II

The 5 Actions of Smart Trust

In this section, we'll zero in on the 5 Actions of Smart Trust, the five specific actions that, remarkably, an incredibly diverse variety of high-trust individuals, teams, and organizations from all over the world have in common. We'll look at how Smart Trust leaders consistently perform these 5 Actions:

- **Smart Trust Action 1: Choose to believe in trust** (they create the foundational paradigm out of which all other trust-building behaviors flow).
- **Smart Trust Action 2: Start with self** (they focus first on developing the character and competence—the credibility—that enable them to trust themselves and to also give others a person—or a team, organization, or country—they can trust).
- **Smart Trust Action 3: Declare their intent . . . and assume positive intent in others** (they signal goals and intended actions—both what and why—clearly in advance and generally assume that others also have good intent and want to be worthy of trust).
- **Smart Trust Action 4: Do what they say they're going to do** (they follow through and act to carry out their declared intent; they walk their talk).
- **Smart Trust Action 5: Lead out in extending trust to others** (they are the first to extend trust and initiate the upward virtuous cycle that leads to prosperity, energy, and joy).

We'll also note the principles on which these 5 Actions are based, as well as their opposites and counterfeits. The counterfeits are particularly dangerous because although the opposites are self-evident, counterfeit actions—like counterfeit money—appear to be real but on closer inspection reveal themselves as disingenuous. Whether engaged in knowingly or unconsciously, counterfeits are often the most prevalent actions in teams, organizations, and relationships of all kinds. They are also the actions most likely to diminish trust.

The good news is that there is a dramatically increasing number of people and organizations everywhere engaging in the 5 Actions of Smart Trust—thereby avoiding their opposites and counterfeits—and getting remarkable results. And their stories are enormously inspiring. As you can see from the relatively few we've included in this book, they not only demonstrate the power of the 5 Actions, they provide deeply personal inspiration and confirm the reality of the renaissance of trust.

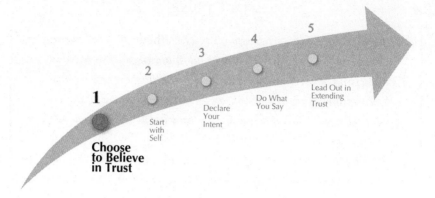

CHAPTER FOUR

Smart Trust Action 1:
Choose to Believe in Trust

So much of long-term success is based on intangibles.
Beliefs and ideas. Invisible concepts.
ISADORE SHARP
Founder and CEO, Four Seasons Hotels and Resorts

The outer conditions of a person's life will always
be found to reflect their inner beliefs.
JAMES ALLEN

Stephen:

One night I was talking with my eight year-old daughter, Arden,
about writing this book. As I explained a little about Smart Trust,
she excitedly said, "Oh, that's like Ping in The Empty Pot!*" She*
ran to get the book—one of her favorites—and we sat down to read
it together. It's the beautifully illustrated story of an emperor who

(continued on next page)

needed to choose a successor to his throne. Because he loved flowers so much, he decided to give every child in the kingdom some flower seeds, and whoever produced the best results in a year's time would succeed him to the throne. All the children were excited, but Ping was the most excited of all because he, too, loved flowers and was very good at growing them.

Ping filled his pot with rich soil and planted his seed carefully. He watered it and nurtured it and watched it every day, but no flowers appeared. He replanted it in a bigger pot, and still nothing happened. When the day came for the children to bring their pots to the emperor, Ping was embarrassed. All the other children's pots were filled with beautiful flowers, but his was empty. The emperor looked at each of the pots, saying nothing until he got to Ping's. Then he looked at Ping and asked why he had brought an empty pot. Ping tearfully explained all he had done to make the seeds grow, but to no avail. The emperor smiled and said, "I have found him! I have found the one person worthy of being emperor!" He then told Ping that the seeds he had given the children had all been cooked and could not possibly have grown flowers. Because Ping had the courage to be honest and bring his empty pot, he was rewarded with the entire kingdom and was made emperor over all the land.

As we finished reading the book, Arden exclaimed, "See, Dad? The emperor knew if he could find a person he could trust, then that person would be the best emperor. Isn't that what Smart Trust is all about?"

I assured her that, indeed, it was.

In the story of *The Empty Pot*, the emperor set up the test the way he did because he *believed* in trust. He *believed* that the person best qualified to be emperor would be someone who was worthy of trust. He *believed* that by extending trust to Ping, he would create the best possibility that his kingdom would be filled with prosperity, energy, and joy. And his beliefs guided his actions.

Belief is critical to getting results in any area of life. Our work with leaders, teams, and organizations around the world has convinced us that belief is the foundational platform for sustainable success. In fact, what we *believe* is even more important than what we *know* because beliefs drive our behavior and our actions. An increasing body of scientific evidence validates this important principle. In *The Biology of Belief,* Dr. Bruce Lipton put it this way: "[B]eliefs control behavior . . . and consequently, the unfolding of our lives." And this is the case whether our beliefs are accurate or not.

Perhaps you're aware of a story that is loosely based on the movie scene from Neil Simon's play *The Prisoner of Second Avenue.* It's about a man who was visiting New York City. Having been warned by a friend about the dangers of being mugged on the streets, he was nervous. Nevertheless, he decided to go for a walk downtown. Sure enough, it wasn't long before he was bumped by a jogger, and when he recovered his balance, he discovered that his wallet was no longer in his back pocket. He immediately took off running after the thief, and when he reached him, he grabbed him by the shirt, shook him roughly, and demanded, "Give me that wallet!" Clearly frightened, the thief immediately handed over the wallet, and as soon as the man let him go, he turned and ran away. The man returned to his hotel, irate that that someone would be so dishonest and disrespectful as to take another person's wallet but glad that he had at least been forewarned. He opened the door to his room, and as he walked over to the dresser to set down his room key, he suddenly stopped in dismay. There on the dresser was his own wallet, lying where he'd left it that morning. He had taken the jogger's wallet!

This man's belief drove his actions—*even though his belief was wrong*—and caused him to unwittingly become the very thing he feared: a rude, insolent thief. Similarly, a belief in distrust can drive actions that also bring unwanted outcomes. This is why the first Smart Trust action is so important. Deciding to believe in trust is a choice, the fundamental choice out of which all other Smart Trust actions flow. In the very act of choosing to believe in trust, we inspire ourselves to take the actions necessary to extend Smart Trust. And this holds true in teams, organizations, and even countries. Consistently applied, our belief in trust transforms our ability to create the conditions that generate prosperity, energy, and joy in all that we do.

> *Your beliefs become your thoughts. Your thoughts become your words. Your words become your actions. Your actions become your habits. Your habits become your values. Your values become your destiny.*
>
> MAHATMA GANDHI

Understanding Your Beliefs About Trust

To choose to believe in trust is to enhance your natural propensity to trust. This action is based on the *principles* of belief and trust. The *opposite* is *not* to believe in trust or to believe in distrust—to believe in the expediency of treating other people with suspicion or doing whatever it takes to get ahead. *Counterfeits* include giving lip service to trust when it is popular, being a "fair-weather" believer based on situation, opportunity, and convenience, using trust as a "technique" rather than choosing it as a core belief, and faking a belief in trust in order to manipulate others.

For some, believing in trust is difficult. Like the man who accosted the jogger in New York, many of us have been preconditioned to be

DILBERT © 2008 Scott Adams. Used by permission of UNIVERSAL UCLICK. All rights reserved.

distrustful, so we automatically look at every situation through glasses of suspicion. Or we've had experiences when we've extended trust but have been seriously burned in doing so. Maybe a work colleague betrayed us. Perhaps we've been through a painful divorce. Maybe we've seen others around us lie, cheat, and steal and get away with it, making it appear that since "everybody's doing it," such behavior is a more expedient and efficient way of getting things done in today's world. Maybe we fear that by trusting we will lose control or that trusting is just too risky. Whatever the reason, many of us don't genuinely believe in trust, or we might believe in it as a nice, idealistic platitude, but we don't believe it works—or, particularly, that it will work for us. The underlying issue behind many of these scenarios is fear—fear of being taken advantage of, of being hurt, of taking that shaky step outside the box, of not being able to succeed.

For others, a belief in trust comes more easily. Maybe we were raised in a high-trust family, neighborhood, or society. Maybe we had positive models and mentors as we were growing up. Maybe we entered into a high-trust friendship or marriage, or we had the opportunity to work for a boss who trusted us or on a high-trust team or in a high-trust company where we experienced firsthand the rich benefits of trust. Maybe we've become aware of examples of trust that have inspired us, led us to decide to trust, and opened the door to possibilities that would not have existed without trust.

Whatever our situation, the choice to believe in trust increases our propensity to trust. It is the foundational action that leads to all other Smart Trust actions, and those actions are what lead to the prosperity, energy, and joy we desire. It's not enough to merely give lip service to the idea of trust. It's not enough to use trust as a pragmatic technique in certain situations when it's to our advantage. It's not enough to trust only once in a while, when we think there is no risk involved. The greatest and lasting dividends of trust come only when we choose trust as our underlying approach—the operating system, if you will, that consistently governs our day-in, day-out choices and decisions.

The good news is that whatever our scripting or past experience, we have the capacity to make that choice and to change the results we're getting in our lives. It is to that end that we share the stories in this book of leaders and individuals around the world who have made this choice. It's our intent that as you read their stories, you will begin to develop a more accurate and powerful belief in trust.

Three Beliefs About Trust

As we work and interact with high-trust individuals, teams, and organizations worldwide, it's become increasingly clear to us that their actions grow out of three specific beliefs about trust:

1. A belief in being worthy of trust
2. A belief that most people can be trusted
3. A belief that extending trust is a better way to lead

Let's look at each of these beliefs in turn.

1. A Belief in Being Worthy of Trust

At the root of the belief in trust is a belief in trustworthiness or credibility—in the importance of acting with character and competence so that both you and others know that you can be trusted. This belief is manifest in some of the examples of successful people and companies we've already highlighted, such as Azim Premji, who fired a general manager of Wipro due to a small indiscretion in inflating a travel bill and refused to bribe officials to release a critical consignment at a lower duty rate. Or Jon Huntsman, Sr., who chose to conclude a deal with less favorable terms rather than create stress for a man whose wife was dying of cancer and sold a business at a $3 million loss rather than pay government kickbacks he considered to be "nothing more than extortion." Or Warren Buffett, who tells his employees, "Let's be sure that everything we do in business can be reported on the front page of a national newspaper in an article written by an unfriendly but intelligent reporter." Another standout is Isadore Sharp, founder and CEO of the Four

Seasons hotel chain. In his book *Four Seasons,* he tells the story of his father's decision to become a plastering contractor. His father had emigrated from Poland to Canada and was struggling to learn the English language. According to Sharp:

> *On his first job, he misread the plans. He didn't realize that the plans showed only half the building, because the other half, as the plans explained, was identical; this was a common practice then. As a result, his quote— readily accepted, of course—was 50 percent too low.*
>
> *He didn't comprehend this until he was well into the job. He could have picked up his tools and walked away, leaving someone else to finish it. But he had made a commitment and felt honor-bound to keep it. So he finished the house without lowering quality and worked for the next several years paying off his resulting debt. I was only told of this later, but it became for me an invaluable lesson in business ethics that I have remembered throughout my career.*

Out of that experience, Sharp gained a belief in being worthy of trust that helped him develop his highly successful luxury hotel chain.

As the experience of these and countless other leaders show, those who have a core belief in trustworthiness do not consider that belief as merely a practical option or as a technique to get what they want in a particular situation. Rather, they are committed to being trustworthy even when it's hard, even when there's a price to pay. In fact, we might say that the real *test* of trustworthiness and credibility is doing the right thing, especially when there's a cost or consequence.

2. A Belief That Most People Can Be Trusted

Successful high-trust people and companies create their success by choosing to believe that most people can be trusted—not *all* people (that wouldn't be smart), but *most* people. They refuse to allow the small minority who can't be trusted to define the vast majority who can. As part of their analysis, they find ways to isolate the few so that they can run with a high-trust belief in the many. And they apply this belief to all stakeholders—customers, partners, investors, team members, and also family and friends.

You can see this in stories we've previously shared such as that of Muhammad Yunus, who—against all advice—set up high-trust micro-loans to poor people with no collateral yet achieved a 98 percent re-payment rate. Yunus expressed his belief in his customers as follows: "Grameen assumes that every borrower is honest." You can see it in Pierre Omidyar, who set up eBay on the premise that most people are basi-cally good, enabling more than a million successful transactions daily between buyers and sellers who are complete strangers to each other. Former CEO Meg Whitman captured the essence of the eBay belief in these words: "Pierre showed me that choosing to view our community as full of good people who generally wanted to create an honest place to do business was essential to our enterprise. . . . It became deeply woven into our culture—a fundamental component of how we treated one another internally as well as how we treated eBay users and partners."

You can see it in Netflix, which not only trusts its millions of subscrib-ers by mailing returnable DVDs directly to their homes but also trusts its employees to choose how to take their pay (in either cash or stock) and to take as much vacation time as they need. Or in Google, which trusts its engineers to spend 20 percent of their time working on projects of their choosing. As Vice President Marissa Mayer put it: "20 percent time sends a strong message of trust to the engineers." Or in L.L.Bean, which trusts customers with a service guarantee of "100% satisfaction in every way" and encourages them to "return anything purchased from us at any time if it proves otherwise." Or in Zappos, which trusts customer service reps to handle customers without scripts and trusts customers with a 365-day return policy with free shipping both ways.

Another organization that strongly believes in trust is W. L. Gore & Associates, a company that specializes in products that are derived from fluoropolymers, such as Gore-Tex fabrics. Diane Davidson, who works in market development, said, "When I arrived at Gore, I didn't know who did what. I wondered how anything got done here. It was driving me crazy. 'Who's my boss?' I kept asking." "Stop using the B-word," her sponsor replied. The reason for Davidson's confusion was that in the early days of the company, its founder, Bill Gore, believed in trust so strongly that he set up a "lattice organization" that persists in the company to this day. Workers are considered "associates" and are expected to grow their contribution by thirty peers who rank one another's contributions, much as in a professional partnership in a law firm. It takes time to earn the trust and credibility to be given responsibilities at Gore. As one associate explained, "We vote with our feet. If you call a meeting and no one shows up, you're probably not a leader because no one is willing to follow you."

Gore does, of course, have a CEO. When Chuck Carroll retired from that position in 2005, the board of directors asked a wide range of Gore employees who they would be willing to follow. As London Business School's Gary Hamel noted in *The Future of Management,* one of the employees, Terri Kelly, was surprised when she learned she'd been chosen as the new CEO. Kelly leads the firm today as it continues to grow with more than nine thousand employees in thirty countries around the world, generating nearly $3 billion in annual revenue and is often referred to as "the world's most innovative company." And Gore is consistently listed as one of the best companies to work for worldwide.

When companies and leaders choose to believe that most people can be trusted, it plays out in organizational design, affecting systems, processes, structures, and even strategies. Just imagine the difference in designing an organization from scratch on the presumption of high trust—as Bill Gore did—rather than low trust or distrust. What kind of expense reimbursement system would you design for people you trust versus people you don't? What different kinds of rules, policies, and procedures would you set up? What effect would the presumption of high trust have on policies for blogging and tweeting? And what about structure?

In speaking of Gore's release style management structure, Hamel offered this insight:

> *Like fish that can't conceive of a world not immersed in water, most of us can't envision management practices that don't correspond to the norms of our own experience. Even our language is hostage to our paradigmatic beliefs. Consider, for example, how thoroughly the notion of hierarchy has infiltrated*

the lexicon of management. "Chain of command." "Pyramid." "Boss." "Subor-
dinate." "Direct reports." "Organizational level." "Top-down." "Bottom-up."
"Cascade." All these terms connote a formal scale of power and authority.

Top-down hierarchical structures tend to be based on control and
on the belief that most people can't be trusted—or, perhaps more accurately, on the belief that because we can't trust the small minority, we also
can't trust the large majority. That is because people sometimes confuse
control and trust, thinking that if we trust, we're not in control. As a
result, the most common response to trust violations is to throw more
rules at the problem—which mostly punishes the many because of the
actions of a few.

But as Jeff Jarvis pointed out in *What Would Google Do?*, "There is an
inverse correlation between control and trust." The highest form of control actually comes from having a high-trust culture, not from excessive
rules. When we start with the belief that most people can be trusted, we
have options we didn't have before, as the example of W. L. Gore clearly
shows.

> The more you control, the less you will be trusted; the more
> you hand over control, the more trust you will earn.
>
> JEFF JARVIS
> JOURNALIST AND AUTHOR

Another prime illustration is Nordstrom's "One Rule" approach,
which, better than a thousand rules, incents employees to remain worthy
of trust and to ensure that their colleagues not only "get it" but "keep it."
Yet another illustration is Chaparral Steel, whose former CEO Gordon
Forward said:

> *We felt that a lot of the procedures in many organizations were designed
> to catch the 3 percent who were trying to cheat in one way or another. We
> decided to design our rules for the 97 percent we can trust. The others would*

stand out like sore thumbs, we figured, and they'd eventually leave. That's exactly what happened.

Again, we're talking about Smart Trust, not blind trust, so our analysis of the situation and risk in a particular circumstance may tell us that we're dealing with the equivalent of nuclear submarines rather than newspapers and that exercising good judgment demands a more conditionally trusting response. And there are clearly cultures (whether an organization such as Enron or whatever country is ranked dead last on the Corruption Perceptions Index) where the "most people can be trusted" ratio may have shifted enough to warrant a different Smart Trust starting belief. But in the vast majority of situations, starting with the belief that most people can be trusted is a far better starting point than the other way around.

3. A Belief That Extending Trust Is a Better Way to Lead

Successful high-trust leaders believe that extending trust is a better way to lead, primarily because trust inspires people to perform, it's reciprocated, and it ultimately leads to greater prosperity, energy, and joy.

This belief was clearly manifested by BestBuy.com, which experienced a 35 percent jump in productivity after extending trust to employees to work whenever and wherever they liked, as long as their jobs were done well and on time. And by Warren Buffett, who told his managers regarding the 257,000 people in the seventy-seven companies that are part of Berkshire Hathaway: "Somebody is doing something today at Berkshire that you and I would be unhappy about if we knew of it"—yet still chooses to operate based on "deserved trust" rather than distrust. And by Wegmans, whose high-trust culture enables the company to engage employees in such a way that turnover is less than 3 percent in an industry averaging 47 percent.

In 2007, Ross Smith acted on his belief that trust could make a big difference in the productivity of his eighty-five-member Microsoft Windows Security Test Team. He renamed the team "42Projects" to help bridge the generation gap by capturing the imagination of the twentysomethings familiar with Douglas Adams's *The Hitchhiker's Guide to the Galaxy*, in which the number 42 is defined as the universal truth. Ross described the challenge in these words:

> *We knew we couldn't simply send a memo to the team inviting them to "trust us." At this stage, trust was a brand new, awkward, and potentially emotional topic. How could we convince people that trust was a good thing to actually spend their time on? No one disagreed with the notion that more trust was better than less, but to actually take time away from "real work" to build trust was a dubious proposal. We had already established a weekly forum where we bought pizza and invited team members to come and share—ideas, projects, proposals, and research. So we used one of these "pizza meetings" to brainstorm the list of behaviors that influence trust. Participants came up with about 150 trust-influencing behaviors.*

The team also came up with various games to keep score of their progress, improve collaboration, and prioritize behaviors. The project was entirely voluntary, and team members created a wiki to encourage participation. Ross reports the impact: based on various metrics, a 20 to 50 percent increase in retention compared to the team's history and peer teams and a 10 to 60 percent increase in productivity. The team also improved its position in the war for talent by creating what Ross called "a virtuous circle." According to Ross, "Talented, happy people contribute great ideas, and new thinking attracts new recruits." One team member, Marc McDonald, Microsoft's first employee and a high school friend of Bill Gates, said, "42Projects tries to recapture the feeling and passion you have at a small start-up or at the beginning of an industry by breaking down the stratification of a large organization."*

You can see a belief in trust manifested on a larger scale across the board in customer service expert Jeanne Bliss's book *"I Love You More than My Dog,"* in which she identifies decisions of leaders and organiza-

---

* For a complimentary Trust Index to help you assess the current level of trust on your team, go to SmartTrustBook.com.

tions that make companies "beloved" and drive extreme customer loyalty in good times and bad. One of them is what she calls "Decide to Believe." She says:

> *Inside the beloved companies, they decide to* believe. *They believe their employees and they believe their customers. Trust and belief are cornerstones of their relationships. By deciding to trust customers, they are freed from extra rules, policies, and layers of bureaucracy that create a barrier between them and their customers. And by deciding to believe that employees can and will do the right thing, second-guessing, reviewing every action, and the diminishing ability of employees to think on their feet is replaced with shared energy, ideas, and a desire to stick around. There is an energy that comes from being believed, from being trusted, and from sending that trust back to customers and employees.*

You can also see it in an inspiring story shared by our colleague Jose Gabriel "Pepe" Miralles, who runs FranklinCovey Latin America:

> *When I was about twelve years old, my parents moved to Puerto Armuelles, Panama, a small city whose main business was exporting bananas. This was the place my family was originally from, and my parents had always wanted to return. They saved money and started their own business—a small supermarket, where we all worked.*
>
> *At the time they set up the store, there was a group of street kids, about twenty-five of them in all, between the ages of eight and sixteen. They would wander around town day and night and were known for being sailors' guides and thieves. They were viewed by almost everyone as scum, like an unpleasant black stain on someone's white shirt.*
>
> *All the merchants were very cautious of these kids. They were not allowed into any of the stores—except for ours. From the beginning my mother spoke to each of them—at times in small groups, at times individually. The message was consistent: "You are a worthwhile individual. You will be allowed to come into my store anytime you want, and you will not be watched. However, you will be expected to honor the trust I am placing in you." This was the first time some of these kids had ever been affirmed as worthwhile.*

The results were both immediate and positive. These kids that would steal from anyone else would come into our store and be respectful and decent. None of them ever stole anything from us. In fact, they would even warn us if they saw any suspicious people come into the store.

As time went on, many of these kids got onto the right track. Some of them are now professionals. Others are blue-collar workers. Most are decent citizens with families. My mother's initial act of trust opened them up so that they could receive more words of encouragement and advice and act upon them, which they did.

The reason my mother extended trust to these kids was because she had a belief in trust. She believed that most people are inspired by being trusted and that these kids would return the trust given to them. And they did.

As Miralles's experience shows, one of the most important reasons that extending trust is a better way to lead is that it inspires both trustworthiness and reciprocity. When others trust us, we want to live up to that trust. When we give trust to others, they tend to give it back in return.

> *If you give respect, you'll get respect. The same goes for loyalty, and trust and all the other virtues that I believe great leaders have to offer.*
>
> JOHN WOODEN
> LEGENDARY UCLA BASKETBALL COACH

Belief in Trust as a Management Philosophy

In July 2005, Dr. Kai-Fu Lee, the corporate vice president of interactive services at Microsoft, became a focus of media attention when he left Microsoft to become president of Google Greater China. Lee capsulized what he felt were the elements of Google's strength in a formula that he put on a Chinese website read by thousands of young engineering students: "Youth + freedom + transparency + new model + the general public's benefit + *belief in trust* = the Miracle of Google."

With Google, as with all the successful people and organizations whose stories we've shared in this chapter and throughout this book, a belief in trust is not a technique or situational practice, it is a foundational operating system that generates prosperity, energy, and joy. The following chart is a summary of how some of the leaders and companies we've already talked about, as well as others, have expressed this philosophy with regard to their lives and organizations.

Leaders/Companies	Management Philosophy/Operating System
Isadore Sharp, Four Seasons Hotels and Resorts	Trust was the emotional capital of Four Seasons, our ethical imperative for long-lasting success, a code and a compass enshrined in the corporate culture. . . . [It] had been the primary reason for our success, crucial to the reputation that precedes us in every deal, in every hotel opening, and in all our operations. . . . Like the invisible hand that regulates the free market, the invisible hand of trust had been our guide and our dynamic. And every year, as trust rose, our reputation rose with it.
Al Carey, Frito-Lay	Our team trusts each other. We move faster on difficult decisions. So when you trust each other there's no need for all the extra bureaucracy. It can allow you to reduce layers of management. It can allow you to move directly to decisions quicker, because you trust each other. You don't have multiple groups overlooking each other to make sure that people are doing things the right way.
Andrea Jung, Avon	Our entire model has been build around personal relationships with our customers, and that is based on trust. The power of those relationships is the key to our success and to the future.

(continued on next page)

Leaders/Companies	Management Philosophy/Operating System
Charlie Munger, Berkshire Hathaway	Our model is a seamless web of trust that's deserved on both sides. That's what we're aiming for. . . . Not much procedure, just totally reliable people correctly trusting one another.
Meg Whitman, eBay	More than a decade later, I still believe that Pierre [Omidyar] was right: the fundamental reason eBay worked was that people everywhere are basically good. We provided the tools and reinforced the values, but our users built eBay. Our community's willingness to trust eBay—and one another—was the foundation of eBay's success. . . . eBay is all about trust.
Muhammad Yunus, Grameen Bank	We were convinced that the bank should be built on human trust, not on meaningless paper contracts. . . . People everywhere prefer to live in an environment of trust.
Jim Goodnight, SAS Institute	I believe management must trust the people who work for them. You have to treat people like they make a difference. And if you do, they will. . . . When you trust people to do their best, the revenue takes care of itself, even in challenging economic times.
Azim Premji, Wipro	Values are a matter of trust. They must be reflected in each one of your actions. Trust takes a long time to build but can be lost quickly by just one inconsistent act.
Terri Kelly, W. L. Gore & Associates	[T]here are some fundamental things that hold Gore together. One is the values to which we all subscribe, in terms of how we're going to treat each other—there's a huge trust element in the Gore culture.
Tony Hsieh, Zappos	We trust our employees to use their best judgment when dealing with each and every customer.

Leaders/Companies	Management Philosophy/Operating System
Ken Chenault, American Express	The competitive advantage of trust has never been more important or more valuable.
John Wooden, UCLA	I believe the following: "It is better to trust and be disappointed occasionally than to mistrust and be miserable all the time."
Google	Too many companies have been built on not trusting people but on making rules and prohibitions, telling customers what they cannot do, and penalizing them for doing wrong. Google has built its empire on trusting us. (Jeff Jarvis, *What Would Google Do?*)

A Leap of Trust

If you've seen the 1989 movie *Indiana Jones and the Last Crusade,* you probably remember the climactic, nerve-rattling scene where Jones, an archaeologist and adventurer extraordinaire, stands perspiring on the edge of a chasm that plunges hundreds of feet. In order to save his dying father, who has been shot by the "bad guys," he has to quickly cross the chasm and get the Holy Grail. But there is no visible way to cross. As he hurriedly refers to some clues his father (also an archaeologist) wrote in a small notebook, he sees the words "Only in the leap from the lion's head will he prove his worth." As he grasps the meaning, his face registers shock and fear. But then his expression shifts to determination, and to the movie watcher's bated breath, he takes a step—a leap of faith—out into the thin air. Miraculously, a bridge suddenly appears beneath his foot. To the viewer's enormous relief, Jones is able to cross the chasm and retrieve the Holy Grail.

As we noted in chapter three, there are times when extending trust requires a leap. And although a leap of trust is rarely as dramatic as Indiana Jones's leap into thin air, it is nevertheless a sometimes difficult and often defining moment.

For example, in 2007 Ted Morgan, the CEO of an unknown location-finding technology company called Skyhook, had been trying for months to get major companies to use his technology. Then one day when Morgan checked his voice mail, he found that a caller had left the following message: "Ted, this is Steve Jobs from Apple. I'd like to talk to you about Skyhook. Call me at . . ." Thinking the message was a joke played by someone on his team, Morgan deleted it. Later that day, he told Mike Shean, Skyhook's cofounder, "Good try, but you gave it away by pretending to be Steve Jobs. You should have said you were Scott or one of the other managers we just met at Apple." Shean said he knew nothing about the message. When Morgan realized that the call had actually been from Steve Jobs, the CEO of Apple, asking to meet with him, he sat up in a hurry.

Morgan returned the call and met with Jobs, and things started happening quickly. It looked as though a great deal was in the making. Then one day Jobs called Morgan and said that Apple had a big Macworld event coming up, that it was close to doing a deal with Skyhook, and that he wanted to model Skyhook's technology at the event—but he couldn't do it without Skyhook's code. So Jobs asked Morgan to give him the code. While still on the phone, Morgan turned to his management team and whispered, "He's wanting our code." The immediate response of the team was "No! No! No!" Morgan said to Jobs, "Steve, as you might imagine, we're never given out our code. That code is our intellectual property. It's everything we have." Jobs replied, "I know that. You're just going to have to trust me."

Against the advice of his team, Morgan gave Jobs the code. We later asked Morgan, "What do you think would have happened if you had said, 'Steve, I just can't'?" He replied, "You never know. But personally, I don't think he would have done the deal. I think Steve would have moved on." Instead, Jobs rewarded Morgan by personally demonstrating Skyhook's technology at Macworld in January 2008, giving an animated explanation of how the technology worked and adding, "Isn't that cool? It's really cool." Morgan called Jobs's spotlight on Skyhook "the biggest publicity event any company can have."*

---

*To view video of Jobs's spotlight on Skyhook at Macworld, go to SmartTrustBook.com.

Skyhook's WPS became the primary location engine for Google Maps and other applications used by both the iPhone and iPod Touch until April 2010, and the company continues to provide location-based services for Apple as well as other technology giants such as Samsung, Motorola, Dell, Qualcomm, and Texas Instruments. Its software powers thousands of mobile applications and is being used on tens of millions of devices around the globe. Morgan's leap of trust turned out to be a huge positive game changer for Skyhook. It also affirms that although there is risk in trusting, there is often greater risk in not trusting.

> *The man who trusts men will make fewer mistakes than he who distrusts them.*
>
> Camillo Benso di Cavour
> Italian statesman

McDonald's took a leap of trust with Cordia Harrington, now known as "the Bun Lady" because she runs the $60 million bakery that supplies buns to McDonald's and other restaurants. In the 1990s she was a single mom struggling to take care of her three sons and pay her bills. She bought a McDonald's franchise in Illinois, but because of its poor location, business was slow. Not to be deterred, she bought a Greyhound bus franchise and changed the route so that it would run past her restaurant, providing from sixty-eight to a hundred buses daily filled with hungry customers.

When Harrington learned that McDonald's needed a bun supplier, she started working to convince the corporate office that she could do the job, even though she'd had no prior bakery experience. Four years and thirty-two interviews later, she managed to earn McDonald's trust, and the deal was sealed with a handshake. The deal has lasted for sixteen years. Harrington says, "This relationship is very sacred. We have no contract, we have a handshake. It's important that my handshake is worthy of their trust."

When a handshake is given, it must be honored—at all costs. Tough bargaining occurs only before the deal is agreed to. When you shake hands, the negotiating is over. Your word is your greatest asset; honesty is your greatest virtue.

Jon Huntsman, Sr.
Founder, Huntsman Corporation

In order to fund her enterprise, Harrington borrowed money from the bank. Based on her work ethic and the credibility she had established, the bank gave her a $13 million loan, again on a handshake. In a keynote speech to the Maryland Women's Conference, Harrington told women, "Get yourself a banker you trust and who trusts you and develop a plan." She also said, "It doesn't always take money. It takes creativity. . . . I was told no 31 times, but if you have your dream in your gut, you stay with it. I thought these bankers were nuts when they gave me a $13 million loan, on a handshake, for a bakery." From the bankers' perspective, they weren't totally nuts. Their analysis showed that Cordia had tremendous credibility, a great track record of results, and an agreement with McDonald's that included significant advance orders.

Novartis, the world's third largest pharmaceutical company, took a leap of trust by announcing plans to invest $1.25 billion over the next five years in two research and development centers in China. Risky? Yes, particularly with China's traditionally cavalier attitude regarding intellectual property rights. Smart Trust? Maybe. Novartis has obviously combined its propensity to trust with thorough analysis. Its sales in China have been rising at a rate of 30 percent annually, and a massive expansion of health care coverage is under way. According to Novartis chairman Daniel Vasella, China will be among the top three markets in five to seven years. In Vasella's words:

Look at the big picture: The U.S. is overly indebted, has invested a high percentage in health care, and has an aging population, so the health bill will increase. So a counter movement will be cost containment. China has a dynamically growing economy, and they have lots of money and no debt. And then you have the willingness of the government to cover many more of its citizens. There will be growth.

In addition, government efforts to encourage people to study English (the international business language) and sciences such as chemistry and engineering have created a strong talent base from which Novartis can recruit. Also, though protection of intellectual property rights has traditionally been a challenge, the Chinese government has begun cracking down on pharmaceutical piracy. As Vasella says, "Ultimately, locating our new R&D center in China is an expression of trust—trust that the government and the people we hire will respect our property and work together to build a global scientific center of excellence."

It will be fascinating to see if China reciprocates Novartis's extension of trust. It will be equally fascinating to watch what happens in coming years as an increasing number of people and companies like Novartis begin to take calculated leaps of trust, not only in China but all over the world.

The Decision to Believe

Perhaps the most important belief for many of us is the belief that we *can* develop a belief in trust—that despite whatever negative scripting or experience we may have had and despite the crisis of trust that surrounds us, we *can* decide to make trust our fundamental paradigm—our personal operating system—and that we can thereby increase the prosperity, energy, and joy in our lives and in our relationships.

One of our colleagues told us about an experience he'd had in leading a two-day program for a group of nurse managers, administrators, and teams that work with veterans:

The first morning, I asked everyone what they hoped to take away at the end of the program. "Clint," who works with the homeless vets, said, "I'd like to learn how to trust again." When I asked him to say more, he replied,

"After what happened in Afghanistan, it's hard for me to trust anybody." He then told us his story.

After a twenty-two-year military career, two deployments to Iraq, and two to Afghanistan, he was sent on a final tour in Afghanistan, where he led a unit that was training the Afghan army to take over security when the U.S. troops left. Clint and his men worked side by side with the Afghans for weeks, training, eating, sleeping, and fighting together. Then, one day, the Afghan soldiers turned their weapons on their American trainers. Clint was severely wounded in the firefight. "That's why I can't trust anybody," he concluded. "It can get you killed." I could tell from his sharing that his trust issues were deeply affecting his relationships at home, especially with his son.

Sobered, I told Clint that I couldn't begin to understand what he'd gone through, but I asked him to stay open with the hope that over the next two days he might find some tools and language that might help him feel more safe by beginning to trust again. He said he would. He stayed the two days and worked hard, sharing his opinions and ideas and interacting with the group. I got him to lead a few of the exercises, and I wondered how far this class could move someone with his experience of betrayal.

At the close of day two, I asked the class what had worked for them. Answers came back: the time together to share common concerns, the videos, the exercises, the cards describing behaviors that create trust. And then Clint raised his hand and said, "I'll tell you what. There are four of those cards waiting on my son's bed when he gets home from school today. And we're gonna talk!" The class gave a huge cheer.

Several months later, I ran into Clint again, and the change in the man was phenomenal. He'd just returned from a camping trip with his son where the two of them had enjoyed a great time together. Clint looked like a different person altogether. He'd changed from gruff, ominous, and intimidating to warm, open, and approachable, and it was clear he'd built a great relationship of trust with his son—and likely with others as well.

Sometimes it's incredibly hard to overcome intense experiences that can script us for a lifetime. But it's possible. Even if all we can start with is a bias to believe, we can work on building that bias. We can put on our trust glasses and look more thoughtfully at the world around us. We can analyze how trust plays out in other people's lives and relationships as well as in our own. We can study it. We can test it. We can take steps to build trust—and perhaps even take an occasional leap of trust—and notice the results. Based on everything the two of us have seen and experienced both personally and professionally in our work with individuals, leaders, and organizations everywhere, we are convinced that developing a belief in trust is the most powerful thing people can do to begin to access the benefits of trust in their lives.

> *If I have the belief that I can do it, I shall surely acquire the capacity to do it even though I may not have it at the beginning.*
>
> MAHATMA GANDHI

As you read the next four chapters and see four additional actions leaders are taking to create high trust in their relationships, teams, organizations, and countries, we encourage you to think about how their belief in trust is at the root of each one. We also encourage you to think of the opportunities they might have missed—in fact, might not have even seen—had they not taken that first action to choose to believe in trust.

QUESTIONS TO CONSIDER

- What do your actions reveal concerning your fundamental beliefs about trust? How might your beliefs be affecting the results you're getting in your life?
- What evidence do you see—or might others see—to suggest that you believe one or more of the following?
  - It's important to be worthy of trust.

- Most people can be trusted.
- Extending trust is a better way to lead.

- What evidence do you see that might cause you or others to think that you have different beliefs?
- What effect do you think your beliefs are having on the way you interact with others and on your prosperity, energy, and joy?

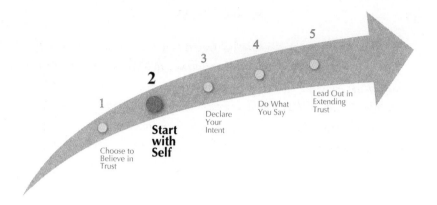

CHAPTER FIVE

Smart Trust Action 2: Start with Self

Trust yourself, and you will know how to live.
GOETHE

The only way we can expect others to trust us is, we need to be trustworthy ourselves, and especially to ourselves.
SIDNEY MADWED
Author and communications expert

R ecently a friend and business colleague of ours, Roger Merrill, shared this experience:

During my growing-up years, my dad served as CEO of a dry foods company he founded in California. At one point, the company had heavily invested in a new product that was doing very well when the market suddenly fell apart. Several advisers suggested that Dad declare bankruptcy, but he would have none of it. Though it took a long time, he personally made sure that every penny that was owed was paid—sooner or later, one way or another.

After I graduated from college, I went back to California to work with him in another company. During the time he was training me, we were awarded a large government contract to supply cocoa beverage powder for the troops in Vietnam. In order to secure funds to fulfill the contract, he took me to the bank with him one day. As we sat down with the branch manager, who was also a senior officer with the bank, he said, "How much do you need?" Dad told him the amount, and the manager said, "Fine. When do you need it?" My dad replied, "As soon as possible." The manager said, "Would in the morning be all right?" Dad said, "Fine," and that was the end of the conversation. As we started to leave, the bank manager pulled me aside and said, "Son, you need to understand that I would give your dad any amount within my power at any time and under any circumstances because of what I've seen him do when he didn't have to. This is a legacy he has earned."

As critical as it is to choose to believe in trust, that's not enough. Individuals, leaders, teams, and organizations that operate successfully in today's world also behave in ways that grow out of that belief. They develop the character and competence that enable them to both trust themselves and earn the trust of others. And the credibility that emerges provides a strength and confidence that open the door to enhanced prosperity, greater energy, and increased joy.

In our work with client organizations, we have developed 6 Key Processes to help people and organizations establish, grow, extend, and restore trust. Though each of these processes involves several steps, the first step in each is always the same: *Start with Self.* In other words, look in the mirror. Assess your own credibility. Can you trust yourself? Are you giving others a person, a leader, a team, a company, a country they can trust? The act of starting with self and asking these two vital questions will affect every other step you take and every decision you make in creating and restoring trust because your credibility is the foundation of all the other Smart Trust actions.

"Start with self" is based on the principles of responsibility and credibility. The *opposite* is to wait for others to change or take responsibility. It's failing to take responsibility for your own credibility and success. *Counterfeits* include pretending (seeming rather than being), faking credibility when you haven't earned it ("Trust me!"), taking credit for success while blaming others for failure ("I did what I was supposed to do; it's their fault we failed"), starting with self-*ish* (doing what you want to do, regardless of the consequences or effect on others), and using ego and arrogance as a prosthesis for genuine self-trust.

Character and Competence

As we pointed out in Part I, credibility is one of the three vital variables of Smart Trust analysis. And again, credibility is a function of two things: character and competence. *Character* involves your integrity (honesty and congruence) and your intent (motive and agenda). Obviously it's easier for people to trust you if they see you as honest, straightforward, dependable, and genuinely concerned about their welfare rather than dishonest, deceitful, manipulative, and self-serving. But character alone is insufficient. Credibility also requires *competence,* which involves your capabilities (talents, skills, and expertise) and your results (track record and performance). Again, it's easier for people to trust you if they see you as knowledgeable, skilled, successful, and deeply engaged in continuous improvement rather than as someone who doesn't perform, who is irrelevant or inexperienced, or whose skills are outdated.

So character and competence are both necessary. It's the combination of the two that makes a person, a team, an organization, or a government credible and trusted. Consider how the emergence of Singapore as a powerhouse nation has come about through the performance of the government and country. Over the last several decades both its character (demonstrated by its low corruption and mentality of national service) and its competence (demonstrated by the way the country has reinvented itself while simultaneously increasing productivity and competitiveness) have made Singapore highly credible and given its citizens and the world a country they can trust.

We need new leadership: authentic leaders, people of the highest integrity, committed to building enduring organizations . . . leaders who have the courage to build companies to meet the needs of all their stakeholders, and who recognize the importance of their service to society.

BILL GEORGE
FORMER CEO, MEDTRONIC;
HARVARD BUSINESS SCHOOL PROFESSOR

It's the combination of character and competence that gives us the confidence to trust ourselves and enables us to inspire others to trust us. This combination plays an integral role in our ability to answer the two key questions in this chapter: "Do I trust myself?" and "Do I give others a person they can trust?"

Do I Trust Myself?

During a break in one of our presentations, a man came up to us and said, "I can't tell you how valuable your presentation has been in helping me recognize my problem. For years, things have not been going as well as I wanted them to in my career, in my organization, in my personal life. And I've been blaming everyone else for it. 'I can't trust my manager.' 'I can't trust the company.' 'I can't trust my people.' 'I can't trust my boss.' 'I can't trust my spouse.' But as I've thought about what you've been saying, I've finally realized that that's not the problem." He looked around to make sure no one was looking, and then he leaned in and whispered, "The problem is that *I don't trust myself.* And that's what I'm projecting onto others. It's hard for me to see other people as trustworthy when I know I am not. The problem is me, and it's being reflected in the way that I see and interact with everyone else."

Distrust is often a projection of missing self-trust.

FERNANDO FLORES AND ROBERT SOLOMON

BUSINESS AUTHORS

Just consider the impact that man's insight could have in his life. His epiphany was not just about some technique or skill to handle a situation differently; it was about literally seeing *everything—every* situation, *every* problem, *every* opportunity, *every* relationship, including his relationship with himself—through different glasses. That is because self-trust affects not only our worthiness to be trusted, it also affects the way we see and interact with others—and, reciprocally, how others see and interact with us. Just think of the difference it would make if that man had the confidence that he could trust himself—if he knew he could make and keep promises to himself and to others; if he knew he could act based on his principles and values instead of reacting to moods or circumstances; if he knew he could be honest and comfortable in transparency; and if he had developed the knowledge and skills to be competent along with a track record of results to validate that confidence. Can you imagine the extent to which that kind of self-trust would affect the way he would see and interact with others?

A man who doesn't trust himself can never really trust anyone else.

CARDINAL DE RETZ

SEVENTEENTH-CENTURY FRENCH CLERGYMAN

The personal congruence that leads to self-trust instills in us the confidence and credibility to inspire others. The two of us have seen countless examples of leaders—many times informal ones—who reach inside themselves, rise to the occasion, and turn the tide in leading a team or organization. One of the more inspiring stories we recall to illustrate this point is from the NBA basketball championship series of 1980. The Los Angeles Lakers led the Philadelphia 76ers three games to two in a best-of-seven series. The Lakers' star player, seven-foot, two-inch center Kareem Abdul-Jabbar, had severely sprained his ankle in game five and would not be traveling with the team to Philadelphia for game six in the hope that he could heal enough to play in game seven, if necessary.

An unlikely hero presented himself in the form of a nineteen-year-old rookie just drafted from Michigan State University, Earvin "Magic" Johnson. Johnson sensed fear and hopelessness in his more experienced and somewhat jaded teammates, who had relied on Kareem for the entire season and had just watched him miraculously score fourteen points in the fourth quarter on a badly sprained ankle to win game five. In the words of coach Pat Riley, as recorded in *Tell to Win* by Peter Guber, when Johnson heard his teammates say they were going to lose, he said, "I know what the problem is. All you guys are afraid because Kareem isn't here. Well, I'll be Kareem." Riley continued, "We get on the plane for Philadelphia, and 1A is Kareem's seat. Even when he was sick, nobody ever sat in 1A. He'd put a sign there: DON'T SIT IN MY SEAT. I'M KAREEM. But Magic sat in his seat and said, 'Hey, I'm Kareem. I'm here.'" According to the NBA encyclopedia:

> *Johnson's confidence lifted his team's spirits, and then he backed it up with one of the most remarkable games in NBA Playoff history. He began by jumping the opening tap in Abdul-Jabbar's place, then went on to play every position on the floor at one time or another, from his customary point guard role to Abdul-Jabbar's pivot spot. Johnson scored 42 points, grabbed 15 rebounds and handed out 7 assists as the Lakers stunned the 76ers 123-107 to clinch the first of his five NBA championships. After the game, he looked into the TV cameras and sent a message to Abdul-Jabbar back in his Bel-Air home: "This one's for you, Big Fella!"*

Magic's confidence was not about himself; it was about his desire to rise to the occasion and draw on his trust in his own character and competence to inspire his team. As Guber commented, "The irony is, Earvin

Johnson's greatest act of magic was the story he told to move his team into believing he was their hero. It was a pretty gutsy story for a rookie, but he pulled it off because he knew he was up to the role and because his ultimate goal was to benefit them all." That Johnson's character and competence typified him over time is evidenced in a *New York Times* article written eleven years later: "Magic Johnson gained the respect of many because, among other things, he devoted much of his off-the-court time to raising money for charities. On the court, he kept making himself better in his profession, no matter how good he got. And that, too, seemed to indicate the heart and mind of the man."

To be clear, self-trust is not ego, arrogance, or unwarranted bravado. It's a quiet inner confidence that reflects our awareness of the most important kind of prosperity we will ever have—a high balance in our own personal trust account. And whatever our current balance (or the balance of our team or organization) may be, the good news is that we can increase it significantly by making regular deposits through behaviors that both develop and demonstrate character and competence.

Keep in mind that actions and behaviors are things we can choose to change. As the renowned executive coach Marshall Goldsmith said, "When people ask me if the leaders I coach can really change their behavior, my answer is this: As we advance in our careers, behavioral changes are often the only significant changes we can make."

> Self-trust is the first secret of success . . . the essence of heroism. . . . In self-trust, all the virtues are comprehended.
> RALPH WALDO EMERSON

Do I Give Others a Person They Can Trust?

The second key question—do I give others a person they can trust?—can be asked in a variety of ways. A manager of a team could ask, "Do I give my team a leader they can trust?" A company could ask, "Do we give our employees, our customers, and our partners a company they can trust?" Leaders of a country could ask, "Do we give our citizens and the world a country they can trust?" And a parent could ask, "Do I give my children a parent they can trust?" The extent to which we demonstrate character and competence through behavior is the extent to which we give others a person, team, organization, country, or parent they can trust.*

> In the end, the degree to which you succeed in forming trusting partnerships is less a reflection of . . . their trustworthiness than of your own.
>
> RODD WAGNER AND GALE MULLER
> GALLUP EXECUTIVES AND AUTHORS

In the rest of this chapter, we'd like to share with you just a few of hundreds of illustrations. It's our hope that these stories will not only inspire you but also give you a greater sense of how the credibility of others enables you to trust them and how your own credibility can inspire others to trust you. That is why credibility is critical to Smart Trust analysis. In addition, we hope these stories will spark personal insight as you engage in lateral thinking. It constantly amazes us to see how people in one sector creatively apply trust-building principles used by people in a completely different sector, such as the physicians you'll read about who significantly reduced errors in cardiac surgery by implementing the trust-based system they saw demonstrated in Grand Prix racing. So even though some of the examples may be out of your box—your discipline, your industry, your pay grade, your country—we encourage you to keep your eyes open for insights that will be helpful in your situation.

---

*"Got Trust?" Find out who trusts you by having friends and associates answer seven brief questions on our Facebook app. Go to SmartTrustBook.com.

Giving Employees a Leader They Can Trust

Peter Aceto is the president and CEO of ING Direct Canada, a major division of the largest banking/financial company in the world. One year after Aceto became CEO, he sent out the following e-mail to the company's approximately one thousand employees. The subject line read, "Leadership: Your Call."

Dear Teammates,

True leaders are not chosen to lead by Boards of Directors and Shareholders. True leaders are chosen by their teammates based upon the respect they have earned, results achieved and the confidence the team has that the team will win with that leader in place. I was chosen by the Shareholders and our Board to be your leader. I was not chosen by you. May 1st was my 1-year anniversary as your CEO and enough time has elapsed for you to decide whether you would like me to lead this great ING Direct team.

Please click on this link and tell me if you want me to remain the CEO as well as any constructive comments you may have for our business or for my leadership. If I do not have your collective vote of confidence, I will move along.

This survey is anonymous, so please be honest. If you choose for me to remain, this will be your free choice and I will be honored to continue to lead with all of my energy and ability.

Please respond on or before Tuesday, May 12th for your vote to be counted.

Thanks,

Peter

The response rate to Aceto's e-mail was over 95 percent, and of those who responded, an amazing 97 percent said he should stay while only 3 percent said he should leave. (As the two of us thought about those percentages, we were impressed—particularly when we surmised that if we did the same thing in our families, we'd be lucky if 50 percent of our kids wanted us to stay!) As former U.S. attorney general Robert F. Kennedy once said, "About one-fifth of the people are against everything all of the time!"

So what was it that enabled Peter Aceto to take such a bold action? As we talked with him, it became clear to us that he trusted himself and had given his employees a leader they could trust. He knew it, and they knew it. His credibility had been proven. He didn't solicit his employees' evaluation blind. He did so with high awareness and the kind of self-confidence that comes through significant credibility and consistent behavior. It was also clear that he believed that by involving his people in this way—in a sense, giving them a chance to select him as their leader—those who voted for him would become even more committed to him, and those who didn't would likely have some fairly good advice for him on what he might do better. Another reason for Aceto's boldness was that his organization, ING Direct, had significant credibility and self-trust. In speaking at a conference on social media, Aceto said:

> *If you or your business is willing to be authentic, if you are willing to tell the truth, if you're willing to be real and you can deliver on that promise every day, then that . . . will build trust and will serve you well in all relationships. . . .*
>
> *I am honoured to work for a business that can open the front door and the back door and the side doors and share what it is that we do. You have to have those values. You have to be willing to be open and honest and you may discover things that you didn't know and be willing to do something about it. If you can't live up to that commitment then you probably shouldn't be there.*

Aceto's e-mail gave his employees the same opportunity that elected lawmakers in many nations have to express trust (or lack of trust) in their leadership through a parliamentary motion or vote of confidence/no confidence. In some circumstances, no-confidence motions or votes result in the resignation or replacement of a leader or parliamentary dissolution and a request for a general election. Aceto's "vote of confidence" clearly reflected the high trust his people at ING Direct had in him and his leadership.

Giving Players and Fans a Coach They Could Trust

John Wooden is one of the most successful and revered coaches in sports history. During his twenty-seven-year career of coaching men's basketball at UCLA, he led the Bruins to an eighty-eight-game winning streak during the early 1970s and ten NCAA national championships in a twelve-year period, including an unmatched seven in a row. He was named national coach of the year six times and was inducted into the Basketball Hall of Fame as both a player and a coach—the first person (and one of only three ever) to be honored in both categories. ESPN named Coach Wooden "the Greatest Coach of the 20th Century."

Even more impressive than *what* John Wooden accomplished, however, was *how* he accomplished it. He taught his players how to be successful not only in basketball but also in life. He encouraged teamwork ("The star of the team is the team. 'We' supersedes 'me.'"), loyalty ("Be true to yourself. Be true to those you lead."), character ("Be more concerned with your character than your reputation, because your character is what you really are, while your reputation is merely what others think you are.") and selfless giving ("You can't live a perfect day without doing something for someone who will never be able to repay you."). He firmly believed in trust ("I believe the following: 'It is better to trust and be disappointed occasionally than to mistrust and be miserable all the time.'"), and what he taught—and lived—consistently built trust.

One example of personal trustworthiness demonstrated early in his career was reported in a brief review of his life distributed by the Associated Press at the time of his death at the age of ninety-nine in 2010:

> *The bespectacled former high school teacher ended up at UCLA almost by accident. Wooden was awaiting a call from the University of Minnesota for its head coaching job and thought he had been passed over when it didn't come. In the meantime, UCLA called, and he accepted the job in Los Angeles.*
>
> *Minnesota officials called later that night, saying they couldn't get through earlier because of a snowstorm, and offered him the job. Though Wooden wanted it more than the UCLA job, he told them he already had given UCLA his word and could not break it.*

Although the prosperity John Wooden gained from his career in coaching was not primarily economic (he never earned more than $35,000 in a season, and early in his career he worked two jobs to make ends meet), he gained enormous wealth in terms of the respect and appreciation he earned from his players and from people in all walks of life. Following his passing, outpourings of appreciation came from people everywhere. In the words of Duke basketball coach Mike Krzyzewski, "Many have called Coach Wooden the 'gold standard' of coaches. I believe he was the 'gold standard' of people."

In addition, Wooden found great energy and joy in what he did. Bill Walton, one of Wooden's championship team players who moved on to a highly successful career as an NBA player and sports broadcaster, wrote this about Wooden in 2000:

> *At 89, John Wooden is happier, more positive, more upbeat than ever. . . .*
>
> *The joy and happiness in John Wooden's life comes today, as it always has, from the success of others. He regularly tells us that what he learned from his two favorite teachers, Abraham Lincoln and Mother Teresa, is that a life not lived for others is not a life. . . .*
>
> *[H]e still has the enthusiasm, energy, industriousness, initiative and love of life that allows him to get up every day, quite early I must add, even though the legs are now failing him, with the attitude of "we get to play basketball today. Lets [sic] go." . . .*
>
> *I thank John Wooden every day for all his selfless gifts, his lessons, his time, his vision and especially his patience.*
>
> *This is why we call him coach.*

Ability may get you to the top, but character keeps you there.
JOHN WOODEN

Giving Patients a Doctor They Can Trust

Every year, the Australian *Reader's Digest* conducts a survey to determine "The Most Trusted Person in Australia." For five years in a row, the honor has gone to Dr. Fiona Wood, the head of Royal Perth Hospital's Burns Unit. Dr. Wood was thrust into the international spotlight in 2002 when twenty-eight people were rushed to the Burns Unit in the aftermath of a terrorist bombing in Bali. She led a team that worked day and night to save the patients, who were suffering from whole-body burns, deadly infections, and life-threatening shock. Miraculously, all twenty-eight survived. Wood has said, "It's exciting to . . . see that at the end of the day we could actually influence the outcome in the scar. And scar to me isn't its appearance. It's how you move, how you function."

She has developed a technique of spraying skin cells cultured from the patient's own skin directly onto the burn, which reduces the culture time for new skin from weeks to just five days. She is dedicated to a future of "scarless wound healing." She also says, "I firmly believe that every day we go to work, we should be looking for opportunities to improve the outcome such that tomorrow's a better day. The day that you think, 'That's as good as it gets,' is retirement day." Imagine you were a burn victim. If you were making a choice, who would you trust to work on you?

Giving a Community a Leader It Can Trust

Geoffrey Canada grew up in the South Bronx, New York, in the 1950s and '60s, in the midst of poverty and violence. Raised by a single, divorced mother, he learned firsthand what it is like for a child to grow up "poor, segregated from other races, ethnic groups, and economic classes." With the help of a teenage friend, he learned how to fight with his fists, how to hide feelings of weakness, how to survive. When Canada reached his midteens, his mother sent him to Freeport, Long Island, to live with his grandparents. Swimming upstream against his background, he was able to get good grades and earn a college scholarship. He ended up with a BA in psychology and sociology from Bowdoin College in

Maine, a master's degree from the Harvard Graduate School of Education in Massachusetts—and a passionate desire to help other kids who came from poor, embattled neighborhoods.

In 1990, Canada became president and CEO of the Rheedlen Centers for Children and Families in New York City. Seven years later, he launched the HCZ (Harlem Children's Zone). He marked out twenty-four (now almost a hundred) city blocks in Harlem, one of the most impoverished areas in the United States, and began, a block at a time, a house at a time, a child at a time, to engage the community in a radical program to end the cycle of generational poverty. He told parents, "If your child comes to this school, we will guarantee that we will get your child into college. We will be with you with your child from the moment they enter our school till the moment they graduate from college."

Called by some "the Harlem Miracle," Canada's program has produced dramatic results in bringing a huge percentage of students up to grade level. Astonishing to many, it has virtually eliminated what has been called the "black-white achievement gap." In addition to academic services, HCZ provides social services, including debt relief counseling, domestic crisis resolution, and access to legal guidance, and health care, including special childhood obesity and asthma initiatives—nearly one in three children under the age of thirteen in Central Harlem has asthma. All services are offered to HCZ residents free of charge. According to *The New York Times Magazine:*

> Canada's new program combines educational, social and medical services. It starts at birth and follows children to college. It meshes those services into an interlocking web, and then it drops that web over an entire neighborhood. . . . The objective is to create a safety net woven so tightly that children in the neighborhood just can't slip through.

HCZ has received significant national media attention, including recognition by *The New York Times Magazine* as "one of the most ambitious social experiments of our time," and it serves as the model for an additional twenty-one "Promise Neighborhoods" now being planned across the United States, with the hope of more to come. Canada has been given a number of prestigious awards and several honorary degrees and was named as one of America's Best Leaders by *U.S. News & World Report* in 2005.

Geoffrey Canada's impressive track record of results, combined with his demonstrated intent to elevate others, makes him credible. He gives the Harlem community a leader it can trust. His charge to others is to do the same: "There are enough children who need our help that each one of us can find the right match, very likely close to home, and go to work to build trust and offer support in order to make a real difference in the life of a child."

> We do not believe in ourselves until someone reveals that deep inside us something is valuable, worth listening to, worthy of our trust, sacred to our touch. Once we believe in ourselves we can risk curiosity, wonder, spontaneous delight or any experience that reveals the human spirit.
>
> E. E. CUMMINGS
> POET, ESSAYIST, AUTHOR, AND PLAYWRIGHT

Giving Society a Business/Thought Leader They Can Trust

Harvard Business School's Bill George is the former chairman and CEO of Medtronic, a company that produces medical devices. In 2004, he was named one of the 25 Most Influential Business Persons of the Past 25 Years by PBS. He told a 2011 graduating class of MBAs that when he had received his MBA, he'd had two goals: first, to be a values-centered leader of an organization making significant contributions to society, and second, to have some modest influence on other business leaders as values-centered leaders. He also described a personal moment of creating self-trust:

My defining moment came in the fall of 1988, driving home around Lake of Isles [in Minneapolis, Minnesota] when I looked in the mirror and saw a very unhappy person. Outwardly, I was doing well: Penny and I had been married for nearly twenty years, our sons Jeff and Jon were thriving in school, and we had been part of the Twin Cities community since 1970. I was one of the leading candidates to become Honeywell's next CEO. But in that "flash in the mirror," I recognized I was striving so hard to become CEO by trying to impress others that I was losing sight of my True North—my inner moral compass—and failing to be that values-centered leader. I wasn't passionate about my work, and I was even less happy with myself. I drove home and told Penny, who concurred with my critical self-assessment. She recommended I reconsider the offer to join Medtronic as president I had recently turned down. Months later, when I walked through Medtronic's door for the first time, I felt like I was coming home—home to a place where I could be that values-centered leader, working with the remarkable people of Medtronic to make significant contributions by restoring millions of people to fuller life and health.

Not only did George and Medtronic make significant contributions to the health of millions through their work in medical devices and technology, the company also achieved extraordinary financial results. Under George's leadership, Medtronic's market capitalization grew from $1.1 billion to $60 billion, averaging a staggering 35 percent per year growth in market value.

Later, to reach his second goal, George retired from his successful career at Medtronic to teach leadership at Harvard Business School. He now also serves as a director on several boards, as well as of the Carnegie Endowment for International Peace and the World Economic Forum. He has written several best-selling and highly regarded business books, including *Authentic Leadership* and *True North*. As a prolific thought leader, George has also written numerous articles and blog posts teaching high-ground leadership principles.

George's trust-inspiring influence is further reflected in another remark he made to the freshly minted MBAs:

We have also learned that "rock star" CEOs selected for their charisma, style and image, *especially those from outside the organization, result in choosing the wrong leaders. Today's leaders are being selected for their* character, substance and integrity, *over 80 percent from inside the company. These new leaders are focusing on achieving high performance by being values-centered and customer-centric, rather than catering to short-term shareholders.*

Giving the World a Nonprofit Leader It Can Trust

Years ago the late Peter Drucker, the "Father of Modern Management," was asked to identify the person he thought was the greatest leader in the United States. His immediate reply was "Frances Hesselbein." At the time, Hesselbein was the CEO of the Girl Scouts of the USA. When the journalist who asked the question inquired if he might perhaps be referring to the greatest leader in the nonprofit world, Drucker replied, "Frances Hesselbein could manage any company in America."

Hesselbein accepted the role of CEO of the Girl Scouts at a time when the organization was still grappling with the impact of the social changes of the 1960s and early '70s. Despite the fact that the Girl Scouts was the largest organization for girls and women in the world, it was becoming irrelevant and fading into insignificance. Membership had been in decline for eight years in a row. But Hesselbein took on the challenge of making the organization relevant by leading a "total transformation of a great movement," revamping the curriculum, and redesigning the handbook so that any young girl who opened it, from "a Navajo girl on a reservation to a blue-eyed girl in a New England home with picket fences," could see herself in it. When she retired in 1990, the organization had the highest membership in history and had tripled its minority membership. Reflecting on her role as the leader of this transformation, Hesselbein told us, "They trusted me, and I trusted them. When trust is not just a word but is in every action, everything we do, we live by our values. Our people watch us. And when they know they can trust us, the possibilities have no limits."

Hesselbein went on to become the founding president of the Peter F. Drucker Foundation for Nonprofit Management (now the Leader to Leader Institute) and currently serves as its president and CEO. In 1996 she was awarded the Presidential Medal of Freedom, the United States' highest civilian honor, in recognition of her service as "a pioneer for women, volunteerism, diversity and opportunity." She has also been appointed to two presidential commissions, received numerous awards, coauthored two books on leadership, coedited twenty-seven books, and been awarded twenty honorary doctoral degrees.

Hesselbein's commitment to the importance of building trust and starting with self is evident not only in her life but also in her writing. She co-edited a book her Leader to Leader Institute put out that espoused the following:

> How can we . . . regain the trust and respect that American business enjoyed for years, as well as the freedom business had to essentially self-regulate? Current initiatives of whistle-blowing or CEOs issuing a few memos a year fall far short of the ethical revolution that is required to preserve the free enterprise system that has served us so well for so long. Responsibility for reform must start in the boardroom and the office of the CEO.

Her life and words also reflect her awareness of the prosperity, energy, and joy that come from high-trust relationships and organizations—not only in her enthusiasm and sparkle when she speaks of her own joy in her work, but also in her advice to leaders:

> Will it be the leader of a dispirited, demoralized workforce who leads the pack or will it be the new leader, building from vision, principle, and values, who builds trust and releases the energy and creativity of the workforce? . . .
>
> I challenge us to measure the performance of a team whose work is underscored by trust, civility, and good manners against a team where mistrust, disrespect, and lack of consideration are the rule of the day. No contest. Spirit, motivation, respect, and appreciation win every time. Dispirited, unmotivated, unappreciated workers cannot compete in a highly competitive world.

> *Few delights can equal the mere presence of one whom we trust utterly.*
>
> GEORGE MACDONALD

Giving Children a Parent They Can Trust

On May 7, 2010, the celebrity chef Emeril Lagasse led a television production crew into the lobby of the Saint Vincent Health Center in Erie, Pennsylvania, where he surprised a small Ethiopian cleaning lady named Almaz Gebremedhin with the announcement that out of thousands of nominees, she had been selected as *Good Morning America's* Woman of the Year and was to receive a Mother's Day breakfast in bed. Having been nominated by the nurses in the maternity ward where she worked, Gebremedhin was so shocked and shy that she could hardly look at Emeril or the camera.

As her story came out, viewers learned that Gebremedhin had spent her childhood as a refugee living in Sudan and by the age of fifteen was in an arranged marriage. She soon had five children, and when the family emigrated to Pennsylvania in 1993, her husband abandoned her. She was alone in a new country with the five children and a young nephew to care for. Determined that she would not live on welfare, Gebremedhin took three cleaning jobs and worked more than sixteen hours a day. But despite the continuing struggle to make ends meet, her children said of her:

> *"She taught us how to respect people."*
> *"She taught us how to work hard."*
> *"She taught us how to love unconditionally."*
> *"She taught us how to give."*
> *"She taught us never to quit and to follow your dream."*

As a result, all five of her children graduated at the top of their high school classes and all attended Penn State University on scholarships, and in 2005, she and her children all became citizens of the United States.

Like many people worldwide, through her sacrifice and devotion, Almaz Gebremedhin gave her children a parent they could trust.

"Start with Self" to Create Customer Trust

"Start with self" is the foundational action to create trust not only in ourselves as individuals but also in our organizations. This is clearly evident in building trust with customers. Consider Apple, one of the most innovative companies in the world. Starting in computers and software, Apple has reinvented itself time and again over the last decade to become extraordinarily relevant to consumers of all ages and to businesses and organizations everywhere. Today it is one of the top two most valuable companies in the world in terms of market capitalization and has been named the number one brand in the world by numerous evaluators of global brands.

After Apple was ranked the Most Admired Company in the World, *Fortune* magazine commented as follows:

> *What makes Apple so admired? Product, product, product. This is the company that changed the way we do everything from buy music to design products to engage with the world around us. Its track record for innovation and fierce consumer loyalty translates into tremendous respect across business' highest ranks.*

As BMW CEO Norbert Reithofer puts it:

> *The whole world held its breath before the iPad was announced. That's brand management at its very best.*

As well as producing high-quality, innovative products known for elegant design ("insanely great" is the term the company uses to describe its products), Apple provides superb real-time, hands-on consumer support through its "genius bars," where "geniuses" interact with customers, answer their questions, and help them with their problems—almost always without charge. In addition, the company provides in-store classes and training and typically overstaffs its stores to enable customers to get help quickly. And the layout of the stores encourages shoppers to sample the products. As a result, Apple enjoys the highest sales per square foot of any bricks-and-mortar retailer in the world by far. Apple stores average $4,323 per square foot annually, compared to a U.S. mall average of $386 per square foot. Though the company doesn't give out specific store figures, at least one analyst estimates that the Apple store on Fifth Avenue in New York City is doing $35,000 in sales per square foot each year.

The most significant benefit of all of Apple's innovations is tremendous customer trust. Whenever Apple has a release of a new product or an upgrade to an existing one, the release typically commands significant anticipation, as customers have learned that when Apple puts something out, they can trust that it's going to be, as Steve Jobs likes to say, "pretty cool." Jobs says, "One of the keys to Apple is that we build products that really turn us on."

Another standout is the Great Ormond Street Hospital for Children in London, England. Dr. Martin Elliott, the director of the Cardiorespiratory Unit, told us about his team's experience in reducing infant deaths following cardiac surgery. From studies, they had learned that the most critical time for patients was during the transfer from the surgical team to the critical care team. Elliott said:

> You have to disconnect the baby from a lot of kit and quickly transfer a lot of information about the baby from one tired team to a fresh new team. You can do the best operation you have ever done in your life and have the best intensive care team waiting to receive the baby, but you can completely screw up in the two-minute period when you move the baby from one place to another.

One night, as Elliott and his team sat in the break room next to the operating room, Formula One racing came on the television. When the Ferrari team came into a pit stop, Elliott noticed how the high-trust multispecialist crew worked effectively together to change the tires, fill the car with fuel, exchange information with the driver, and get the car off again in 6.8 seconds. He said:

> *What was happening in the pit stop seemed to us to be remarkably similar to what was happening at the hospital—but there was a big difference. When a patient would come back from the operating room to the Intensive Care Unit, we were all rushing around the bed, talking fast, and getting in each other's way. The Formula One pit crew, on the other hand, clearly worked as a high-trust team. They each knew their job, and they did it silently and got of the way, trusting the other members of the team to do their jobs.*

Elliott arranged to have his team flown to Maranello, Italy, to meet with the Ferrari team. As a result of implementing what they learned from that meeting, the flow of information and the speed with which children could be safely transferred between surgery and intensive care at Great Ormond Street Hospital improved dramatically. Errors during handoffs decreased by 42 percent, and information handover omissions were reduced by 49 percent. When we asked Elliott about his greatest lesson from the experience, he replied, "I think that trust is critical, I have to trust that other people will do their job well, and my public demonstration of that trust is to step back out of the way."

Costco also gives customers a company they can trust. Operating in nine countries, it's the ninth largest retailer in the world. According to CEO Jim Sinegal, the key to Costco's success over the years is the trust the company has created with members and the bonds it has developed with its workers. In Sinegal's words, "Our members trust us, so we're always looking for ways to exceed their expectations. As for our employees . . . I've always had the attitude that if you have good people and provide them with good wages and a career, then good things will happen in the business."

Sinegal is hard-line about providing low prices for Costco's 44 million members. According to one account in *The New York Times*:

> *Tim Rose, Costco's senior vice president for food merchandising, recalled a time when Starbucks did not pass along savings from a drop in coffee bean*

prices. Though he is a friend of the Starbucks chairman, Howard Schultz, Mr. Sinegal warned he would remove Starbucks coffee from his stores unless it cut its prices.

Starbucks relented.

"Howard said, 'Who do you think you are? The price police?'" Mr. Rose recalled, adding that Mr. Sinegal replied emphatically that he was.

Sinegal is also hard line about providing top wages and high benefits for his employees. In response to critics who have said it's better to be a customer or an employee of Costco than a shareholder, Sinegal has said, "On Wall Street, they're in the business of making money between now and next Thursday. I don't say that with any bitterness, but we can't take that view. We want to build a company that will still be here fifty and sixty years from now." (He might also smile quietly about the fact that Costco's stock price doubled over the five-year period between 2005 and 2010 and that the company has the lowest employee turnover in the retail industry.) Sinegal sets a personal example that inspires trust, wearing a name tag that simply says "Jim," answering his own phone, and listing his name alphabetically (and thus near the end) on the list of executive officers on the corporate website. He is one of the few CEOs cited by Warren Buffett as best of breed. When Buffett's partner Charlie Munger was asked about his favorite company outside Berkshire, he replied, "That's easy. It's Costco. It's one of the most admirable capitalistic institutions in the world. And its CEO, Jim Sinegal, is one of the most admirable retailers to ever live on this planet."

"Start with Self" to Create Employee Trust

As Costco and other organizations show, "Start with Self" is the foundational action of building trust with employees as well as customers. In defining employee trust, one Ritz-Carlton general manager put it this way:

It all starts with "Do I trust you? Do I trust you to create an environment and a workplace that made me feel that I belong and that I make a differ-

ence? Do I trust you to tell the truth and demonstrate a frank leadership style? Will you take the time to get to know me and go beyond preventing my disengagement but instead chase my strengths because the strengths of a team will offset our individual weaknesses?" We can make leadership so complicated, but really it comes down to whether we are earning the trust of our people or are simply asking for their compliance as a result of our ascribed authority.

Consider SAS, the world's largest privately held software business, whose systems are used in virtually every industry worldwide. CEO Jim Goodnight is fond of saying, "My chief assets drive out the gate every day. My job is to make sure they come back." In keeping with that priority, company leadership works to ensure the prosperity, energy, and joy of every employee in the company. The company has beautiful on-site exercise facilities as well as health care offices; child care facilities, parking, and food services are available on an equal basis to senior leaders and service workers. It places significant emphasis on free and open communication and on appreciation of employees' innovations and contributions.

As a result, employee turnover is significantly below the industry average (2 percent compared to the 22 percent industry average), the number of job applicants is extremely high (26,432 for 156 jobs filled in 2010), and SAS has been financially successful every year during the thirty-four years of its existence. During the global economic crisis, when technology companies everywhere were laying people off, Goodnight declared clearly to his people, "There will be no layoffs. . . . It's acceptable to me to take slightly less profit in order to keep our people." There has never been a layoff in the company's thirty-four-year history.

A number of companies have attempted to duplicate the remarkable culture at SAS without success. According to the 2010 Great Place to Work report:

> *The difference at SAS is that what is "spoken" with respect to people, quality and service is supported by behavior that reinforces every message. The words are not empty, they are full. And because the words are full employees trust their leaders. They have confidence in the long-term success of their organization and are able to focus on the quality of their work. They*

know they will be treated fairly, offered professional development and learning opportunities and will be supported in their personal lives. Employees know that they are critical to the success of SAS and they give their ideas, creativity, and thoughtful consideration to their work, their peers and the entire organization.

Employees also take pride in knowing they are contributing to sustainability and social well-being through their company's extensive social corporate responsibility efforts, including SAS's sustainability software.

Another outlier is the Mayo Clinic, a not-for-profit medical practice and research group that specializes in hard-to-treat diseases. Established in 1889, the Mayo Clinic has a distinctive high-trust culture rooted in the enduring hallmarks of its founders, including being patient-centered, collaborative, informed and improved by research and medical education, and committed to professional growth by making the best use of the latest advances for the improvement of public health.

This culture is the key to engaging the hearts and minds of all employees. The Mayo Clinic philosophy is that it takes a team to care for a patient and that every job counts. When Berkshire Hathaway's Charlie Munger delivered the 2007 Law School commencement address at the University of Southern California, he closed his remarks with the following: "The highest form a civilization can reach is correctly trusting one another. That's the way an operating room works at the Mayo Clinic."

This kind of employee trust has placed Mayo on *Fortune's* list of 100 Best Companies to Work For eight years in a row. In 2010 Mayo was ranked as the number two hospital overall in the United States for the twenty-second consecutive year. It was also ranked number three in non-profit brands in the Harris Interactive EquiTrend study measuring trust in over a thousand brands across forty-two categories. As well as inspiring employee trust, this kind of credibility plays a huge role when donors decide to whom they will make out their checks.*

---

*For a complimentary Trust Index to help you measure the current level of trust in your organization, go to SmartTrustBook.com.

> *If you have a workforce that enjoys each other, they trust each other, they trust management, they're proud of where they work—then they're going to deliver a good product. You can lecture and train, but unless they really believe in who they work for and are proud of who they work for, and trust each other and trust management, you won't get that.*
>
> JEFF SMISEK
> CEO, UNITED AIRLINES

"Start with Self" to Create Investor Trust

Laura Rittenhouse, the founder of the New York–based investor relations firm Rittenhouse Rankings, told us that companies with CEOs who talk straight to their investors earn greater investor trust and deliver better results. The firm's research shows a direct bottom-line difference between companies whose annual CEO letters to shareholders clearly spell out the company's goals and objectives as well as their track record of performance and addressing problems—and those that don't. Rittenhouse suggests, "If the letter is full of jargon, generalities and gobbledygook, then it could be time to look for another investment. If you, as a reader, can't understand what the CEO is talking about, you have to wonder if the employees can. Do a fog check. If the fog is so thick you have to listen for the foghorn, it's probably time to move on." In Rittenhouse's CEO Candor Surveys for nine of the past ten years, top-ranked companies, whose letters scored highest on trust-building qualities such as candor and accountability, have outperformed bottom-ranked companies by 18 percent on average in investor returns. In 2010, the top-quartile companies outperformed the bottom-quartile companies by 31 percent.

"Start with Self" Works with Countries, Too

Some might not think of the importance of a country providing to its citizens and to the world a country they can trust, but this has enormous impact, not only on the economic and political decisions made by other countries, companies, and tourists with respect to that nation but also on the prosperity, energy, and joy of the citizens of the nation itself.

Consider Denmark. To say that the Danes believe in trust is an understatement. Trust literally defines how they view the world. According to the 2011 Corruption Perceptions Index, Denmark ties with New Zealand and Singapore for recognition as the nation with the least corruption in the world, and it has consistently ranked in the top ten every year since the inception of the Index. The trustworthiness reflected by these and other rankings enables the Danish people to comfortably extend trust to one another and to all society. According to a 2008 OECD survey, 88.8 percent of Danes, the highest percentage of all nations in the world, express a high level of trust in others.

What's particularly remarkable about the Kingdom of Denmark is how abundantly the outcomes of prosperity, energy, and joy manifest themselves in the society. Despite a population of only 5.5 million, Denmark is among the most productive nations in the world, ranking near the top globally on the World Competitiveness Scoreboard put out each year by IMD (based in Switzerland, one of the top business schools in the world). The country also has an extremely high GDP, the fifth highest in the world, and was ranked number two on the 2010 Legatum Prosperity Index. In terms of energy, Denmark comes in near the top on most measures of health and engagement. IMD ranked the country number one in the world on the criteria statement, "Worker motivation is very high." Joy is where Denmark really stands out. The country was recognized as the happiest nation on Earth in the Gallup World Poll and at or near the top in numerous other studies and indices.

There are many reasons trust is so high in Denmark: historical, cultural, demographic, political, environmental, and behavioral. In any event, by both being trustworthy and extending trust, Denmark gives its citizens and the world a nation they can trust.

The Constant Opportunity/The Constant Challenge

Maintaining credibility and giving people a person, a leader, or a company they can trust is a constant challenge in today's world. Some who achieve it in one situation fail to do so in another. Others who achieve it through exemplary behavior at one point find that they lose it through misbehavior at another.

When seven people died from taking Tylenol that had been laced with cyanide in 1982, Johnson & Johnson became the textbook example of trustworthy crisis management. The company took full responsibility—among other things, immediately alerting customers, recalling more than $100 million worth of Tylenol, offering to exchange additional millions of dollars' worth of capsules that had already been purchased for tablets, and developing a tamper-proof seal for all Tylenol products. But in 2008, when the company discovered a possible potency problem in some improperly dissolving Motrin tablets made by its McNeil division, the company responded entirely differently. In the words of one *USA Today* editorial, "executives forgot to read their own textbook." Instead of making a public announcement and issuing a recall, the company leadership tried to hide the problem by hiring a contractor to instruct workers to act like regular customers and quietly buy up the defective product. When a more serious problem developed leading to the recall of 130 million bottles of children's and infant's liquid medicines in 2010, an investigation uncovered the Motrin problem as well. In his testimony to the House Committee on Oversight and Government Reform, Johnson & Johnson CEO William Weldon said:

> *I know that we let the public down. We did not maintain our high quality standards, and as a result, children do not have access to our important medicines. . . . [W]e recognize now, that we need to do better, and we will work hard to restore the public's trust and faith in Johnson & Johnson, and strive to ensure that something like this never happens again.*

Another example is Toyota. With its strong history of quality and dependability, Toyota was ranked number one in the Harris Interactive

EquiTrend study of automotive manufacturers in 2010. However, the study was taken just prior to Toyota's recall of 2.3 million cars and trucks because of a problem with an accelerator pedal that was sticking and causing the vehicles to unintentionally speed up. The recall followed closely on the heels of a recall of 4.2 million vehicles for the same problem.

In a press release dated February 24, 2010, Harris Interactive noted, "One company to carefully monitor is Toyota, which is in the midst of dealing with unprecedented product safety and consumer trust related issues. Given that EquiTrend® was conducted just prior to Toyota's major recall, the study provides a valuable baseline upon which to monitor change in equity."

The following month, it said, "We will be closely monitoring levels of consumer trust in automotive brands, especially as it relates to perceptions of personal safety and product quality. The recent crisis highlights just how quickly a foundation of trust can be shattered."

In January 2011, speaking at the World Economic Forum in Davos, Switzerland, Toyota CEO Akio Toyoda, a grandson of the company's founder, took responsibility and apologized to customers for causing them worry. "I am deeply sorry," he said. "Truly we think of our customers as a priority and we guarantee their safety. I would like for the people to trust us."

Restoring trust is usually far more difficult than establishing trust in the first place. But what both Toyota and Johnson & Johnson have going for them is years—even decades—of behaving in ways that have built trust and delivered results. Because of this, both companies have built up sizable "trust accounts" with consumers, partners, and the public, and those trust accounts put them into a position to behave themselves out of the problems they have behaved themselves into.

That is the operating principle behind restoring trust: *You can't talk yourself out of a problem you behaved yourself into. The only way out is to behave your way out.*

One person who did so in a remarkable way was Frank Abagnale, Jr. Following his parents' divorce when he was sixteen years old, Abagnale ran away from home and became one of the most notorious con artists in history. Before his arrest at age twenty-one, he successfully impersonated an airline pilot and was estimated by Pan American World Airways to have flown more than a million miles on more than 250 flights to twenty-six countries by "deadheading" (faking employee status to fly free). For nearly a year he impersonated a doctor, temporarily replacing the chief resident pediatrician in a Georgia hospital until a permanent replacement could be found. At age nineteen he forged a Harvard University law transcript, passed the state bar, and worked in the office of the state attorney general of Louisiana. And during his five-year crime spree, he passed approximately $2.5 million in forged checks around the world.

However, following his capture and arrest in 1969 and prison terms in France, Sweden, and the United States, Abagnale turned his life around and, amazingly, was able to restore trust. Accepting the conditions of his early release, which were to help federal authorities with crimes committed by con artists and report in once a week, he approached banks to hire him as a security consultant. Though skeptical at first, they were ultimately persuaded by his competence in detecting scams and by his repeated trustworthy actions to reassess his credibility. That enabled them to gain confidence in him and in the company he later founded, Abagnale & Associates, which advises businesses on fraud prevention. Today Abagnale is a trusted security adviser, a consultant and lecturer for the FBI, a devoted husband and father of three, and a legitimate millionaire. His exploits were the subject of his book *Catch Me If You Can*, as well as the 2002 movie and 2011 Broadway play by the same name. In writing of his past, he said:

> *We all grow up. Hopefully we get wiser. Age brings wisdom and fatherhood changes one's life completely. I consider my past immoral, unethical and illegal. It is something I am not proud of. I am proud that I have been able to turn my life around and in the past 25 years, helped my government, my clients, thousands of corporations and consumers deal with the problems of white collar crime and fraud.*

One company that started with self to restore trust is Nike, the world's leading supplier of athletic shoes and apparel and a major manufacturer of sports equipment. In the 1990s Nike was roundly criticized for not being sufficiently socially responsible because conditions in some of its partners' foreign manufacturing plants were substandard. Initially defensive, the company finally decided to take on the issue head-on. Chairman Phil Knight apologized for the initial defensiveness, calling it "a bumpy original response, an error for which yours truly was responsible." But going beyond mere words, Nike translated its response into actions and behaviors. The company enacted higher standards, insisted on compliance, and increased transparency. Those behaviors not only improved Nike, they elevated the entire industry. Today Nike is a widely recognized leader in corporate social responsibility, having been ranked number ten on *Corporate Responsibility Magazine*'s 2011 list of 100 Best Corporate Citizens. Through its behavior, Nike restored trust to a level higher than it had ever been.

In some situations, the opportunity to restore trust may never come. That ship may have sailed. But in the majority of cases, restoring trust is possible. It isn't easy, and it can't be done through words alone. Though words are helpful in signifying intent, restoration of trust ultimately requires consistent trust-building behavior over time.

Moments of Trust

Almost daily, most of us have what we could call "moments of trust," single instances in which our behavior enables us to build, extend, or restore trust or to diminish it. How we respond in those key moments, large or small, often has a disproportionate impact, sometimes beyond our wildest imagination.

One remarkable moment of trust occurred for Mark Zuckerberg right after his social networking service, Facebook (then called Thefacebook), was launched in 2004. Zuckerberg had entered into a verbal agreement for critically needed funding with Donald Graham, the chairman and CEO of the Washington Post Company. Just a few weeks later, the Accel Partners venture capital firm bettered the offer by $4 million. At a dinner with one of Accel's co–managing partners, who was trying to close the deal, Zuckerberg appeared to tune out of the conversation. He left to go to the bathroom and didn't come back. In *The Facebook Effect*, David Kirkpatrick wrote:

> *Cohler [one of the first executives hired by Zuckerberg] got up to see if everything was okay. There, on the floor of the men's room with his head down, was Zuckerberg. And he was crying. "Through his tears he was saying, 'This is wrong. I can't do this. I gave my word!'" recollects Cohler. . . . "So I said, 'Why don't you just call Don up and ask him what he thinks?'" Zuckerberg took a while to compose himself and returned to the table.*
>
> *The next morning he did call Graham. "Don, I haven't talked to you since we agreed on terms, and since then I've had a much higher offer from a venture capital firm out here. And I feel I have a moral dilemma," Zuckerberg began.*
>
> *Graham had already talked to Breyer, so he was disappointed but not surprised. But he was also impressed. "I just thought to myself, 'Wow, for twenty years old that is impressive—he's not calling to tell me he's taking the other guy's money. He's calling me to talk it out.'" Graham knew that even his first offer was very high for a company so tiny and so young. . . .*
>
> *"Mark, does the money matter to you?" Graham asked. Zuckerberg said that it did. It could, he went on, be the one thing that could prevent Thefacebook from going into the red or having to borrow money. . . .*
>
> *"Mark, I'll release you from your moral dilemma," said Graham after a twenty-minute conversation. "Go ahead and take their money and develop the company, and all the best." For Zuckerberg it was a huge relief. And it further increased his respect and admiration for Graham.*

Obviously, Zuckerberg has many years still ahead of him, but what has happened following that "moment of trust" has been nothing short of astounding. Today Facebook has more than 800 million active users worldwide and is literally redefining our world in ways both small and great, from enabling youths to share everyday thoughts with friends to fueling massive social movements, such as the 2011 democracy uprising in Egypt. In 2010 Zuckerberg was named *Time* magazine's Person of the Year, and today the company is valued at more than $80 billion and continues to rise.

However, as Zuckerberg's example and the examples of companies such as Johnson & Johnson and Toyota clearly show, maintaining character, competence, and credibility is an ongoing challenge—but it is one to which we can and must rise. Our credibility is critical to people's willingness to place their trust in us and in our organizations. And our capacity to assess credibility in others is critical to our exercising informed judgment in extending Smart Trust.

It's our hope that our sharing many of the remarkable positive examples that exist in today's world—both in creating trust and in restoring trust—will help increase trust in the world of tomorrow. Whatever other insights can be gleaned from the people and companies whose stories are included in this chapter, it's clear that the place to start is with self—to be able to look into the mirror, trust what we see, and give others a person, a leader, an organization, or a country they can trust.

QUESTIONS TO CONSIDER

- To what extent are you giving people (including yourself) a person, a parent, a company, a charity, or a government they can trust?
- What steps could you take to improve your character or competence (or the character and competence of your team or organization) and increase the likelihood that people will extend trust to you?

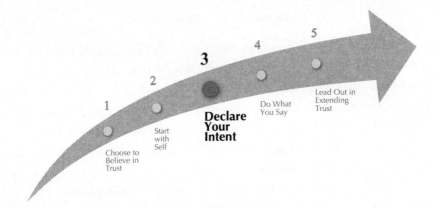

CHAPTER SIX

Smart Trust Action 3: Declare Your Intent . . . and Assume Positive Intent in Others

What is the quality of your intent?
THURGOOD MARSHALL
Former U.S. Supreme Court justice

Stephen:

Recently I had the exhilarating experience of being driven down the streets of Bangalore, India. Though I never saw an accident, I witnessed hundreds of breathtaking near misses. There were no clear lane markers; drivers simply jerked into and out of traffic, anticipating openings and gunning it. I was never quite sure if someone was going to suddenly zip into the lane in front of us, so it seemed best to assume that they probably would.

Given the norm, the expertise of the local drivers was amazing, and I suppose that if they had been too cautious they would have been a hazard to everyone else. But to outsiders like me, the situation appeared totally chaotic. I did notice after a while that most drivers would at least honk their horns as they were zipping in and out, but that gave me little comfort. Most of the time I just closed my eyes, tightened my seat belt, and hoped I was not going to die.

In a saner moment, I compared that experience to driving in Switzerland, where the roads and lanes are precisely marked and the rules are very clear. Among other things, Swiss drivers tend to turn on their blinkers in an orderly manner before changing lanes. The reason they signal is not for themselves; they already know what they're going to do. They signal to communicate their intent so that other drivers can anticipate the move, be prepared for it, and adapt accordingly.

The more I compared the two experiences, the more I realized that drivers in both places were communicating their intent—through either honking or signaling. The intent was just clearer and more understandable to me in Switzerland than it was in Bangalore.

In a very real sense, "declaring your intent" is signaling your behavior to others. It's like turning on your blinker or honking. It's telling people what you intend to do—and, done most effectively, it's also telling them *why* you intend to do it.

There are two parts to this action. The first (declare your intent) is based on the *principles* of purpose and intention. The *opposite* is to fail to declare intent or to simply assume your intent is clear. *Counterfeits* include hiding or disguising your intent, operating with hidden agendas, "spinning" or misleading, pretending, creating illusion, and overpromising,

The second part (assume positive intent in others) is based on the *principles* of trust and positive expectation. The *opposite* is to assume negative intent. *Counterfeits* include giving lip service to positive intent while secretly harboring suspicion or ill will and appearing to trust people to their faces while sneaking behind their backs to check up on them.

We consistently find the twin behaviors of *declaring intent* and *assuming positive intent* to be two of the most neglected yet highest leveraged actions leaders and organizations can take to create Smart Trust. Yet these actions are not a shortcut to trust; they are extraordinary *accelerators* of trust. Let's take a look at why.

The Two Halves of Declaring Intent: *What* and *Why*

There are two parts to effectively declaring intent: stating *what* we want to do and stating *why* we want to do it. Both halves are vital. Most managers are fairly good at declaring the *what* (e.g., "Here's our action plan to cut costs") but very poor at declaring the *why* ("Here's our motive and the intent behind our thinking"). Sharing the why behind the what makes a profound difference in how others interpret our communication up front, as well as how they interpret our subsequent behavior.

The reality is that we tend to judge ourselves by our intent and others by their observable behavior. Therefore, when people distrust us, it's most often because of the conclusions they draw about what they see us do. By declaring our intent—both the what and the why—we can actively influence the conclusions others draw and therefore increase the probability that we'll be able to gain and keep their trust.

Declaring intent smartly in negotiations is a powerful game changer. The leaders of one company we worked with told us of an experience they'd had when they were about to enter into significant contract negotiations with a major partner. They had been through the process before, and the previous negotiations had been basically transactional—the typical tit-for-tat, "you give some and I'll give some" mating dance ritual. They usually ended up with an agreement, but at various times along the way, both parties wondered if they getting the short end of the negotiating stick.

In this case, the leaders of our client company had just immersed themselves in Smart Trust training and decided to test it. Right up front, they declared to their partner their intent to negotiate in a different manner. Rather than playing the traditional game of withholding information and guessing what would be the highest acceptable compromise, they deliberately led off with a full disclosure of their objectives and an offer of their best deal. They shared what mattered most to them, why it mattered, and even what didn't matter. They told their partner they didn't want to do a deal unless it was a major win for both parties, and rather than starting high and ending up in the middle, they would present their best deal up front—a deal that they would be excited to do. Their partner then had a choice: they could see this disclosure as weakness and try to use the information to their advantage in negotiating a better deal for themselves, or they could reciprocate the trust, declaring its own intent of what mattered to it, what didn't, and why. The partner chose the latter option, and the result was that both companies ended up with what they saw as their best deal ever, much faster, and with a higher trust relationship to boot. Those outcomes emerged from the fact that both parties declared their intent, opened their agendas, and acted with transparency.

Yes, there's some risk to this kind of approach, but there's also the possibility of a much higher return. What wouldn't work in a situation like this would be to go into the negotiating strategy without first signaling your intent—i.e., to be transparent on every deal point unilaterally without first having declared your intent to negotiate in a completely different manner.

How Declaring Intent Can Build Trust

Several years ago, Doug Whittaker, the administrator of Charlotte County Public Schools in Florida, shared the following experience with us.

> *Our school district had made a commitment to change how we did business with our unions, but before we could actually get into the bargaining for the coming year, hurricane Charley hit. We knew that we were facing a major catastrophe. Eight of our twenty-one facilities were unusable. We had children out of school, teachers out of work, and people whose homes were destroyed.*

Our superintendent, Dr. Dave Gaylor, called a meeting. In addition to the district administrator, he invited others, including the two union presidents, which was a bold step. He announced that our top priority was to make sure that everybody got paid as soon as possible, even though they wouldn't be working. He also made a commitment that regardless of what happened, we were not going to reduce force. Following the meeting, Dr. Gaylor went on the television and radio channels that were working and announced that we would be paying our employees on Tuesday. Teams of union and administrative representatives went out together and made sure those paychecks got delivered.

As damage assessments came in, we realized that we were probably going to have a permanent loss of six of our schools and that two would be re-pairable. We waived parts of the union contract, set up a memorandum of understanding to address the critical changes that had to be made, and set up a plan to go on double sessions immediately. Within two weeks of the hurricane, children were back in school, and teachers and administrators were back at work. Within three months, we were able to bring in relocat-able buildings, rebuild temporary campuses, and back off the double sessions.

As a result of all these things, the school district built incredible trust with our employees. We also built trust with the community as people came to see the school system as a focal point of recovery. And when it came time for financial negotiations with the union, our finance officer put the figures up on the screen and said, "Here's what we have available, and here's how that might look over a three-year implementation." From that point, the negotiation, which would normally have taken months, took only two hours. There was no caucusing. There were no threats. There was no question that the data on the screen was correct. The discussion was simply around minor adjustments to make it work.

I think we had all anticipated that building trust with our employees and the unions was going to be a very slow process over a long period of time. But when the hurricane hit, the pretense was gone. It was no longer "I'm an administrator and you're a teacher," it was "I'm Joe, who owns the house that just got destroyed" and "You're Sam, who owns the house where the roof caved in." We all came together. We said, "We do have a mutual interest here. This is our employment. This is our contribution to our community. We have kids to think about. We have parents to think about. We've got to put the old stuff aside." And it was amazing; both sides really did.

As Whitaker shared his experience, it became apparent to everyone that one of the primary reasons for the school administrators' success—both in the short run and in future negotiations with the unions—was Dr. Gaylor's clear declaration of intent. Right up front, Dr. Gaylor declared that the top priority was to make sure all the teachers were paid, that no one would be fired, and that paychecks would not be reduced. Not only did he make the declaration at the meeting, he also went on television and radio to declare the intent directly to the teachers and the public in general. This declaration immediately reduced stress and gave people hope in a very challenging situation. It also communicated that people cared. The administrators' immediate follow-through then validated the fact that the people making the promises were worthy of trust and created the high-trust relationship that led to the incredible speed in negotiating the contract.

I, for one, begin with intent.

TOMMY FRANK
GENERAL, U.S. ARMY

The experience of the Charlotte County school district administrators clearly shows how declaring intent builds trust. Another illustration is the way in which the Illinois State Toll Highway Authority completed a $729 million systemwide conversion to open road tolling (ORT), a feat that had never before been attempted on such a large scale. Based on industry standards, a project of this magnitude would typically take up to ten years to complete. At the very outset, however, department leaders said, "We want to do this differently. We want to collaborate. We want to build a relationship of trust and partnership, and we want to have a different type of exchange among the multiple players involved." They forged collaborative partnerships with designers, engineers, contractors, and tollway staff to expedite and streamline the concept, design, bidding, and construction. By doing so, they were able to manage twenty projects simultaneously, coordinating the development of new building concepts, infrastructure, plaza geometry, signing and review processes, and contract management. With trusted collaboration as their operating paradigm from the outset, they were able to move much faster than under normal conditions, and the project was completed in an unprecedented twenty-two months, much to the joy of the 1.3 million commuters who now enjoy a nonstop travel corridor from Wisconsin to Indiana.

A Performance Multiplier

Declaring intent multiplies performance in a number of ways. It creates context. It inspires hope. It's authentic and transparent, which connects us with people not only intellectually but also emotionally. It gives us the confidence that we are acting intentionally and with purpose. It encourages reciprocity. It facilitates and accelerates the achievement of our goals. It shows respect for others and involves them in the process. It typically causes people to listen to us more fully and with greater empathy.

When we do not declare our intent, we leave others to guess or to wonder, "Where is she going with this?" "What is he up to?" This fear of the unknown at worst causes confrontation and at best impairs the ability of others to listen openly to what is being said.

> People need to find their own language for describing the intent of their efforts in ways that work in their own context, as part of developing their own strategies and leadership practices. How we talk about our work matters.
>
> PETER SENGE
> THE FIFTH DISCIPLINE

The reality is that when people trust someone else's motive or agenda (or at least understand it), they respond differently than when they don't.

So how can we inspire trust in our motive or agenda? By declaring it. By being transparent about it. By letting people know that our agenda is open—not hidden.

DILBERT © 1999 Scott Adams. Used by permission of UNIVERSAL UCLICK. All rights reserved.

Former U.S. president John F. Kennedy is remembered for declaring his intent on May 25, 1961, when he said, "I believe this nation should commit itself . . . to achieving the goal, before this decade is out, of landing a man on the moon and returning him safely to the Earth." That was the *what.* He later declared the *why:* "We choose to go to the moon in this decade . . . not because [it is] easy, but because [it is] hard, because that goal will serve to organize and measure the best of our energies and skills, because that challenge is one that we are willing to accept, one we are unwilling to postpone, and one which we intend to win."

To many, Kennedy's intent seemed bizarre and unachievable, but just short of a decade later Neil Armstrong and Buzz Aldrin stepped out of their spacecraft and onto the surface of the moon, almost a quarter-million miles above the earth. According to the National Aeronautics and Space Administration, "NASA's overall human spaceflight efforts were guided by Kennedy's speech."

On the lighter side, the legendary baseball player Babe Ruth is remembered for declaring his intent by making a pointing gesture with his bat toward the center-field bleachers when he was up to bat during the fifth inning of game three of the 1932 World Series. To the delight of media and fans, on the next pitch he hit a home run to deep center field, sending the ball flying almost five hundred feet to land in the temporary seating in the streets.

Muriel Summers was the principal of the lowest-performing school in the Wake County Public School System of North Carolina in 1999. She recently told us about the impact of declaring her intent when she faced the challenge of saving the school's magnet* status by coming up with a new learning model different from that of any other school in the nation and using no additional budget or staff—in only one week. The challenge was particularly difficult because A. B. Combs Elementary included students from fifty-eight countries who spoke twenty-seven different languages, only 67 percent of whom were performing at or above grade level and 45 percent of whom were receiving federal aid for school lunches.

After researching the issue, Summers declared her intent to make A. B. Combs the first elementary *leadership* school in the nation. The school's declared mission became "to develop leaders, one child at a time." Due to the efforts of Summers and her staff to fulfill that intent, the school soon became the top-performing school in the district and was recognized by the Magnet Schools of America as the top magnet school in the nation in 2006, with 97 percent of students performing at or above grade level and students astonishing adults with their ability to articulate and implement powerful leadership principles, both at school and at home. Today, the A. B. Combs mission has been enlarged: "to develop *global* leaders, one child at a time."

In 2010, Warren Buffett and Bill and Melinda Gates joined forces in asking hundreds of billionaires to declare their intent to give away at least half of their wealth to charity in their lifetimes or at death. As of the one-year anniversary of their "Giving Pledge," sixty-nine had signed, the youngest being Facebook cofounders Dustin Moskovitz and Mark Zuckerberg. While CNN founder Ted Turner similarly contributed and challenged others to do the same over a decade ago, what Buffett and

---

*A magnet school is one that offers special curriculum designed to draw students from across the normal geographical boundaries defined by authorities.

the Gateses have done differently is to elevate the challenge to a formal declaration of intent, which is creating a greater, farther-reaching impact. In asking his fellow billionaires to sign the Giving Pledge, Buffett said:

> *I think it is fitting that I reiterate my intentions and explain the thinking that lies behind them.*
>
> *First, my pledge. More than 99% of my wealth will go to philanthropy during my lifetime or at death. . . .*
>
> *The reaction of my family and me to our extraordinary good fortune is not guilt, but rather gratitude. Were we to use more than 1% of my claim checks on ourselves, neither our happiness nor our well-being would be enhanced. In contrast, that remaining 99% can have a huge effect on the health and welfare of others. That reality sets an obvious course for me and my family: Keep all we can conceivably need and distribute the rest to society, for its needs. My pledge starts us down that course.*

Declarations of intent such as these engage people and enable them to make more informed decisions concerning the people and organizations they choose to trust with their time, money, and energy.

Declaring Intent: An Accelerator of Trust

In addition to creating hope and helping us achieve our goals, declaring intent also multiplies our performance by enabling us to increase trust faster. The leadership of one consumer products manufacturing company we worked with decided to build trust in its culture by declaring its intent to open its books, making all its financial information available to everyone in the company and asking for their help in improving the business. Because it was a private company, that was not something the leaders were required to do, but they believed that being transparent would build trust, increase engagement, improve performance, and create a more rewarding work experience for everyone.

At first people wondered what the leaders were up to. They questioned the accuracy of the financials. They projected possible motives. But the leaders stuck with it. They were open, honest, and transparent and kept reiterating their intent, telling people what they were doing and why. Within a few months, people realized that the numbers were real. There was no hidden agenda. The leaders sincerely wanted to involve people in the business, to engage them as stakeholders, and to get their ideas for improvement. Though opening the books might not be an appropriate trust-building approach for some organizations, the leaders of this company reported that this single practice of openness and transparency had built trust better and faster than anything else they had ever done.

> *We've learned that the best way of building trust is by letting people see for themselves what we're doing.*
>
> JOHN LECHLEITER
> CHAIRMAN AND CEO, ELI LILLY

When We Don't Declare Intent

When people work interdependently, most want to be aware of the intentions and motives of the others involved. The best way to address this issue is simply to declare intent. Doing so increases awareness and diminishes suspicion.

When we don't tell people what we're going to do, they're often not aware of it or looking for it. Therefore they may not recognize its fulfillment as a trust-building promise kept or as evidence that we (or our team or our organization) behave in a manner they can count on. In addition, they're missing an important piece of information they need to assess credibility and make informed decisions. Though it's clearly better not to declare intent and deliver anyway than to declare intent and not deliver, our failure to declare intent may cause us to come across as someone who stands for nothing—someone with no promise, no purpose, no hope to offer, no brand, or no value. And in today's crowded marketplace that decreases trust.

Also, when we don't declare intent, people typically respond in one of two ways: either they *guess* our intent, or they *project* their own intent on our behavior. In that way, they attempt to fill in the missing piece. Unfortunately, in a low-trust organization, people typically guess worst case rather than best case. In a low-trust relationship, they project fears, suspicions, and worries more often than hopes, dreams, and wishes. People are guessing and projecting daily in every dimension of life—in families, personal relationships, companies, teams, and governments. As a result, they make judgments and decisions based on inaccurate information— and more often than not, it damages trust.

> *The moment there is suspicion about a person's motives, everything he does becomes tainted.*
>
> MAHATMA GANDHI

A few years ago, a translator for CNN mistranslated one important word in a speech given by President Mahmoud Ahmadinejad of Iran. Instead of developing "nuclear *technology*," President Ahmadinejad was reported to have talked about developing "nuclear *weapons*." In the already highly charged political environment surrounding Iran's nuclear interests, CNN was immediately thrown out of Iran. Hossein Shariatmadari, the chief editor of the *Kayhan* newspaper, said, "*The distortion was deliberate* with the aim of preventing the impact of the president's comments on the public opinion." Following a public apology, CNN was allowed back into Iran, but it was interesting how, in the low-trust environment and in the absence of a declaration of intent, malicious intent was instantly ascribed to the incident.

Mistakenly ascribing neglectful intent sparked an international debate in May 1997 when a Danish woman was arrested for leaving her fourteen-month-old daughter in a stroller just outside the window of an East Village restaurant in New York while she had a drink. Responding to a call from a customer, the police had entered the restaurant, handcuffed, jailed, and filed criminal charges against the woman and put the child into protective foster care. After four days, she was allowed to be with her daughter, but only on a supervised basis, until several days later, when a Criminal Court judge told her the charges would be dropped if she "remained out of trouble for six months." Both the woman and many people from Denmark were incensed. As it turned out, parents leaving children outside while they ate or shopped is not uncommon in high-trust Denmark, as they believe that *frisk luft*, or fresh air, is one of the most important things they could give a child. The woman argued that she could easily see the stroller out the window at all times and felt she was taking good care of her daughter.

What was the intent of the police? To protect the child against abuse. What was the intent of the customer who called the police? To ensure the safety of the little girl. What was the intent of the woman? To avoid having to take her baby into a stuffy, crowded restaurant—as was the custom of many good parents in Denmark at the time. All were well intended, but because they did not understand each other's intent, they inaccurately ascribed malintent.

When we don't declare intent, we risk not just the *possibility* but more likely the *probability* that our motives will be misunderstood. When we do declare intent, we eliminate the need for ascribing motive by guessing or projecting. We don't leave people to wonder because they hear it straight from us. If the relationship is low trust, they may not believe us at first. They may say things such as "What are they up to now?" or "What's their agenda here?" or "What are they *really* trying to do?" But the best leaders stay at it, making sincere efforts to authentically, transparently, and clearly communicate so that no one is left in doubt. They create open agendas, not hidden agendas, because there's nothing to hide. As well as being transparent, they openly declare transparency. They signal transparent behavior.

> I'm out talking about this company seven days a week, 24 hours a day, with nothing to hide. We're a 130-year-old company that has a great record of high-quality leadership and a culture of integrity.
>
> JEFFREY IMMELT
> CHAIRMAN AND CEO, GE

Like a child's fear of the "monsters under the bed" that disappears when the light is turned on, people's fear of what you may be trying to do and why dissipates when you transparently declare your intent and shine a light on your agenda and motive.

Motive Matters

There are three people in my department that I don't trust, and I've thought and thought about why. They pretty much meet deadlines, do what they say they are going to do, and are very competent as teachers and program coordinators. However, I don't trust them because without fail they will always take care of themselves before someone else, and even at someone else's expense. Their motives are very clear. They want what is best for them, and hopefully that will not interfere with what is best for others. They never sacrifice for something else, even if it would benefit someone or something more than themselves. Their motives are selfish. It is hard for me to trust that they will represent my program accurately, want the great things that I want for my team, or do me any favors. I don't trust they have anyone's best interest in mind but their own.

PAM MCGEE
PROFESSOR AND CONSULTANT

Declaring intent builds trust fastest, of course, if the intent is based on caring and mutual benefit. If you really don't care or if you have self-serving interests or hidden agendas that would embarrass you if they were made known ("My intent is to win everything, and I really don't care if you win or lose"), you're generally better off *not* declaring your intent until you refine it. It's certainly okay for you to win. No one begrudges that. They just don't want you to win at their expense. They also want to know that you sincerely care about them as individuals or as clients or as

a team—about their interests and their objectives. No motive will build
trust as quickly and deeply as the motive of caring. As an illustration,
nurses are typically ranked even higher than doctors in terms of trust in
the medical profession. Both are seen as competent, but nurses are generally seen as having more caring intent. In addition, firefighting has been
ranked as the most trusted profession in the world for several years in a
row. No one questions the caring intent or motive of firefighters, who put
their lives on the line to help others for very little pay.

A caring motive is a powerful performance multiplier. One great illustration is the experience of Erik Weihenmayer, the only blind person to
ever reach the top of Mount Everest. His ascent in May 2001 was considered perhaps the most successful ascent ever, as nineteen climbers made
it to the top, the most from one team ever to reach the top in a single
day. Erik later told us, "Being roped together when crossing an ice field
riddled with crevasses is the ultimate trust scenario. In the mountains,
my life is often in my teammates' hands and theirs in mine."

Michael Brown, the filmmaker who documented the event, said:

> *What I find to be really intriguing about that milestone is that everybody
> on the team put aside their own self-serving need to get to the top to get be-
> hind Erik's summit. And when that team was able to get behind a singular
> vision, we were all about to get to the top. So we had this huge success as a
> team because we were able to put aside our individual needs. Most of the
> time on Everest, it's every man or woman for himself, saying "I want to be
> on top." Everybody wants to be on the top, so they're not being encouraging
> and supportive and really wanting the expedition to work. They're more just
> concerned about "Well, am I going to reach my goals?" . . . Our team had
> a loftier goal, to get behind Erik and make sure he was able to safely get to
> the top and back down. As a result of that, everybody on the team was able
> to get to the top.*

Greg:

Some years ago, I participated in a six-day residential leadership course, and on the first morning we all went for a run. The instructions were simple: "Run 'all out' for one mile, time yourself, and record your time." That was easier said than done. Most of us were painfully out of shape. Nevertheless, the peer pressure ensured an all-out effort.

The second day the instructions were the same, with one small addition: "This time, make a point of cheering on and encouraging the other runners." Counterintuitively, and to our collective surprise, in spite of excruciating muscle pain from the previous day, our times improved! By getting out of our heads and focusing on the needs of others, we actually performed better and with seemingly less effort.

You can see a caring motive—and its results—manifested in the actions of successful companies such as GlaxoSmithKline, a pharmaceutical company that pledged to keep the prices of its drugs in poor countries to 25 percent of the amount charged in rich ones, to donate one-fifth of all profits made in poor countries toward building their health care systems, and to open their database freely to others researching causes and cures of malaria. This was an extraordinary declaration of intent for a pharmaceutical company. What was its motive? To build business, of course, but also to make a difference. CEO Andrew Witty declared:

I want GSK to be a very successful company, but not by leaving the population of Africa behind. In any village hospital, you can see the beds filled with women and babies severely febrile with malaria, staring into space, and you wonder: Who's taking care of the other children? It's so obvious, the damage that's being done.

John Mackey, CEO of Whole Foods Market, declared a remarkably caring, trust-building intent in his 2006 letter to his employees. He wrote:

> *The tremendous success of Whole Foods Market has provided me with far more money than I ever dreamed I'd have and far more than is necessary for either my financial security or personal happiness. . . . I am now 53 years old and I have reached a place in my life where I no longer want to work for money, but simply for the joy of the work itself and to better answer the call to service that I feel so clearly in my own heart. Beginning on January 1, 2007, my salary will be reduced to $1, and I will no longer take any other cash compensation. . . . The intention of the board of directors is for Whole Foods Market to donate all of the future stock options I would be eligible to receive to our two company foundations.*
>
> *One other important item to communicate to you is, in light of my decision to forego any future [pay], our board of directors has decided that Whole Foods Market will contribute $100,000 annually to a new Global Team Member Emergency Fund. This money will be distributed to team members throughout the company based on need. . . . The first $100,000 will be deposited on January 1, 2007, and requests will be considered after that date.*
>
> *With much love,*
John Mackey

The intent of Whole Foods is expressed clearly in the title of its mission statement—its "Declaration of Interdependence." In an article for the Huffington Post entitled "Creating a High Trust Organization," Mackey noted that fulfilling that mission requires a caring motive. "Ultimately we cannot create high trust organizations without creating cultures based on love and care." He then made several suggestions to stimulate thinking on the issue, including the following:

> *The leadership must embody genuine love and care. This cannot be faked. If the leadership doesn't express love and care in their actions then love and care will not flourish in the organization. As Gandhi said: "We must be the change that we wish to see in the world." . . .*

We should consider the virtues of love and care in all of our leadership promotion decisions. We shouldn't just promote the most competent, but also the most loving and caring. Our organizations need both and we should promote leaders who embody both.

In *Delivering Happiness,* Zappos CEO Tony Hsieh declared the caring intent of his company: "Zappos is about delivering happiness to the world." The company's intent to make customers happy is clearly manifest in its "free shipping both ways" and "365-day return" policies, its encouragement of customer service reps to spend whatever time is needed to make a customer happy, and the plethora of positive customer responses on its blog site. Its intent to make employees happy is manifest in its high-trust, empowerment-oriented, "quirky, happy culture" where "Employees enjoy free lunches, no-charge vending machines, a full-time life coach on hand, and 'create fun and a little weirdness' as one of the company's guiding tenets."

Hsieh also declared a caring intent in writing his book:

I wanted to write this book . . . to contribute to a happiness movement to help make the world a better place.

My hope is that through this book, established businesses will look to change the way they are doing things, and entrepreneurs will be inspired to start new companies with happiness at the core of their business models, taking with them some of the lessons I've learned personally as well as the lessons that we've collectively learned at Zappos. My hope is that more and more companies will start to apply some of the findings coming out of the research in the science of happiness field to make their business better and their customers and employees happier.

My hope is this will not only bring you happiness, but also enable you to bring other people more happiness.

If happiness is everyone's ultimate goal, wouldn't it be great if we could change the world and get everyone and every business thinking in that context and that framework?

Perhaps Hsieh's most notable declaration of caring intent came as a result of the global financial crisis that hit hard in the fall of 2008. Zappos responded to the crisis by reluctantly cutting 8 percent of its workforce. Rather than "spinning" this decision, Hsieh openly and transparently declared his intent and his reasoning—the why behind the what that had led to the decision. In a letter to employees (which was also published for the public in his blog), he communicated sincere regret and genuine caring. In addition, he shared an explanation of the significantly higher-than-normal-for-the-times severance benefits for those who had to be let go, which included two months–plus (rather than the typical two weeks) of severance pay and reimbursement for up to six months of COBRA insurance payments. He also provided a URL containing information on a relevant meeting with one of Zappos' major investors that had led to the decision and another on how to deal with the overall situation. Finally, Hsieh said:

> *I know that many tears were shed today, both by laid-off and non-laid-off employees alike. Given our family culture, our layoffs are much tougher emotionally than they would be at many other companies. . . .*
>
> *These are tough times for everyone, and I'm sure there will be many follow up questions to this email. If you have any questions about your specific job or department, please talk to your department manager. For all other questions, comments, or thoughts, please feel free to email me.*

The overwhelming blog response to Hsieh's letter included not only sympathy and regret but also enormous respect, understanding, and support for Zappos' decision from customers and employees alike.

When you get down to it, one of the few things we can actually guarantee is motive. A leader can't always guarantee specific performance or that the market won't change, banks won't fail, or someone won't come along with a new product or service that forces a company to reinvent and restructure. But leaders *can* guarantee that they care—about the company, the people, the industry, the world—and that they will put forth every reasonable effort to translate that caring into action and behavior that will create prosperity, energy, and joy for all concerned. And declaring that intent creates trust.

> *Whether you're a CEO, salesperson, volunteer organizer, or small business owner, your listeners will never fully connect to you, buy into your proposition, or join your parade unless they can trust you. And only if they respect your motives and empathize with you as a fellow human being will they feel that trust.*
>
> PETER GUBER
> FORMER CEO, SONY ENTERTAINMENT

The Bottom Line

Bottom line—in good times and bad—is that the motive that best builds trust is caring; the motive that destroys trust is exclusive self-interest. The agenda that best builds trust is mutual benefit; the agenda that destroys trust is "win at all costs." And the test of both caring and agenda is transparency: How would people feel—and how would you would feel—if your true intent were published to all the world? And how would it affect people's willingness to extend trust to you?

That said, there may be times when declaring self-serving intent openly and transparently may be better than not declaring it at all simply because transparency and authenticity build trust. Even if people don't agree with your motive or your approach, the fact that you are open and transparent about your intentions will in some cases encourage people to be more trusting toward you because they know what the reality is and that they're not dealing in any deception. One blogger recently wrote to another with whom he disagreed, "Your decision to NOT hide things makes you trustworthy." Although most people would agree that "trustworthy" would be too positive a term to describe someone with self-serving intent, most would also agree that the behavior of creating transparency powerfully affects the trust people have in us. One humorous reflection of self-serving intent hangs on a sign outside the Giggling Marlin restaurant in Cabo San Lucas, Mexico: "If our Food, Drinks and Service are not up to your standards, please lower your standards."

> *A fraudulent intent, however carefully concealed at the outset, will generally, in the end, betray itself.*
>
> TITUS LIVIUS
> ANCIENT ROMAN HISTORIAN

But by and large, the best approach to declaring intent in trust-building ways is this: If you believe your intent would build trust, then declare it. If you don't, but you still want to build trust, refine your intent and then declare it. So how can we refine our intent? We can start by doing a self-check reality test to question our intentions and examine our real motives. One way is to use the "five whys" process developed by Japanese businessman Taiichi Ohno for Toyota. According to Ohno, by asking "Why?" and then asking "Why?" to that answer and to each subsequent answer until you've done it five times, "the nature of the problem as well as its solution becomes clear." The idea is that with each successive "Why?" we get closer and closer to truly understanding and then being able to either refine or declare our intent.

When we do declare trustworthy intent with openness and transparency—and then follow through on that intent (which is the subject of our next chapter)—people are far more willing to extend trust to us. The keys are to be wise so that we don't overpromise and underdeliver, thereby diminishing trust, and to be clear in communicating—in other words, to communicate our intent so clearly that it cannot be misunderstood. By making sure our intent is clear, we enable people who are assessing our credibility to make better-informed decisions.

Declaring Intent Through Statements of Purpose, Mission, Vision, and Values

One effective way many leaders in organizations, companies, NGOs, and government agencies have found to declare intent is through mission, vision, and value statements. In formulating such statements, leaders not only give people bases for informed judgment; they also create vision, hope, and possibilities that may not have existed otherwise. When such statements are backed up by congruent actions and behaviors, trust flourishes.

Though many organizations have become good at declaring their intent to their customers and shareholders and a growing number are becoming fairly good at declaring their intent to their partners—and increasingly to society—far too many are still mediocre or poor in declaring their intent to their own people. With today's emphasis on "all stakeholders," however, leaders are discovering that this, too, is a critical element of effectively declaring intent.

PepsiCo is a great example of a company that declares its intent to all of its stakeholders. It is the largest food and beverage business in North America and the second largest in the world. Under the leadership of CEO Indra Nooyi, PepsiCo is in the midst of a transformation from being viewed essentially as a "junk food" company to one that provides consumers with multiple options, including a vast array of more healthful products. Currently $10 billion in revenues come from their "good for you" category, and PepsiCo is now pointing the bat to intentionally grow that to $30 billion by 2020. PepsiCo's new mantra is "Performance with Purpose"—as opposed to the "performance at any cost" mantra that drives many organizations.

The Promise of PepsiCo

At PepsiCo, "Performance with Purpose" means delivering sustainable growth by investing in a healthier future for people and our planet.

As a global food and beverage company with brands that stand for quality and are respected household names—Quaker Oats, Tropicana, Gatorade, Frito-Lay and Pepsi-Cola, to name a few—

(continued on next page)

we will continue to build a portfolio of enjoyable and wholesome foods and beverages; find innovative ways to reduce the use of energy, water and packaging; and provide a great workplace for our associates. Additionally, we will respect, support and invest in the local communities where we operate, by hiring local people, creating products designed for local tastes and partnering with local farmers, governments and community groups. Because a healthier future for all people and our planet means a more successful future for PepsiCo. This is our promise.

In addition to PepsiCo's general promise to all stakeholders, in its 2009 annual report the company explicitly declared its intent to each of its stakeholders with very specific promises:

- **To its investors: Performance:** *"To strive to deliver superior, sustainable financial performance."* This promise is accompanied by a list of measurable goals concerning elements such as growth of revenues, market shares, brand equity, and cash flow.
- **To the people of the world: Human sustainability:** *"To encourage people to live healthier by offering a portfolio of both enjoyable and wholesome foods and beverages."* This promise is accompanied by a list of industry-leading nutrition goals (which is rare for a snack food company).
- **To the planet we all share: Environmental sustainability:** *"To be a good citizen of the world, protecting the Earth's natural resources through innovation and more efficient use of land, energy, water and packaging in our operations."* This promise is accompanied by a list of measurable, time-bound goals and commitments, including providing access to safe water in developing countries, avoiding the creation of a billion pounds of landfill waste, and reducing the company's carbon footprint and greenhouse gas emissions.
- **To the associates of PepsiCo: Talent sustainability:** *"To invest in our associates to help them succeed and develop the skills needed to*

drive the company's growth, while creating employment opportunities in the communities we serve." This promise is accompanied by specific goals and commitments that enable the company to provide a supportive and empowering culture, provide opportunities that develop skills and capabilities, and contribute to better living standards in the communities they serve.

Since Nooyi became CEO, PepsiCo has not only performed well financially (outperforming the S&P 500 by two to one), it has also climbed measurably in Harris Interactive's Reputation Quotient and the 100 Best Corporate Citizens list. In addition, Nooyi has been named the number one most powerful woman in business by *Fortune* magazine for the past five years in a row and the fourth most powerful woman in the world by *Forbes* in 2011.

Another company that declares intent to all stakeholders is Procter & Gamble—a 175-year-old global company producing more than fifty leading brands for home, personal, and baby care products. The company's PVPs (Purpose, Values and Principles) are not just a nice set of platitudes; they describe the reality of how business is done and how people behave (and are expected to behave) at P&G. For an employee to be out of sync with the PVPs is a very serious offense, even if he or she is otherwise performing well. While many organizations merely talk the talk, P&G means it. As former CEO A. G. Lafley said, "While we value and expect business results, we place equal value on how we achieve those results."

P&G declares its intent to provide products that "improve the lives of the world's consumers, now and for generations to come." This declaration has become not only the driving purpose for P&G but also the guidance for its overall growth strategy—what current CEO, Bob Mc-Donald, calls "purpose-inspired growth." One extraordinary example of how P&G carries out this intent grew out of the company's efforts to create a commercial market for its water purification powder. When the project proved relatively unsuccessful in the marketplace, the company decided to give the product away and created the Children's Safe Drinking Water Program, a nonprofit initiative targeting the millions of children in the developing world who die each year from drinking unsafe water. P&G's Pur powder and water filters quickly turn contaminated water into clean drinking water and, since 2004, have provided nearly 4 billion liters of clean drinking water to people in need. The company has boldly declared its intent "to save one life every hour by delivering more than 2 billion liters of clean drinking water every year by 2020." Could there be a better illustration of P&G's declared intent to "improve the lives of the world's consumers, now and for generations to come"?

Southwest Airlines also declares its intent to multiple stakeholders and is particularly good at declaring intent to its employees. This is evident in the way cofounder Herb Kelleher has placed employees first in the corporate hierarchy, with customers second and shareholders last. Yet, more than any other airline, Southwest has also delivered to its shareholders, with an unmatched thirty-eight straight years of profitability in a sometimes brutal industry. Kelleher said:

> It used to be regarded as sort of . . . an analyst's or a business school conundrum. People would ask me when I was talking at business school or to an analyst group, "Which comes first, your employees, your customers or your shareholders?" And you know for a long time . . . I've been telling them that it isn't a conundrum. That if you treat your employees right, they're happy and proud and participate with respect to what they're doing. They manifest that attitude to your customers and your customers come back. And what's business all about but having your customers come back, which makes the shareholders happy?

Southwest recently updated its mission to include declarations of intent to its employees as well as "to our communities, to our planet, and to our stakeholders." In part, the declared intent for employees is to have a fun experience in doing their work and in creating fun travel experiences for their customers, as manifested throughout the culture in what they call a "Fun-LUVing Attitude." Current CEO Gary Kelly says: "We credit our success to our employees."

By transparently declaring their intent to all stakeholders, companies such as PepsiCo, P&G, and Southwest are giving people context and perspective that helps them decide what products and services they want to buy, where they would like to work, and where they want to invest their money.

Making the Creation of Trust an Explicit Objective

Top leaders and organizations have learned that one of the most effective things they can do in declaring intent is to make the creation of trust an explicit objective. They don't want trust to be seen merely as the by-product or natural outgrowth of whatever else they may be doing but rather as a specific outcome they're targeting, just as they would target market share or profit margin. They declare their intent to build a high-trust team or a high-trust culture and then deliberately focus on it. They engage everyone in it. They measure it and watch the needle move toward it. In other words, they grow trust on purpose.

One great place to set the creation of trust as an explicit objective is in negotiation. Another great place is in sales. The most effective approach in both cases is always to seek two outcomes: (1) to get a mutually beneficial deal and (2) to build a relationship of trust. If we get the deal but don't get the trust, the value of the deal is significantly diminished. In fact, lack of trust will hamper execution of the deal as well as the opportunity for future deals and negotiations. However, if we can get the deal in a way that also builds a relationship of trust, our ability to execute on the deal and to negotiate effectively on any changes and/or future deals goes up considerably. The president of Coca-Cola Philippines told us in 2011 that owing to its extraordinary relationship of trust, its deal with its largest client, McDonald's, continues to live on in the form of a handshake.

Doing deals in ways that build relationships of trust is especially critical in today's fluid and changing world, where predictability is hard to pin down. In outsourcing deals, for example, it has become increasingly difficult to envision and capture up front all the specifics that will need to be addressed in a long-term relationship—especially with new, disruptive technologies such as cloud computing. So what is needed even more than an impossibly precise contract is a relationship of trust that enables people to address shifting realities in mutually beneficial ways. One study out of the U.K. shows that outsourcing deals based primarily on a relationship of trust outperform deals based primarily on a contract (service-level agreement) by up to 40 percent of the total value of the contract.

Doug Conant, CEO of Campbell Soup Company, has been able to achieve world-class levels of engagement with his employees by deliberately declaring his intent to build trust and in the process has turned the iconic food company around, reversing a serious decline in market value and "delivering cumulative shareholder returns in the top tier of the global food industry." Conant told us that in both new and existing relationships with employees, customers, suppliers, and even investors, he frequently declares his intent—what he calls "Declare yourself!"—with words to this effect: "It is important to me that we build a relationship of trust. That is an explicit objective of mine because if we can trust each other, everything is better for both of us. So I want you to be able to trust me, and I, in turn, want to trust you. But I'll lead out first."

Conant then signals his behavior—in other words, he tells people what to look for:

> So, here's what you can know about me. If I tell you something, you can know that I'm telling you the truth. I'll talk straight, and I won't spin or twist it. If I have an agenda, it'll be an open, transparent agenda; it won't be hidden. If I make a commitment, you can know that I'm going to keep it—or else I won't make the commitment in the first place. So you can count on these and other such behaviors from me. You can know that I will behave with you in a way that will earn your trust. And I hope you'll reciprocate with me because my goal is to build a high-trust relationship that will benefit us both.

Conant then follows through on his declaration. He walks his talk. Now imagine if you were on the other side of a relationship with Doug Conant as an associate, supplier, customer, or investor. Is he a leader you would want to follow? Is he a leader you'd want to do business with? The result of Conant's approach can be seen in Campbell's world-class employee engagement and cumulative total shareholder returns in the top tier of the global food industry.

Another CEO who declares intent to build trust is Barry Salzberg of Deloitte LLP. Acknowledging the challenges of building trust inherent in the digital age, when rumors and hearsay take on the status of truth and are passed quickly through tweets and blogs, Salzberg observes, "Never is the truth more at risk than during tough times, with layoffs in the headlines and uppermost on employees' minds. At such times leaders need to redouble their efforts to tell employees the truth, balancing candor with compassion and hope with honesty." In response to the challenge, Salzberg has invested significant time in the company's "Straight Talk" program, traveling to regional offices and holding town hall meetings in which "no question is out of bounds." According to Salzberg:

> *Hardballs, softballs, anything goes. Everyone else in the organization is invited to dial in and listen. And the sessions and additional questions and answers are posted on a site available 24/7. . . .*
>
> *Online surveys and e-mails show that the response is overwhelmingly positive, notably for the candor of the answers, the opportunity for employees to offer direct feedback, and the willingness of the CEO to be unguarded and available.*

Regarding the importance of trust, Salzberg observes:

> *Trust is like oxygen for a business. When it's in short supply, the effect— for employees and customers alike—can be like a loss of cabin pressure on an aircraft. And never has the danger been higher than it is now in the viral conditions of the Twitter Age.*
>
> *Against these seemingly unstoppable high-tech forces, I am heartened that even today, trust and transparency still can emanate from the ultimate in low-tech: a leader standing flat-footed in a room, listening and offering, as best he or she can, the plain, unvarnished truth.*

Other Ways to Declare Intent

Other ways to declare intent include oaths, official declarations, constitutions, and vows. The MBA Oath is a voluntary pledge that was created by the 2009 graduating class of the Harvard Business School to help restore accountability and trust in business leadership. It is now supported by more than three hundred business schools and has been signed by thousands of graduating MBA students worldwide.

Predating the MBA Oath by three years, the Thunderbird International Business School instituted an Oath of Honor that reads, "As a Thunderbird and a global citizen, I promise: I will strive to act with honesty and integrity, I will respect the rights and dignity of all people, I will strive to create sustainable prosperity worldwide, I will oppose all forms of corruption and exploitation, and I will take responsibility for my actions. As I hold true to these principles, it is my hope that I may enjoy an honorable reputation and peace of conscience. This pledge I make freely and upon my honor."

Similarly, the Columbia Business School created a pledge to uphold its succinct Honor Code: "As a lifelong member of the Columbia Business School community, I adhere to the principles of truth, integrity, and respect. I will not lie, cheat, steal, or tolerate those who do."

Many medical school graduates take the Hippocratic Oath, which provides the opportunity for them to publicly declare their intent to practice medicine ethically. The Olympic Oath is taken during the opening ceremony at each of the Olympic Games by one athlete representing all participating athletes and one judge representing all participating judges. For the athletes, it is a commitment to rule-abiding drug-free participation and sportsmanship; for the judges, it is a commitment to impartiality and respect for the Olympic rules. Both the athlete and the judge are from the host country, and each holds a corner of the Olympic flag while reciting the oath.

Declarations of intent are also found in oaths such as those taken by political, military, and some religious leaders and others entering into public service, and also in statements such as political platforms and national constitutions. Effective declarations of intent can also be made in expressions such as personal mission statements, marriage vows, and family mission statements—or in any situation where someone clearly communicates intended purpose, motive, and behavior.

As well as to an overall purpose, relationship, office, or role, a declaration of intent may apply to a specific event or situation. One example is the "Commander's Intent," which was first articulated by the Prussians after a resounding defeat by Napoleon in 1806 and adopted by the U.S. Army in the 1980s. This is a results-oriented declaration that defines the purpose of a specific operation so that a subordinate can quickly grasp the vision of the end in mind and his or her part in achieving it but also gives the subordinate flexibility in planning and execution to enable the most effective response to whatever the troops might actually face, including unanticipated enemy maneuvers and challenges created by the weather or terrain.

According to General Gordon Sullivan, a retired U.S. Army chief of staff:

> *The competitive advantage is nullified when you try to run decisions up and down the chain of command. All platoons and tank crews have real-time information on what is going on around them, the location of the enemy, and the nature and targeting of the enemy's weapons system. Once the commander's intent is understood, decisions must be devolved to the lowest possible level to allow these frontline soldiers to exploit the opportunities that develop.*

West Point's Colonel Thomas Kolditz points out another powerful advantage of Commander's Intent. "As a commander," he says, "I could spend a lot of time enumerating every specific task, but as soon as people know what the *intent* is they begin generating their own solutions." The results of this kind of engagement can be seen in examples we've mentioned earlier in this chapter, such as President John F. Kennedy's "Man on the Moon" speech and Muriel Summers's transformation of A. B. Combs Leadership Magnet Elementary School.

Assuming Positive Intent in Others

> *Treat people as if they were what they ought to be, and you*
> *will help them to become what they are capable of being.*
>   GOETHE

Up to this point in this chapter, we've focused on how declaring intent can build trust. Let's look now at the other side of the coin: how assuming positive intent in others can also build trust. Just as we don't want others to assume the worst about us, others don't appreciate it when we automatically assume the worst about them. It damages trust. Especially in the absence of a declaration of intent, the best place to start with a person—and the way we'd want others to start with us—is to assume positive intent.

When PepsiCo CEO Indra Nooyi was asked, "What is the best advice you ever got?" she responded:

> *My father was an absolutely wonderful human being. From him I learned to always assume positive intent. Whatever anybody says or does, assume positive intent. You will be amazed at how your whole approach to a person or problem becomes very different. When you assume negative intent, you're angry. If you take away that anger and assume positive intent, you will be amazed. Your emotional quotient goes up because you are no longer almost random in your response. You don't get defensive. You don't scream. You are trying to understand and listen because at your basic core you are saying, "Maybe they are saying something to me that I'm not hearing." So "assume positive intent" has been a huge piece of advice for me.*

Most effective leaders assume positive intent. It's an extension of trust. It flows from our propensity to trust. It opens up possibilities that may not otherwise be seen. Assuming positive intent doesn't mean that we eliminate analysis, only that we suspend it as our starting point in most situations.

Muhammad Yunus assumed positive intent in believing that the reason the poor people of Bangledesh wanted to borrow money was to help lift themselves and their families out of poverty and that they sincerely wanted to pay back their loans in a responsible, timely manner. Even when they couldn't pay, he did not assume that they were derelicts and cheaters; he assumed that there was some valid circumstance that was preventing them from paying and that they would pay as soon as they could. Yunus's assumption of good intent enabled him to move beyond the myopic paradigm through which most people saw an unsolvable social problem to a visionary paradigm that changed the world. Pierre Omidyar's assumption that "most people are basically good" enabled eBay to shift the way the world conducts transactions to an entirely new dimension, and Google's assumption of good employee intent led to the "20% time" and other practices that have yielded some of the company's most profitable products. The assumption of good intent opens the door to high-trust relationships, creative partnerships, and productivity-enhancing practices such as flexible work hours and telecommuting.

Of course there's risk in assuming good intent. Some people may have ulterior motives. They may try to cheat you. They may try to upstage you, undercut you, or steal your ideas and claim them as their own. That's why this book is about "Smart Trust"—about engaging your propensity to trust *and* effective analysis in making trust choices. But keep in mind that the acts of the small percentage of violators who receive the huge percentage of media coverage and mind share are not necessarily representative of the norm. Also keep in mind that although there's risk in assuming good intent, there's usually a greater risk in assuming bad intent. In doing so, you cut yourself off from infinite creative possibilities and from the productivity and the prosperity, energy, and joy inherent in high-trust relationships.

The very act of assuming good intent changes the dynamic of a relationship. It inspires reciprocity. It leads to trust-building behaviors. It creates a virtuous upward cycle of trust and confidence rather than a vicious downward cycle of suspicion and distrust.

PepsiCo CEO Indra Nooyi told us, "I have an amazing executive management team, all thirteen of them. And the best thing about them is that I know every one of them wants me to succeed." That is certainly not typical in a low-trust organization, where CEOs are often looking anxiously over their shoulders at ambitious executive team members who have their eyes on the CEO's job. But because Nooyi assumes positive intent and freely extends trust to the members of her team, they reciprocate in kind. One trust-building behavior that grows out Nooyi's assumption is her practice of sending letters to the parents of the members of her team. She says, "These parents have never gotten a report card on their kids since the kids were in school, and now here they are in their forties and fifties. These parents need to hear about all the wonderful things their kids are doing. In the letters, I focus on the positive—on the reasons why I have them on my team and how grateful I am to them, as parents, for raising a wonderful child who has become such a positive influence to me and to our company." The upward cycle grows even more as Nooyi encourages her team to do the same for their reports.

A Better Place to Start

When people in one department of an organization are asked to interface with people in another department, both often start with the assumption of negative intent: "What's your hidden agenda? What's your real motive here? I think you're trying to get more of the pie (read 'budget'). You're trying to position yourself, your group, your team in a way that you'll get more and we'll get less." But think about it: when you're working on interdependent teams with people who have been hired by the same company that hired you, isn't a better starting point to assume positive intent—to assume that they have character and competence just as you do and that you're both trying to help the company succeed in a way so that everyone can win?

> *We have confidence in each other's capabilities and intentions.*
> From P&G's Purpose, Values and Principles

Some people might say this approach is naive. But our observation is that the best leaders, the best teams, the best companies start from that premise and doing so creates the very behavior they're seeking. Those who initially assume negative intent often create the very thing they fear. They torpedo the opportunity to create prosperity, energy, and joy and frequently end up with a shipwrecked deal.

In analyzing a particular situation, we may discover that someone's lack of credibility or the level of risk involved may make it smart *not* to assume good intent or to be cautious about how far and fast we move. But as a general rule, assuming positive intent with coworkers, teams, organizations, partners, suppliers, spouses, children, and others is clearly a better place—a more prosperous, energetic, and joyful place—to start.

QUESTIONS TO CONSIDER

- Did you have an experience as a child or as an adult when your intent was not understood? How did it make you feel? What difference would it have made if your intent had been correctly understood?
- Have you ever assumed negative motives on the part of someone else? Have you ever been surprised to discover that your assumption might have been wrong?
- What has been your experience in working with others when people assumed good intent on the part of others? What was your experience when they didn't?
- If you're not satisfied with your intent, how can you change it? Is it worth the cost of changing? Is it worth the cost of *not* changing?

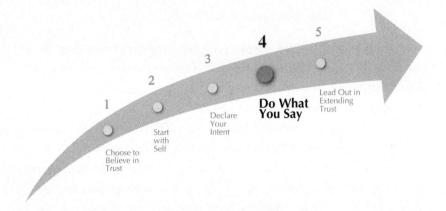

CHAPTER SEVEN

Smart Trust Action 4: Do What You Say You're Going to Do

Follow through on what you say you're going to do. Your credibility can only be built over time, and it is built from the history of your words and actions.

MARIA RAZUMICH-ZEC

Regional vice president, Hongkong and Shanghai Hotels

Power is actualized only when word and deed have not parted company.

HANNAH ARENDT

German political theorist

A s important as the action of declaring your intent is to building trust, it won't work—in fact, it will surely backfire—if you don't follow through on your declaration; in other words, if you don't do what you say you're going to do, if you don't "walk your talk."

In a recent conversation with us, the CEO of a European-based technology group shared a compelling insight. He said:

We do business in 180 countries and employ people of more than fifty different nationalities. Though everyone may agree on a value such as doing what's right, they don't all necessarily agree on what "right" means because their understanding varies based on culture and circumstance. So what we've found that works for us in evaluating personnel is to simply ask, "Do they do what they say they are going to do?" This is a specific behavior that is valued in every culture, in every belief system, and by every nationality. This is what enables us to know whether or not we can trust them. It is the best way we've found to judge the performance of our people and our company against all the different cultural and global expectations.

That CEO's insight matches our experience. We have found that in almost every nation, culture, religion, and philosophy of effective living throughout the world, "Do what you say you're going to do" is recognized as an important value and a significant measure of trust-building behavior in interactions with others.

From Around the World

Islam:	"Fulfill your promises and commitments."
Judaism:	"[Man] shall do all that proceeds out of his mouth."
Christianity:	"Not every one who saith . . . shall enter into the kingdom . . . but he that doeth . . ."
Hinduism:	"I do act as I talk and live up to my words in deed."
Buddhism:	"However many holy words you . . . speak, what good will they do you if you do not act upon them."
Confucianism:	"The superior man is modest in his speech but exceeds in his actions."
Humanism:	"First are the decencies that involve . . . keeping one's promises, honoring pledges, living up to agreements."
Greek Philosophy:	"First say . . . what you would be; and then do what you have to do."
Arabian Proverb:	"Promise is a cloud; fulfillment is rain."

A Global Standard

Because "do what you say you're going to do" is a global standard in building trust, this action has become a key evaluator of performance and enabler of multinational and cultural partnering and collaboration in today's world. It is also a critical element of employee satisfaction worldwide. Anita Borate and Joyoti Banerji of the Great Place to Work Institute identified this connection as one of the key lessons of the 2010 study of India's Best Companies to Work For:

> *The best workplaces have differentiated themselves by ensuring highest level of management credibility. Employees want to work for management that is trustworthy and keeps its commitments. Interestingly, the score of Top 25 companies is 92% higher than that of the bottom 25 on the statement, "Management's actions match its words" and 90% higher on the statement, "Management delivers on its promises."*

"Do what you say you're going to do" is based on the *principles* of integrity and congruence. The *opposite* of this action is *not* to do what you say you will. *Counterfeits* include overpromising and underdelivering, being casual in keeping commitments, justifying poor delivery with excuses, making "soft" commitments that create hope but sidestep real accountability, and delivering activities instead of results.

> *We do what we say we are going to do.*
> LEVI STRAUSS & CO. CODE OF CONDUCT

The most effective leaders and organizations are very aware of the importance of this Smart Trust action. In fact, a track record of doing what they say they're going to do enables people to do things they otherwise couldn't do at anywhere near the same speed—or perhaps not at all. When we asked Grady Rosier, the CEO of McLane Company, how Warren Buffett had had the audacity to make a deal to acquire Rosier's

$23 billion food services company on a handshake—and in less than a month and with no formal due diligence—Rosier told us:

> *Buffett knew what my reputation was. And that reputation is pretty simple. I always do exactly what I tell you I'm going to do, good or bad. And everybody in the company knows that, good or bad, I'm going to do exactly what we say we're going to do as a company. If it costs us money, that's part of the deal. And that's what our reputation is. . . . After the deal was done, a group of us had a dinner just to consummate the deal. And over the dinner, Buffett said of us, "These are good guys, and I trust these guys. And we're going to go down the road and the relationship is going to work," and it has.*

John Mackey notes:

> *As the co-founder and CEO of Whole Foods Market, I'm the most visible person in the company. . . . I know that in virtually everything that I say and do, our Team Members are always studying me, trying to determine whether they can trust me and the mission of the company. I'm always on stage. So walking the talk is very important.*

Delivering promised results—doing what you say you're going to do—generates trust faster than any other action. This is particularly true when circumstances make it difficult.

In *It's Not What You Say . . . It's What You Do,* the management consultant Laurence Haughton tells of a time when Level 3 Communications, a large Internet service provider, did what it said it was going to do, even though it was very difficult. In 1998, Level 3 was called the "best funded start-up in history," having raised $14 billion in an industry that had attracted $757 billion of investment between 1996 and 2000. But then the tech bubble imploded, the market tanked, and scores of fiber-optic communications firms were devastated, nearly all of them declaring bankruptcy. It would have been very easy for Level 3 to do the same, but the company leadership determined that it had a responsibility to its stakeholders. CEO James Crowe explained, "We had an obligation. We owed our investors. We owed our customers. We owed our employees. . . . You do what it is that you say you're going to do." And they did. Although the company's market capitalization has never approached what it was before the bubble burst, Level 3 kept its word. As a result, today Level 3 is one of only six Tier 1 Internet providers in the world, with one of the largest IP transit networks in North America and Europe and revenues in excess of $3.5 billion.

After sharing Level 3's story, Haughton observed, "Commitment means never asking the other side 'to understand.' All managers must be willing to expose themselves . . . and say, 'The robustness and stamina of the follow-through is my responsibility. All our promises have my name on them.'"

Delivering promised results even when it is difficult made a quantitative difference for Firoz "King" Husein, the Indian-born owner of Span Construction in Madera, California. Some years ago, Husein faced a difficult test of trust with a major client, Costco Wholesale. Unforeseen delays had created a challenge for his company in completing a warehouse in the 110 days before the opening date announced by Costco. Husein's personal operating principles included not working his crews on Sundays. Nevertheless, he assured the Costco construction executive team that he would do what he had said he was going to do and complete the project on time by bringing in extra workers and working extra hours. That approach seriously worried the Costco executives, who felt strongly that the Sunday work time would be needed. But Husein stood his ground with such conviction and self-trust that the Costco executives decided to trust him. And Span met the goal. In the words of Husein, "Though it was not my intent at the time, since that day, the respect and trust from the Costco management increased substantially. We met our deadline, but we did not work on Sundays. They know we will not compromise our principles in meeting our commitments."

The trust and credibility Husein established by doing what he said he would do while still honoring his principles resulted in his firm receiving contracts to build more than 59 million square feet of buildings for Costco in North America, Asia, Europe, and Australia over the next two decades.

Keeping my word is a mandate I live by. I can't tell you the number of times I've committed to doing something, then later wanted to get out of it but ended up doing it anyway because, for me, backing out is never an option. If I agree to do something, the only way I'm not going to do it is if I'm too sick to move.

OPRAH WINFREY

The Power of the Say/Do Combination

Smart Trust Actions 3 and 4 are a powerful behavioral duet. They're like a one-two punch: you declare your intent, and then you do what you say you're going to do. It's the combination that has the greatest power to knock out suspicion and distrust.

One of the easiest ways to understand the power of this dual-action approach is to consider the four possible options you have in combining "say" and "do." As you consider each option, keep in mind that *say* is declaring intent; *do* is carrying it out. *Say* is words; *do* is actions. *Say* is talk; *do* is walk. *Say* is promise; *do* is deliver. In the words of our colleague Roger Merrill, "Making commitments (*say*) builds hope; keeping commitments (*do*) builds trust." As you read below, think about how each option might affect someone's evaluation in deciding whether or not to trust you—or how it might affect your evaluation in deciding whether or not to trust someone else.

Option 1: Low Say/Low Do—Underpromise and Underdeliver

This option is where people don't say much and they don't do much, building neither hope nor trust. This includes employees who lie low and try to avoid assignments or underdeliver by design so they will not be assigned again. These are disengaged workers who have "quit but stay," doing the minimum required to remain on the payroll. They have no brand, offer no promise, don't stand for anything, and create no expectations. Their behavior usually creates a slow, rather than sudden, loss of trust.

Option 2: High Say/Low Do—Overpromise and Underdeliver

This option is where people make all kinds of promises and commitments but don't follow through. They don't walk the talk. They're incongruent—their deeds don't match their words; they don't do what they say they value. As they say in Texas, "All hat, no cattle." Ironically, although Option 1 does nothing whatsoever to build trust, in many ways it is better than Option 2, which actually destroys trust by turning whatever hope has been inspired by promises into cynicism.

The most prominent example of overpromising and underdelivering is politicians who make a number of promises in order to get elected but fail to keep those promises once they are in office. According to the 2011 Trust Index published by GfK, Germany's largest market research organization, politicians are the lowest-trusted profession by far of the twenty professions surveyed on a global basis within nineteen countries. Another example is organizations whose mission/value statements are nothing more than platitudes hanging on the wall. Understandably, there are companies that don't yet live their mission/value statements fully but are working hard to close the gap. Their sincere, focused efforts build trust. But to create a mission statement and then disregard it is not harmless; it

DILBERT © 2009 Scott Adams. Used by permission of UNIVERSAL UCLICK. All rights reserved.

actually destroys trust. Just as it would be better to not declare your intent in the first place than to declare it and not follow through, it would be better for a company not to create a mission/value statement in the first place than to create it and ignore it.

> Leaders can foster trust by being trustworthy themselves.
> "Do as I say, not as I do" works no better in organizations
> than it does anywhere else. Mission statements that promise
> integrity, openness, and fairness (as Enron's did) mean
> nothing when leaders' actions are dishonest and corrupt.
>
> KAZUO ICHIJO AND IKUJIRO NONAKA
> BUSINESS AUTHORS

Option 3: Low Say/High Do—Underpromise and Overdeliver

This option is where people don't say much, but they do deliver results. This is actually a fairly good option because it will, in fact, build trust; it just won't build it nearly as fast as Option 4 because others aren't as aware of what's happening and often don't recognize performance as a promise kept. In addition, underpromising typically doesn't break through the noise and clutter of a crowded marketplace, nor does it build much hope. Though it may create some hope in the possibility of repeated delivery in the future, there's not anywhere near the hope (or energy and joy) that's created by individuals and organizations that stand for something, declare it clearly, and fulfill it with excellence. Again, it's much better to underpromise and overdeliver than the other way around; but neither approach will bring the high-trust results of Option 4.

> The old cliché in business is that smart companies under-
> promise and overdeliver. But in a crowded marketplace,
> underpromising is a one-way ticket to oblivion.
>
> RICK BARRERA
> BUSINESS AUTHOR

Option 4: High Say/High Do—Promise and Deliver/Overdeliver

This option is where people *say* what they're going to do and then they *do* it. They walk their talk—tall. They signal their intent (which builds hope), and then they follow through (which builds trust). This is where you find the company that says it's going to get the product to you by the fifteenth of the month—and delivers it by the fifteenth. Or the HR director who promises to review the employee benefits package by the next executive meeting—and comes to the meeting with research done and a proposal in hand. Or the spouse, partner, associate, or friend who agrees to meet you at 6:30 sharp—and arrives at 6:30 or even a few minutes before. Or the parent who promises a child a trip to the park on Saturday—and is there on Saturday with the child, even though other things may have come up in the meantime.

"Promise and deliver" combines the strength of *say* and *do* and increases trust much faster than any of the other approaches because it enables people to anticipate and build hope around what you plan to do and to recognize and celebrate it when you do it. And when the *say*—or declaration of intent—includes a transparent, caring *why* as well as the *what,* it builds trust in your character as well as your competence.

One organizational illustration of "promise and deliver" is Wipro, whose modus operandi, according to *Business Week,* is "to offer something outrageous—significantly higher quality with a massively lower price— and then overdeliver by a mile." Another standout is Apple. Just think of the response when Steve Jobs delivered his trademark line, "And one more thing . . ." near the conclusion of a presentation at Macworld or the Apple Worldwide Developers Conference, almost surely signaling the announcement of another product. Practically every Apple product launch brings enormous interest and excitement, and Apple always delivers— and more—on that excitement with terrific products.

And there are others. BMW, the German auto, motorcycle, and engine manufacturer, creates excitement and hope with its "ultimate driving machine" tagline and then actually delivers (according to Greg) the ultimate driving machine. Ritz-Carlton Hotels declare, "We are ladies and gentlemen serving ladies and gentlemen"—and because they back it up with follow-up involving three explicit service promises and twelve deliberate service values, they enable their employees to deliver on what ladies and gentlemen expect. Visa tells us it's "everywhere you want to be," and in fact it is, being the most widely available and widely used credit card in the world. Clearly, the say/do combination goes a long way toward inspiring trust and creating prosperity, energy, and joy in the marketplace, and we only have to look to our own experience to know that it does the same thing in personal relationships as well.

Greg:

In the last few years both my parents passed away and left their home in Phoenix to my brother and me. Deciding what to do with the home turned out to be an emotional issue for both of us. After months of putting off making a decision, we finally decided to take the situation in hand. So we talked about the possibilities. Trying to maintain the home when neither of us lived in the state was impractical. For a number of reasons, trying to rent didn't seem reasonable either. In the end we decided to sell. But the Arizona real estate market was at a rock-bottom, thirty-year low, and we were concerned about how we were going to make it happen.

My first thought was that we should try to sell the home ourselves and save the commission. My wife, Annie, was quick to tell me that that was not a good idea. She suggested we contact some family friends, a mother-and-daughter team who were in real estate, and give them the job. It was tough for me to let go, but I did trust Joan and Lynn completely, even though I laughed when they told me they would sell the house in less than a month. In the end they proved that I had hugely underestimated how worthy they were of that trust.

Talk about doing what you say you're going to do! Joan and Lynn took my painful problem and taught me what competence is all about. Within hours of taking on the project, a charity crew was

(continued on next page)

there, emptying the balance of the furniture, a painter was handing me his written bid, the carpet guy was measuring for new carpet, and the landscape guy was walking the yard. Within a week, the new carpet was down and the walls were painted. Joan and Lynn brought in accessories for the baths and kitchen and silk plants and other decorator touches to "stage" the house. Within nine days, all the work had been completed and a "For Sale" sign was up in the front yard.

But it gets even better! Remember, this was during the worst real estate market in the history of Phoenix. But within one week—one week!—Joan and Lynn had not one but two offers on the house. They conducted a silent bid, and the extra amount of the winning offer exceeded the money we had reluctantly invested in dressing the home up by several times. This mother/daughter team had sold our home in seven days—for more than the listing price! This experience is on my personal highlight list of Smart Trust examples. To me, it was absolutely euphoric!

What If You Can't Do What You Say You're Going to Do?

What happens if you can't deliver on a promise? What happens if circumstances change or something critical comes up and you absolutely can't do what you've said you're going to do?

One answer is to create, in addition to a contract, a relationship of trust that reflects the reality of today's rapidly changing world. As we mentioned in chapter six due to shifting technologies (both disruptive and otherwise), outsourcing contracts need to be written up differently today than they were in the past. Whereas before, it was possible to accurately predict the vast majority—perhaps 80 to 90 percent—of the contractual services and costs over a five-year period, today that figure may well be less than half. By creating a relationship of trust, we can at least proceed in good faith when we discover that commitments can't be fulfilled. Without trust—or with low trust—new challenges will be viewed through the lens of distrust and suspicion, and new solutions will be much harder to envision, let alone create.

Another answer is to be wise in the kinds of commitments we make. Remember, a leader can't always guarantee specific performance or that the market won't change or that someone won't come along with a new technology that forces a company to reinvent itself. Nevertheless, declaring intent is vital to Smart Trust. So we can be wise and thoughtful in declaring our intent in terms of focus, effort, caring, and achievable outcomes. Gallup research shows that trust is fundamental to good partnerships because of the way in which it enables both parties to "concentrate on their separate responsibilities, confident the other party will come through."

We can also be wise in the number of commitments we make. If we say we're going to do sixteen things but we actually do four, we may feel great about the four we've accomplished, but other people will almost undoubtedly be focused on the twelve that didn't get done. Promising four things—and delivering four things—will create trust much better and faster.

Our colleague Alan Fine suggested to us another helpful idea he calls "SayDoCo": *Say* what you'll do, *Do* what you say, and *Co*mmunicate if you find you can't. By communicating quickly and transparently when you really can't do what you say you're going to do, you not only reframe expectations, you can also engage others productively in renegotiating or helping to find alternative solutions. In *You Already Know How to Be Great,* Alan wrote:

> *SayDoCo is the lifeblood of organizations. It's the key to Decision Velocity (speed and accuracy in decision making) and execution. It's how people interact together to get predictable, sustainable results. When people SayDoCo, empowerment, engagement, trust, and accountability naturally develop or increase. When they don't SayDoCo, these high-performance elements diminish or disappear.*

Bottom line, establish relationships of trust, make only commitments you're confident you can keep, communicate clearly and transparently if you absolutely can't keep them, and reschedule or renegotiate alternative solutions. This preserves trust—with a boss, a team member, a customer, a report, a partner, a child, or a friend.

Reputation and Brand

The reason doing what you say you're going to do makes such a huge difference in your success or your organization's success is that it is the ultimate reputation creator. It defines your personal brand. It defines your company's brand. And brand has never been more important than it is in today's reputation economy, where doing what we say we're going to do—or not—can make or break it. A trusted brand dramatically speeds up the Smart Trust decision-making process.

> A brand for a company is like a reputation for a person. You earn reputation by trying to do hard things well.
>
> JEFF BEZOS
> FOUNDER AND CEO, AMAZON.COM

The openness and transparency of this networked world hold people more accountable for their actions, which in turn reinforces more responsible behavior. Technology authority Tom Hayes put it this way:

> *[I]n a global network economy where billions of impersonal and anonymous interactions take place daily, trust is everything: every breach is a crisis. . . .*
>
> *It's a breathtaking reality: three billion people buying from and selling to each other—directly. No middlemen, arbiters, or government agencies between them . . . .*
>
> *Sellers and buyers earn their reputations. And reputation is one's calling card and bond.*

When participants in a recent Edelman Trust Barometer survey were asked, "When you think of good and responsible companies, how important is each of the following factors to the overall reputation of the company?" 91 percent gave high marks to the response "Is a company I trust."

So what creates a brand that inspires trust? Brand experts point to two key elements, which are represented in the twin behaviors of "say" and "do": *the brand promise* (or the declaration of intent that inspires hope) and *the delivery on that promise* (the fulfillment of the declaration, or doing what they say they're going to do). One company that has built a powerful reputation around this behavioral duet is FedEx, a global company that provides a broad array of supply chain, transportation, business, and information services. When Frederick Smith founded the company in 1971, it was simply a shipping company. Overnight delivery did not exist on a national scale in the United States. But by innovatively applying the model of the telecommunications and banking industries to the transportation industry, Smith found a way to deliver point to point, anywhere in the U.S.—absolutely, positively overnight, giving birth to its tagline promise: "When it absolutely, positively has to get there overnight!" According to Smith:

> *We thought that we were selling the transportation of goods; in fact, we were selling peace of mind. When we finally figured that out, we pursued our goal with a vengeance. We provided each of our drivers with a handheld computer and a transmitting device. We made it possible for our customers to track their packages right from their desktops.*

FedEx backed up the promise of its tagline with its actions. It did what it said it would. It consistently produced results. It built a reputation for reliability that has repeatedly won it recognition as one of the most trusted companies in the world. Today, FedEx ranks in the top ten of *Fortune*'s World's Most Admired Companies.

If you study the lists of the companies on Harris Interactive's Reputation Quotient and *Fortune*'s World's Most Admired Companies, you'll see numerous companies that have built strong reputations through having a clear brand promise and consistently delivering on it. These include companies such as Google (which delivers so well on its brand promise to "provide access to the world's information in one click," it doesn't even need to advertise), Amazon.com (which has gone from "World's Biggest Bookstore" to world's biggest retailer by focusing on becoming the most customer-centric company on the planet), and Coca-Cola (which boasts that although taglines have come and gone, "the brand promise has remained the same—to inspire moments of optimism and uplift.")

> *In virtually every industry, the trusted brand is the most profitable.*
>
> SETH GODIN
> AUTHOR AND MARKETING GURU

The research of Joachim Klewes and Robert Wreschniok from Ketchum Pleon shows that the benefits of reputation for companies include significant competitive advantage in a number of areas, including customer and employee loyalty, stock market performance, and talent and investor attraction. According to Wreschiniok, "A recent study by Harvard Business Manager places reputation among the five most important intangible corporate assets, together with customer satisfaction, employee satisfaction, brand and corporate culture—well ahead of patents and licenses."

In addition, a 2009 study by Concerto Marketing Group found that 83 percent of people who trust a brand will recommend it to others, while 50 percent will actually pay more for its products and services. This remarkable phenomenon is corroborated by the research of former UCLA professor Peter Kollock on the impact of reputation in auction-based Internet markets such as eBay. Kollock observes that in addition to incenting less fraud and a greater number of positively completed trading experiences, a good reputation also affects the price consumers are willing to pay for products. He says:

If these reputation systems do in fact provide useful information and an incentive to behave in a trustworthy manner, buyers should be willing to pay more for a good if it comes from a highly rated seller, at least when the transaction involves significant risk. Preliminary evidence from a quantitative study of reputations on eBay suggests this is in fact the case. At least for some high value goods, the seller's reputation had a positive and statistically significant effect on the price buyers paid for identical goods of equivalent quality.

This is evidenced by the fact that the most trusted brands (think Mercedes, Rolex, Sony, and McKinsey) command higher prices in the marketplace. Trust is obviously paramount in the nonprofit sector as well, where reputations determine funding necessary to fulfill missions—"no margin, no mission." Barbara Stocking, the CEO of Oxfam, an international confederation of fifteen organizations working to find solutions to poverty and injustice, has this to say: "The key to being trusted is demonstrating personal integrity. I don't just mean being honest, what I mean is that you are who you say you are and do what you say you will do."

> The trust that the general public places in non-profits is paramount to their success as enduring and powerful brands. Those that deliver well on their promises and missions stand the test of time.
>
> JUSTIN GREEVES
> SENIOR VICE PRESIDENT, HARRIS INTERACTIVE

Bottom line, a company's ability to declare credible intent and then deliver or overdeliver on that stated intent is critical to a company's reputation or brand, and the company's reputation or brand is critical to the prosperity, energy, and joy of its stakeholders. That is why the most effective leaders and companies take seriously the challenge to create hope through declaring their intent and trust through doing what they say (or even more than they say) they're going to do.

City and Country Reputations and Brands

In a very real sense, the reputations or brands of cities and countries also impact their level of prosperity, energy, and joy. Cities with positive reputations tend to attract talent—what the sociologist Richard Florida calls the "creative class"—that produces synergistic communities, such as the high-tech community in California's Silicon Valley and the banking, business, and technology communities in Singapore. A country's reputation influences what kind of "trust tax" or "trust dividend" it may be assessed when interacting with others in the global society. (See page 135.) A company headquartered in Sweden or Germany typically receives a high-trust dividend, while a company headquartered in Russia pays a low-trust tax.

Brand-building behaviors for a nation include declaring the intent to create the conditions for its citizens to thrive and prosper and then following through with legislation and actions to fulfill that intent. In 2010, *Newsweek* compiled metrics within five categories of national well-being—education, health, quality of life, economic competitiveness, and political environment—across a hundred nations. The question it sought to answer was this: "If you were born today, which country would provide you the very best opportunity to live a healthy, safe, reasonably prosperous, and upwardly mobile life?" Though some responses undoubtedly reflected what mattered most to respondents and where their loyalties lay, the overall rankings based on the criteria showed the top five countries, in order, to be: (1) Finland, (2) Switzerland, (3) Sweden, (4) Australia, and (5) Luxembourg, with the United States coming in at number eleven. Warren Buffett has said, "Anything good that's ever happened to me can be traced back to the fact that I was born in the right country [the United States] at the right time." Obviously, other countries have also risen to create opportunities and choices for their citizens that similarly inspire trust.

Your Personal Reputation/Brand

Reputation also plays a vital role in building trust in individuals—leaders, managers, spouses, partners, parents, and friends. Think about what kind of reputation is being created by the following:

- A boss who sets up one-hour executive team meetings—but is always still talking long after the hour is up
- A manager who keeps agreeing to turn in his reports in on time—but never does
- A parent who frequently tells a three year-old, "Okay, you don't get to watch TV for the rest of the day!"—but repeatedly gives in because it's so much easier than following through
- A teenager who repeatedly makes commitments to clean a room or run an errand or take something over to a neighbor—but keeps "forgetting" to do it

Failing to do what you say you're going to do as an individual creates a personal reputation or brand that diminishes trust. That's why the most effective individuals work hard to declare their intent and do what they say they're going to do in whatever role they're in.

Be impeccable with your word.

DON MIGUEL RUIZ
AUTHOR, *THE FOUR AGREEMENTS*

Stephen:

My wife, Jeri, and I were reminded of how important (and how hard) it is to do what we said we were going to do as parents one time when our son Stephen violated an agreement he'd made with us.

(continued on next page)

To ensure his safety and our sanity when he got his driver's license, we wrote up a one-page contract containing rules we expected him to follow, such as "Drive safely," "Use seat belts," and "Obey the laws." We added that in order to maintain his driving privileges, he would have to fulfill his responsibilities at home and maintain good grades. Less than a month later, we got a phone call around midnight from the police, who had pulled him over for excessive speeding. There was no drinking or anything like that involved; Stephen and his friends had just been discouraged after their football team had been eliminated from the playoffs, and they had gone for a way-too-fast drive.

As we thought about the situation, we felt sorry for Stephen. We wondered how he was ever going to pay the huge fine. We were concerned about what it was going to do to his reputation and his relationship with his friends, as well as his relationship with us. We thought about the inconvenience following through with the consequences would create for us, since he had been providing his own transportation and helping out with errands. But in the end, we realized that we really had no choice. If we didn't follow through, how was Stephen ever going to feel he could trust us? And how could our other kids trust us? Clearly, this was an issue that impacted not only Stephen but the whole family culture as well.

So Stephen paid the ticket. It cost him $555, which took almost all his savings from his summer job. The judge did not suspend his license, but we did for a time, as we had designated in our agreement. It was very, very hard on him. But he learned a lesson, and he's been a model driver ever since. In fact, he gained the reputation as the safe driver among his friends. It actually became a joke with his friends that whenever they were all going somewhere and their parents told them to be careful and safe, the kids would reply, "Don't worry—we're going with Covey!" That clearly meant they would be going the speed limit, wearing seat belts, and obeying the law.

Building Self-Trust

"Declare your intent" and "Do what you say you're going to do" are not only the fastest ways to build reputation and trust with others; they're also the fastest ways to build your reputation and trust with yourself.

> The reason I so rarely break promises to other people? It breaks trust. Without trust there's no relationship. The same is true for our relationships with ourselves. Break enough promises to yourself, and soon you no longer believe your own voice when it says, "I'm going to work out an hour every day and never eat unhealthy food again."
>
> OPRAH WINFREY

In chapter five we shared the story of the man who came up to us during a break and shared his epiphany concerning the reason he couldn't trust others, including his company, his people, his boss, and his spouse. The problem, he said, was that he couldn't trust himself, and this lack of self-trust was being reflected in the way he saw and interacted with everyone else. When the man asked for our advice, we suggested a "make/keep/repeat" approach—that he start where he was and *make* and *keep* one small commitment to himself . . . then another . . . then another . . . and *repeat* the process until he developed the ability to make and keep larger commitments to himself on a regular basis. In our experience, there is nothing people can do to more quickly build personal reputation and self-trust.

When people have a healthy degree of self-trust, they are far more likely to extend trust to others. They also have more confidence in their own abilities.

Greg:

Early in my business career, I worked selling resort condominiums for Snowbird Realty at Snowbird Ski Resort in the Utah Rockies. During the interview, the manager asked me to cut my hair (which was long at the time) so that I could better relate to the high-income doctors, lawyers, and executives who frequented the resort and were most likely to invest. Instead I offered to work for free to prove to him that a youthful twenty-seven-year-old with long hair could be just as credible in the eyes of his prospective clients as any of the other fifteen people on his sales force. He accepted the offer. As a result, I was under enormous pressure to perform.

What made the challenge even more difficult than my appearance was the fact that several of the veteran salespeople had a tendency to exaggerate and project future benefits that were somewhat speculative in order to make it easier to persuade customers to invest. I had recently turned my life around and had made a promise to myself that I would always be honest in all my business affairs. I wondered how I could possibly compete with their sales tactics. Nevertheless, with a personal commitment not to exaggerate and to focus on the aspects of the purchase that directly benefited the customers and their families, I gave it my all.

I quickly discovered that the trust I had gained in making and keeping commitments to myself—doing what I said I was going to do—gave me tremendous confidence in working with customers. When I spoke, I knew without a doubt that I was being truthful and that I had my customers' best interests at heart. And the customers could feel it. To my great relief (and my manager's surprise), I quickly became the company's leading salesperson. And because my clients trusted me, they gave me referrals to their friends, which widened the performance gap with the others even more.

When the other salespeople asked about the secret of my performance, I simply told them it was my experience that you cannot lie with the same intensity with which you can tell the truth. That

> *proved to be a foundation for my future success. It gave me the confidence that I could discipline myself to take the high ground and still accomplish anything.*

Recognizing the importance of doing what you tell yourself you're going to do, Yale University's Dean Karlan, Barry Nalebuff, and Ian Ayres, along with a student, Jordan Goldberg, developed a clever website called stickK to help people make and keep commitments to themselves through what they call Commitment Contracts. People are invited, free of charge, to walk through stickK's four-step process:

- Set a personal goal (such as weight loss).
- Put some money on the line (with a designated recipient such as a least-favored charity).
- Select a referee to monitor progress and confirm reports.
- Enlist supporters to help cheer them on.

According to the site's creators, putting something on the line makes a huge difference in motivating people to actually do what they say they're going to do. When people don't meet their goals, the stakes are surrendered to the designated individuals or charities. When they do meet their goals, they're thirty pounds lighter . . . or they've quit smoking . . . or they've accomplished some other meaningful goal to help make their lives better. In the process, they've increased their personal confidence and self-trust.

> *If you do ANYTHING that requires self-regulation, then that makes it EASIER for you to have self-regulation in EVERYTHING.*
>
> ROY BAUMEISTER
> AUTHOR AND PROFESSOR, FLORIDA STATE UNIVERSITY

Marshall Goldsmith has created a similar process to help senior executives change behavior. For those who want to become more open-minded listeners, Goldsmith imposes a fine of $20 whenever they begin a sentence with the word "no," "but," or "however." Over the years Goldsmith has collected $300,000 for charities through this process. More to the point, his approach incents executives to change because they simply can't stand to lose the money. Even though it's a relatively minor amount at their pay grade, it has the equivalent motivating effect of a small and friendly wager on the golf course. Ultimately this approach motivates leaders to actually change their behavior, become more effective, and increase their self-trust. Goldsmith says:

> There's a reason I devote so much energy to identifying interpersonal challenges in successful people. It's because the higher you go, the more your problems are behavioral.
>
> At the higher levels of organizational life, all the leading players are technically skilled. They're all smart. They're all up to date on the technical aspects of their job. . . .
>
> That's why behavioral issues become so important at the upper rungs of the corporate ladder.

The Fastest Way to Restore Trust

When you step into a new role, such as team leader, manager, CEO, stepparent, or spouse, you may walk into a situation where there's a trust tax—sometimes a huge one—already in place. We call this an "inheritance tax." That is what happened to Gordon Bethune when he joined Continental Airlines in 1994. At that point, Continental was on the brink of its third bankruptcy. It had gone through ten leaders in ten years, had reportedly never met a budget forecast, and was ranked dead last in every measurable performance metric, including customer complaints, mishandled baggage, and on-time performance. Gordon Bethune described the environment he encountered in his book *From Worst to First*:

> The culture at Continental, after years of layoffs and wage freezes and wage cuts and broken promises, was one of backbiting, mistrust, fear, and

loathing. People, to put it mildly, were not happy to come to work. They were surly to customers, surly to each other, and ashamed of their company.

Named CEO only months later, Bethune embarked on a dramatic program to restore trust in Continental, among employees as well as in the marketplace. He observed:

> *Employees of a chronically broken company are kind of like abused children, and any new management team has to view itself like a new adoptive parent. You might have the best intentions in the world. You may be the exact person to stabilize the lives of these children and supply them with three meals a day, loving-kindness, a college education, and a Shetland pony, but when they first meet you they're not going to trust you. Their experience with adults is all bad, and just by being an adult you get their mistrust and disrespect. They figure you're gonna whack them around and yell at them and do all kinds of terrible things to them, just like the others they've known. And they're right to feel that way. It makes sense. I had to figure on this. I had to figure they weren't going to rally around my ideas without some good reason to trust that I was going to be different.*

Bethune gave employees good reason to trust that he was going to be different. At one point, for example, he took stacks of company policy manuals that were filled with minutiae-controlling regulations out to the parking lot and had employees set fire to them. He told them that from now on, instead of following some rigid manual, they were to use their own judgment in solving problems, balancing what was right for the customer and right for the company. Very quickly, Continental was meeting its budget forecasts, and soon the company was number one in the two key airline industry measures: on-time performance and baggage handling. Continental's relentless improvement in performance restored the public's confidence that the airline would do what it said it was going to do.

During the ten years Bethune led Continental, the company went from worst (being ranked last in every measurable performance category) to first (winning more J. D. Power and Associates awards for customer satisfaction than any other airline in the world). Continental's stock price rose from $2 to more than $50 per share. In Bethune's final year as CEO, *Fortune* ranked Continental the No. 1 Most Admired Global Airline.

Inherited trust taxes usually exist because the person who previously fulfilled your role behaved in ways that destroyed trust. Or maybe the tax has been imposed by a low-trust industry or high-compliance environment. As a result, the culture is cynical. You're starting off in the red.

On the other hand, perhaps you have to deal with a tax that is not inherited but self-imposed. Perhaps you yourself have behaved in ways that destroyed trust—in a relationship, on a team, or in your organization. As a result, you and others no longer have the prosperity, energy, and joy that come from high trust.

In either case, it's important to know that doing what you say you're going to do is not only the fastest way to build trust with yourself and with others, it's also the fastest way to restore trust when it has been lost. As we've said, although you can't *talk* yourself out of problems you've behaved yourself into, you can *behave* yourself out of problems that you (or others) have behaved yourself into—and the best way to do it is to do what you say you're going to do.

> I judge people by their feet, not their mouth.
>
> GEORGE BUCKLEY
> CHAIRMAN AND CEO, 3M

One CEO we spoke with had bought a business with about two thousand employees. He was the fourth owner in a three-year period, and the culture had become extremely cynical because the previous three owners had not followed through on what they'd said they would do, including staying with the business for the long haul. Recognizing this, the new owner decided to hold a town hall meeting to listen to people's concerns. After capturing the main points of their concerns, he made fourteen commitments of things he was going to do to address them. People walked out of the meeting very skeptical because, in effect, they'd been to this movie before and they didn't like how it ended.

But two weeks later, he called another meeting and reported back on each of the fourteen commitments. He had met twelve of them, which resulted in immediate, significant changes. The other two were still in progress because of the longer-term nature of the commitments. People walked out of that meeting with a renewed sense of hope and belief. It didn't take long before the company grew to completely trust this new leader. He restored their trust through his behavior—by doing what he said he was going to do.

When customer expectations are violated, it is important for companies to act quickly to restore trust. As Vivian Deuschl, a vice president at the Ritz-Carlton Hotel Company, says:

> *I've come to learn that the least costly solution is the one that happens immediately. The longer and higher a customer complaint lives in an organization, the more it grows. By the time a complaint hits senior leadership, what could have been resolved by getting the guest the amenity he or she requested with a slight enhancement turns into resolutions on a par with an upgraded night on the Club Level.*

Coca-Cola Europe demonstrated its understanding of the importance of quick service recovery recently when more than a hundred people in Belgium and several in France reported developing stomachaches after drinking canned Coke. The company quickly accepted responsibility, apologized, and offered to cover the health care costs of anyone affected. Even though there was no clear evidence that Coke's products were causing the health problems, the company also decided to recall beverages from five European countries—17 million cases in total, making it the biggest recall in Coke's history. CEO Douglas Ivester publicly stated that the quality of its products is Coca-Cola's highest priority. He said, "For 113 years our success has been based on the trust that consumers have in that quality. That trust is sacred to us." It was later established that the reported health problems had not been caused by Coca-Cola products, but by acting swiftly and behaving consistently with its brand promise, the company gained, rather than lost, trust with customers.

Another illustration of how trust can be restored through behavior grew out of the story we shared earlier of Stephen's son's driving experience. As young Stephen behaved himself out of the problem he had behaved himself into, he not only restored trust with his parents, he actually increased it to a higher level than it had ever been before.

> If businesses are to regain trust, they will need to adopt a strategy of Public Engagement. . . . The essence of Public Engagement is the commitment of companies to say—and do as they say.
>
> EDELMAN TRUST BAROMETER, 2009

The Principle of Behavior

The reason doing what you say you're going to do increases trust is because *behavior* increases trust (or destroys it). The reality is that we judge ourselves by our intentions, but others judge us by our actions. So when our actions carry out our declared intent, they close the trust-building loop of promises made and kept.

On an even broader scale, this also applies to expectations created by promises that are implied but not necessarily declared. Your customers expect you to be honest and to provide a quality product or service at a reasonable price. Your reports expect you to be open and transparent with them concerning their jobs. Your spouse expects you to be loyal. Your children expect you to be fair. When you behave in ways that are not honest, reasonable, open, loyal, or fair—*even though you may not have explicitly said that you would*—it can also destroy trust. That's why the most effective leaders and managers work hard to create a culture of clarifying expectations and, in the words of LRN CEO Dov Seidman, "*outbehaving* the competition." In doing so, they create a competitive edge that more quickly leads to greater prosperity, energy, and joy. In *The Speed of Trust* we identified 13 behaviors common to high-trust people throughout the world. Here are a few that particularly apply to doing what you say you're going to do.

A Few Trust-Building Behaviors*

Talk Straight

Be honest. Tell the truth. Let people know where you stand. Use simple language. Call things what they are. Demonstrate integrity. Don't manipulate people or distort facts. Don't spin the truth. Don't leave false impressions.

Create Transparency

Tell the truth in a way people can verify. Get real and genuine. Be open and authentic. Err on the side of disclosure. Operate on the premise of "What you see is what you get." Don't have hidden agendas. Don't hide information.

Clarify Expectations

Disclose and reveal expectations. Discuss them. Validate them. Renegotiate them if needed and possible. Don't violate expectations. Don't assume that expectations are clear or shared.

(continued on next page)

Keep Commitments

Make commitments carefully and keep them at almost all costs—or communicate and renegotiate if you absolutely can't. Making and keeping commitments is a symbol of honor. Don't break confidences. Don't attempt to "PR" your way out of a broken commitment.

* For a summary of the 13 behaviors common to high trust people around the world, go to SmartTrustBook.com.

Other implied promises can be created as a result of the words or actions of others who have preceded you in a particular role, such as a team leader, manager, CEO, parent, or spouse—or from the words or actions of others in similar roles in the industry or culture. Getting those expectations out on the table and clarifying and dealing with them—perhaps through a "What do you think has been said?" audit—can go a long way toward eliminating roadblocks to trust and establishing your personal integrity in the say/do cycle. It can also be helpful to take advantage of new technologies that now make it possible for companies to crawl the Web and evaluate the "Web chatter" about their brand. This enables organizations to increase awareness and determine what steps can be taken to clear up any misunderstandings that might be affecting public perception of their say/do strength.†

It's important to keep in mind that people are generally satisfied to the degree to which their expectations are met. If we want to increase satisfaction and create trust, we need to clarify expectations to ensure that our commitments and people's expectations are aligned and that we consistently do what we say we're going to do.

---

† For a sample report that uses our Trust Brand Analytics to compare levels of trust in twelve industries and measure "Web chatter" about your brand without the bias of surveys, go to SmartTrustBook.com.

QUESTIONS TO CONSIDER

- Think of a time when you were disappointed or lost trust in someone. To what extent was your reaction a result of that person not doing what he or she said he or she was going to do?

- To what extent does it affect others' trust in you when you do what you say you're going to do—or when you don't?

- When you see the phrase "a company you can trust," what do you think? Do you believe it's true? Why—or why not?

- How much confidence do you have that you can make and keep commitments to yourself? How do you think this might be affecting your level of prosperity, energy, and joy? How might it be affecting your ability to trust and work with others?

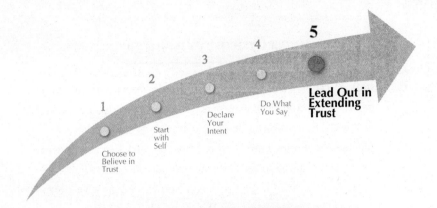

CHAPTER EIGHT

Smart Trust Action 5:
Lead Out in Extending Trust
to Others

Trust men and they will be true to you;
treat them greatly, and they will show themselves great.
RALPH WALDO EMERSON

If you can't trust people, who can you trust?
JOHN WIDDICOMBE

Greg:

During my teenage years, I was a regular hellion—somewhat of a
juvenile delinquent, in fact. Thankfully, by eighteen, I had straight-
ened up a little—enough to manage to get into college and land a job
at a local grocery store to help pay my tuition.

I hadn't been working there for more than a few months when one afternoon, Ralph, the store manager, unexpectedly tossed me the store keys one afternoon and told me to lock up when we closed. I was taken aback. I realized that holding those keys meant that I would be supervising the other employees. It also meant that I would be responsible for handling all the money as I closed out the tills and locked the cash drawers in the safe.

Obviously, I hadn't elaborated on my dubious background when I'd applied for the job. I can only imagine the clue my long, shaggy hair must have given, but if Ralph had had any idea of how untrustworthy I was at that time in my life, he probably never would have tossed me those keys. Nevertheless, I can distinctly remember (after recovering from the shock of the situation) the unfamiliar feeling of responsibility that rose up in me and the gratitude and loyalty I suddenly felt toward this good man. I desperately wanted to prove worthy of his trust in me and absolutely did not want to let him down.

Looking back, I realize that Ralph's simple trust in me that day marked a turning point in my life, a milestone event that has had a profound impact on my entire career. It also gave me a unique desire to look for opportunities to extend trust to others. Understanding firsthand how scared and ill prepared others may feel when asked to "rise to the occasion" inspires me to take the risk and expect the best of people. It gives me the desire to see potential in others, potential they may not yet see in themselves—just as Ralph did for me.

In our work, we often ask leaders and executives around the world to reflect on their lives or careers and to identify a time when someone took a chance on them, extended trust to them, or maybe believed in them even more than they believed in themselves. Whenever we do this, without exception the feeling in the room changes. People become deeply touched and inspired as they recall their experiences and acknowledge with gratitude the impact they have had in their lives. And they become even more inspired when we invite them to share and they take in each other's experiences.

We encourage you to take a minute now and do the same thing. Think of someone who extended trust to you. Who was it? What was the situation? What difference has it made in your life?

Smart Trust managers, parents, and leaders in all walks of life lead out in extending trust to others. In doing so, they build the capacity and confidence of those who are trusted. They unleash human potential and multiply performance. They inspire reciprocal trust in both directions—back to those who extended it and forward to others who could benefit from it. They help create high-trust cultures that generate greater prosperity, energy, and joy.

The Smart Trust Action of extending trust is based on the *principles* of leadership and empowerment. The *opposite* is to withhold trust, attempt to control others, and/or try to do everything yourself. *Counterfeits* include extending "false trust" (giving people responsibility but not authority or resources), extending "fake trust" (acting as though you trust people but then micromanaging and hovering over them), and "managing" or "administering" while thinking you're "leading."

This action is more than choosing to believe. It's choosing to act on that belief—to take the step, to make the leap. The belief that it will pay off is what gives a person the courage and faith to do it. And it's the job of a leader to go first.

Why Is Extending Smart Trust Smart?

There are three primary reasons why extending Smart Trust is smart: (1) it produces results; (2) it increases trust; and (3) it elicits reciprocity. Let's look deeper into each.

1. Extending Smart Trust produces results. Remember the results of building relationships of trust through positive ticketing in the Richmond detachment of the Royal Canadian Mounted Police: a 50 percent reduction in court referrals and juvenile arrests, a drop in recidivism to 5 percent, and a 90 percent reduction in the cost of processing offenders.

Remember the outcome of BestBuy.com's extension of trust to employees, allowing them to work whenever and wherever they like as long as they get the job done: a 35 percent increase in productivity within the first six weeks. Best Buy's headquarters has created a "Results Oriented Work Environment" (ROWE) where performance is based on results, not face time. The culture was described on the cover of *Business Week* as "No meetings. No schedule. (No joke.)" What makes ROWE Smart Trust is crystal-clear expectations and accountability. The result? A 50 percent decrease in turnover and employees working longer hours with no additional pay, while at the same time reporting increased health and happiness. Why does extending Smart Trust create these kinds of results? Because extending trust to people inspires them. It brings out the best in them. It motivates them. In fact, the reason extending trust is so powerful is because *to be trusted is the most compelling and sustainable form of human motivation.*

> Mistrust begets mistrust; trust begets accomplishment.
>
> LAO TZU
> AUTHOR OF *TAO TE CHING*

2. Extending Smart Trust increases trust. It's somewhat ironic that one of the best ways to increase trust is to simply extend it. There are many reasons for this. Trusting people inspires them to want be worthy of that trust. It brings out the best in them. It helps them develop their capabilities. As happened when Ralph, the store manager, threw Greg the keys and trusted him with the responsibility to close the store, people tend to rise to the occasion. They perform, and the results of their performance generate more trust, facilitating an even greater extension of trust to them. The result is increased trust. As Frito-Lay CEO Al Carey told us, "If you trust people, they start leaning in and you see their best self. You see their best work. They bring the best of their abilities to the party. You get 50,000 people working like this, it's going to be great."

> *Trust each other again and again. When the trust level gets*
> *high enough, people transcend apparent limits, discovering*
> *new and awesome abilities for which they were previously*
> *unaware.*
>
> DAVID ARMISTEAD

3. Extending Smart Trust generates reciprocity. As we've said earlier, when we give trust to people, they tend to give it back. When we withhold trust, they withhold it in return. In teams and organizations, giving trust manifests in greater employee engagement and retention, increased customer loyalty and referrals, and other economic benefits. The Paul Zak study we referenced in chapter three showed that sending intentional signals of trust created reciprocity that resulted in a nearly threefold increase in economic returns. Leaders who deliberately extend trust typically find the people in their organizations far more willing to place trust in them and their leadership. Thus the reciprocal process becomes a virtuous upward cycle, all triggered by that first extension (sometimes leap) of trust.

> *The people when rightly and fully trusted will return the trust.*
>
> ABRAHAM LINCOLN

Leaders Go First

In order to increase influence and grow trust in a team, an organization, a community, a family, or a relationship, someone has to take the first step. That's what leaders do. They go first. They lead out in extending trust. In fact, the first job of a leader is to inspire trust, and the second is to extend it. This is true whether a person has a formal leadership role, such as CEO, manager, team leader, or parent, or an informal role of influence, such as work associate, marriage partner, or friend.

In the exercise we described earlier, after asking leaders to reflect on their experience when someone extended trust to them, we then ask, "When have you led out in extending trust to someone else?" This often brings people up short as they realize that they have missed opportunities—sometimes many opportunities—to extend trust, to initiate the upward cycle, to generate prosperity, energy, and joy. You might want to think about your own experience. Have there been times when you extended trust to others and really made a difference in their lives? Have there been times when you didn't but now perhaps wish you had?

Bottom line, if we're not inspiring and extending trust, we're not leading. We might be managing or administering, but we're not *leading*. We manage things, we lead people. And real leadership requires trust. As renowned leadership authority Warren Bennis put it, "Leadership without mutual trust is a contradiction in terms."

> If you give respect, you'll get respect. The same goes for loyalty, and trust and all the other virtues that I believe great leaders have to offer. . . . I also believe the leader, the person in charge, is usually the one who must initiate the process. Don't wait for an employee to respect you before you'll respect him or her.
>
> JOHN WOODEN
> LEGENDARY UCLA BASKETBALL COACH

In *The Truth About Leadership,* James Kouzes and Barry Posner tell the story of Dawn Lindblom, who had recently been appointed regional manager for the Eastern Washington State region of the American Red Cross. Lindblom had been wondering if she could trust Gail McGovern, the woman who had just been put in as president and CEO of the national Red Cross. When someone on McGovern's tour of introduction to the regional leaders asked her point-blank, "Can we trust you?" McGovern replied, "I can't answer that for you, but let me tell you that *I trust each and every one of you.*" As Lindblom told Kouzes and Posner, it made all the difference to her to know that McGovern was willing to go first—that she was willing to take the risk by extending trust to the regional leaders.

> *The only one who earns trust is the one who is prepared to grant trust.*
>
> GUSTAV HEINEMANN
> FORMER PRESIDENT OF THE FEDERAL REPUBLIC OF GERMANY

In 1948 William McKnight, then the president and later the chairman of 3M, led with what was considered at the time a radical philosophy to encourage risk taking in extending trust in organizations. In effect, it was to let go of control in order to grow the organization, speed innovation, and expand the company's influence. McKnight said:

> *As our business grows, it becomes increasingly necessary to delegate responsibility and to encourage men and women to exercise their initiative. This requires considerable tolerance. Those men and women, to whom we delegate authority and responsibility, if they are good people, are going to want to do their jobs in their own way.*
>
> *Mistakes will be made. But if a person is essentially right, the mistakes he or she makes are not as serious in the long run as the mistakes management will make if it undertakes to tell those in authority exactly how they must do their jobs.*
>
> *Management that is destructively critical when mistakes are made kills initiative. And it's essential that we have many people with initiative if we are to continue to grow.*

Operating on this philosophy, 3M has grown from less than $20 million in revenue in 1948 to $26.6 billion in revenue in 2010 and is frequently cited as one of the most innovative companies in the world. The current CEO, George Buckley, recognizes the ongoing relevance of this trust-based philosophy, stating "As a company, while we know pretty clearly where we are going, we must always remember who we are and where we came from."

In *Influencer,* our friends from VitalSmarts shared the story of a woman who led out by making an incredible leap of trust that resulted in the rehabilitation of thousands of people whom most would consider "untrustworthy" thieves, prostitutes, robbers, and murderers. By providing an alternative to prison through work at the Delancey Street Foundation in San Francisco, Dr. Mimi Silbert helped them transform their lives. The rules are strict. There are safeguards in place. It's "trust but verify" at the highest level. But the results are truly amazing.

> *Dr. Silbert's typical new hires have had four felony convictions. They've been homeless for years, and most are lifetime drug addicts. Within hours of joining Delancey, they are working in a restaurant, moving company, car repair shop, or one of the many Delancey companies. And other than Silbert herself, these felons and addicts make up the entire population at Delancey. No therapists. No professional staff. No donations, no grants, no guards— just a remarkable influence strategy that has profoundly changed the lives of 14,000 employees over the past 30 years. Of those who join Delancey, over 90 percent never go back to drugs or crime. Instead they earn degrees, become professionals, and change their lives. Forever.*

When leaders don't extend trust, people often tend to perpetuate vicious, collusive downward cycles of distrust and suspicion. As a result, they become trapped in a world where people don't trust each other— where management doesn't trust employees and employees don't trust management; where unions don't trust management and management doesn't trust unions; where suppliers don't trust partners and partners don't trust suppliers; where companies don't trust customers and customers don't trust companies; where marriage partners don't trust each other; and where parents don't trust their children and children don't trust their parents.

But when leaders take the lead in extending trust—in a relationship, on a team, in an organization, or in a country—negative, collusive cycles of distrust and suspicion can be broken, and the door can be opened to greater prosperity, energy, and joy for all stakeholders.

How Does a Leader Extend "Smart Trust"?

As we acknowledged at the outset, there is risk in extending trust. That's why it takes courage. But there is also risk—often greater risk—in not extending trust. So how do we navigate through the decision-making process and determine whether or not to extend trust, and—if so—how much to extend and under what conditions?

The Smart Trust Matrix we introduced in chapter three identifies the two factors people have found most helpful in making Smart Trust decisions: the *propensity to trust* and *analysis* of opportunity, risk, and credibility. As we explained, it's the combination of the two that creates good judgment.

As we also mentioned, however, creating the highest synergy between these two factors is more of an art than a science. It takes assuming positive intent in others—unless there's good reason to do otherwise. In takes determining when verification will enable trust—or when it will get in the way. It takes discernment and sometimes the willingness to take a leap of trust, sometimes even when "logic" may direct otherwise.

Isabel Blanco, a former deputy director for the Georgia Division of Family and Children Services, shared with us the remarkable story of how she was able to overcome the challenges of a distrustful system and extend Smart Trust to benefit thousands of children at risk in her state. She prefaced her story by telling us that any state agency of child protective services has an extraordinarily high standard of accountability because children's lives are at stake. The high risk puts tremendous pressure on caseworkers and social system leaders to get things right. When an incident is reported to child protective services, it is up to a caseworker to determine whether to refer the case for investigation or work directly with the stakeholders—parents, teachers, administrators, and/or relatives—to remedy the situation. Because of the visible and serious consequences of a child being harmed by being left in an abusive home, the overwhelming tendency of a state or any low-trust bureaucracy is to develop a rule-based system to eliminate human error.

After giving us that background, Blanco described the system she inherited when she assumed her leadership role in the Georgia system in 2004:

> *They had developed policies to cover every possible mistake that could be made and thereby limit the amount of judgment the professionals could utilize by having them speak only to what the policy says. They also had a minutely detailed thirty-two-step tool book to ensure that human judgment could not be blamed.*
>
> *You can just imagine the low trust, the slow, cumbersome process, and the fear. And because of the lack of trust, we weren't making the decisions*

at the front door we needed to. To play it safe, we were assigning everything as an investigation. As a result, when I arrived in 2004, there were 3,711 investigations overdue by ninety days. This meant caseloads of thirty to sixty investigations per caseworker in some urban centers. Because the load was so great, in some instances the caseworkers didn't even know the children's names, so if they read of a child dying in the newspaper, they had to check their case files to see if it was one of theirs.

Blanco recognized that those who had created the process had had a positive intent: to protect children. But unfortunately, the very system that had been designed to protect them was putting even more children at risk by creating huge delays. In addition, the system took a toll on the level of engagement of the case professionals, who started to lose confidence in their professional judgment. Blanco said:

What happens when you have so much policy and so many rules? You clearly send a message to the professionals: "We don't trust you." So what happens? Emotionally, the caseworkers vacate their responsibility, and their judgment begins to reflect it. The system was actually encouraging the exact opposite of what all these other things were designed to ensure. The caseworkers became scared of themselves. So not only was the system causing a crisis of trust, it was also creating a crisis of self-confidence. And the caseworkers were defaulting in picking up the kind of cues in investigations and decisions that would make all the difference.

That human instinct, to be able to come to a conclusion based on one's collective knowledge and judgment, is the art of child welfare. But with all this control and lack of trust to eliminate risk, most systems communicate by sheer rules that the art part of child welfare decision making is not valuable. I would tell you, however, it is extremely valuable.

Conventional wisdom in the agency dictated that the way to solve the backlog problem was to add more caseworkers. But not only was there was no budget to do so, Blanco was convinced that it would not solve the problem.

The reality was I didn't need any more caseworkers. I needed the ones I had to operate on all gears—so why should I get more and only have them operate at 20 percent of their capacity? That's a waste. It was a real "Aha!" moment when we realized we were actually underutilizing the caseworkers' capacity.

Blanco's solution was to extend more trust to the current caseworkers to use their judgment. Given the low tolerance for risk, the various stakeholders initially reacted with fear. Blanco had to convince police and other community stakeholders that trusting caseworkers to make decisions would actually protect more children, not less. It was a hard sell. Surprisingly, her hardest sell was to the distrust-burned caseworkers themselves. Ultimately, she had to get into her car and personally visit workers in the front lines in 159 counties to make it happen.

Eventually, I was able to convince the caseworkers and they were able to be more courageous about trusting themselves, probably because they knew how little trust they had in the validity of misconduct in their caseloads. The backlog was so big, and they knew that 60 percent of the time they were finding nothing. They were investigating, tearing people's lives apart, and then finding nothing, closing the case with no services. They knew the system was broken, and they were more willing to take courageous action in a different direction.

Blanco had two important things going for her in her effort to change the system. The first was her high-trust relationship with her top boss, Commissioner B. J. Walker, whom she was able to engage in her campaign. According to Blanco, every time someone would call Walker and say, "Do you know what your leader out here is saying? You're going to kill babies!" Walker would respond, "No, this is strategic."

The second was her use of Smart Trust. Blanco said:

I was not suggesting that we just blindly trust our caseworkers. We installed processes that supported what we wanted in a very responsible way, and we monitored every decision in a trend line, evaluating our percentage in getting the decision right. The accountability that we held ourselves to was even higher than what the federal government gave us. The federal standard looks at six months, with no further incident to validate a decision. Only six months. We said, "No, no, no, no. Any time we see that child for the rest of our time going forward, we're going to track that child."

Blanco demonstrated superb judgment by combining her strong propensity to trust with equally strong analysis of situation, risk, and credibility. Her determination paid off, and the extension of Smart Trust to caseworkers to use their judgment took root. With this new trust-based approach, and without adding additional staff, in just under six years the case backlog went from 3,711 cases over ninety days down to zero. In the same time period, monthly open investigations dropped by 70 percent, and timely completion rose to 97 percent. In addition, child safety increased by 45 percent. By exercising Smart Trust, Blanco and her team saved lives and started a ripple effect that will continue in Georgia for decades to come.

Stephen:

On a more personal level, in my presentations I sometimes share the story of Anna Humphries, the only girl on a third/fourth-grade Little League flag football team I coached years ago. Anna was a decent player, but she did not have the experience and skills of some of the other players. I had made the decision to play everyone equally, but that decision was really put to the test when our team made it to the final game, when we played another undefeated team for the unofficial "championship." Our opponents were only one point behind, and they were going for two points for the win. With our team goal of winning on the line, I had to decide whether to leave Anna in to finish her turn to play or to replace her with a better player.

In the moment of decision, I determined to extend trust to Anna and leave her in. We all held our breath as the opposing team ran toward Anna's side, but she executed the planned play and pulled the runner's flag (only the second time she had pulled a flag all year) and stopped him just short of the goal. When I saw the exuberant look on Anna's face as she realized what she had done and her joy as she received the enthusiastic congratulations of her teammates and the cheers of a supporting crowd, I was thrilled that I'd decided to extend trust.

As I share this experience, on occasion people will come up to me and say, "It's very convenient for you to call this Smart Trust because it worked, and if it hadn't, you could have said, 'Oh, I exercised too much trust.'" Certainly there's something to be said for the question of accurately labeling a decision "Smart Trust." Making such decisions is a matter of navigating through life and learning how to make good judgment calls. Sometimes we trust too much, sometimes too little. But hopefully, as we become more discerning and capable in considering the opportunity, risk, and credibility of those involved, our judgment calls become better.

In retrospect, however, I have to say that even if Anna hadn't made that winning play and we had lost the game, I still feel it would have been an exercise of Smart Trust to give her the chance. There was more involved than winning the game. Even if we had lost, I believe that everyone on the team would have come out of that experience knowing that they were valuable and that they were believed in and supported as individuals. I think they would have felt good about their efforts and their overall experience in being part of a team.

(continued on next page)

> *Today Anna is a freshman at a major university. She has blossomed into a stunningly talented, beautiful, and confident young woman, an operatic soprano who has performed both locally and nationally. About a year ago, her mother came to my office and said, "You need to see this. I was going through Anna's things, and I found this story she wrote in the fourth grade." It was the story of what happened that year with our football team, and Anna had titled it "The Happiest Thing That Ever Happened To Me." I cannot help but believe that my extension of trust to her made a positive difference in her life.*

Clearly, Smart Trust does not result in a simplistic, "one-size-fits-all" solution for every person or in every situation. What's Smart Trust for one may not be Smart Trust for another. For example, for Warren Buffett to do a deal for a $23 billion company on a handshake with no formal due diligence is not only remarkable, it's Smart Trust for him. He's highly credible. He has a great track record in assessing the credibility of prospective partners. He has a significant platform, and in terms of risk he could afford to have a deal go south. The bottom line is that no one is going to mess with Warren Buffett. But for the two of us to attempt to do the same kind of deal in the same way would probably not be Smart Trust. Without Buffett's platform and track record and with far less margin for risk, our blend of propensity to trust and analysis would almost certainly result in a different Smart Trust approach.

In each situation, Smart Trust requires judgment. It's an integral combination of the wisdom of heart and head—a synergy between the propensity to trust and analysis that is far greater than the sum of its parts. And there are times when others may not understand why we do what we do or the "Smart Trust" label we may put on it. Nevertheless, there are few experiences in life that provide the energy and joy we feel when we know we've made a significant difference in the lives of others by extending trust.

Extending Smart Trust on All Levels

At this point, we'd like to share with you some of the judgments individuals and organizations have made in extending trust to various stakeholders and how it's worked for them. As you read, notice how they integrate their propensity to trust with analysis of opportunity, risk, and credibility and how doing so produces results, increases trust, and inspires reciprocity.

Extending Smart Trust to Customers

Successful organizations lead out in extending Smart Trust to their customers. In addition to the companies we've already highlighted, you can see this manifested in businesses such as Zane's Cycles of Connecticut, one of the three largest bike shops in the United States. Zane's allows customers to go out the door for test drives on their bikes without asking for any identification or collateral. When customers offer to leave their driver's licenses, they are politely refused. The message Zane's communicates to its customers is "Just have a great ride. We trust you." As its founder, Chris Zane, put it, "Why start out that relationship by questioning their integrity? We choose to believe our customers."

The company's high-trust message also communicates clearly to its employees that Zane's is in the business of building customer relationships, not merely selling products. The result is $13 million in annual sales, with a 23 percent average annual growth rate since opening in 1981

DILBERT © 2004 Scott Adams. Used by permission of UNIVERSAL UCLICK. All rights reserved.

and a loss of only five of the 5,000 bikes sold each year to theft. Zane states:

> *Most customers are blown away by how much we trust them, and that goes far in building their confidence in us. As soon as we begin distrusting our customers and treating them like potential thieves, we'll automatically be putting our relationship in jeopardy. . . . Sure, we may lose those five bikes a year, but the other 4,995 that are test ridden do return.*

Zane firmly believes that the customers appreciate being trusted and that they reciprocate that trust by becoming lifelong customers, returning again and again and referring family and friends. So although there's a risk, with the company losing five bikes a year, Zane is convinced that it's Smart Trust because it's selling significantly more bikes than it would without such a high-trust, referral-generating approach.

Another business that leads out in extending trust to customers is the United Services Automobile Association (USAA), a Fortune 500 company providing banking, investing, and insurance services with a focus on people who serve and have served in the U.S. military and their families. Over the years, USAA has earned a remarkable level of customer trust through its extraordinary customer service. During the past several years, the company has ranked number one on the annual Net Promoter index measuring customer loyalty and number one or number two on the list of Bloomberg Businessweek's Customer Service Champs. The company also shows an unbelievable customer retention rate (the ultimate test of value creation and trust) of 97 percent.

What distinguishes USAA is its extension of trust to customers in matters both large and small. Whereas most financial services firms set up cumbersome procedures to protect themselves against fraud, USAA extends trust by allowing its customers to take pictures of their checks and "deposit" them by e-mail. When members call in to say a child is sixteen and an honor student, they receive a discount on auto insurance; the company does not require them to send in their children's report card or a letter from the school principal. In the words of a recently retired vice president, "As a USAA member, until you prove otherwise, we believe what you say. It's about trust. We trust the members, and they trust us."

Carglass, a windshield repair company in Belgium, is another business that leads out with customer trust. At a Smart Trust workshop in Antwerp, one Carglass employee shared with participants how the company had been able to improve a situation dealing with customer complaints by extending trust. Carglass believed that some customers had been less than honest in blaming the company for damage they said had been done by Carglass's repair technicians, when the damage had almost surely occurred in subsequent accidents and was unrelated to the windshield repair. Because every complaint involved significant time and administrative costs, the Carglass complaints department had grown quite large. As company leaders considered options to decrease costs, they finally decided to trust their customers. They offered free repairs to all those who had complaints, even if they had reason to believe they might be attempting to rip them off. As a result, Carglass was able to downsize its complaints department to two people and significantly reduce administrative costs. In addition, the number of people taking advantage decreased significantly, and many who had initially taken advantage turned into regular customers and strong word-of-mouth advocates for the company.

In our travels, we occasionally come across restaurants that have adopted a "pay what you think the meal is worth" approach, where restaurant owners trust customers to determine what they pay based on their own evaluation of the meal/service/experience. Sometimes there is a recommended price, sometimes not. As a result of this approach, some customers pay nothing, most pay something, and some pay significantly more than the normal price of the meal—most likely in delighted response to the trust they've been given. Though the particulars vary, many of the restaurants report equal or, in some cases, significantly higher revenues than they had with their traditional model. For example, Kish, a Persian restaurant in Frankfurt, Germany, increased its revenues by 54 percent after implementing this model. When asked how this could happen, the owner, Pourya Feily, said, "Basically, people are honest. . . . Most people wouldn't want to cheat anybody any more than they would

want to be cheated themselves. And because they set the price themselves, they feel it's a bargain, even if it is just as much as they would have
paid anyway." More than anything, this approach tends to attract and
keep more customers.

In some cases, the focus is less on profit and more on creating energy
and joy. That is the case with the Honesty Coffee Shop on the island of
Batan in the Philippines. The local news media has said:

> *This little store was started by Aling Elena, a retired teacher who decided
> to provide refreshments to townsfolk and travelers in the area. Anybody who
> enters the cafe can get food and drinks and drop whatever payment they feel
> like in a basket. While the items are tagged, the store is not [staffed]. Some
> people drop their payment, others don't. But it's all okay with Aling Elena;
> her ultimate profit is the chance to awaken her customers' consciousness to
> honesty and responsibility and to teach them to live these lessons in the other
> areas of their lives.*

Panera Bread in the United States has a social version of "pay what
you think the meal is worth." Panera Cares Community Cafes, which
effectively serves as a community food kitchen (with no prices or cash
registers), is on a self-sustaining basis because of the donations of others,
using the motto "Take what you need, leave your fair share."

On the Walls of the Honesty Coffee Shop in Batan

We cannot attend to you personally. Get what you wish to par-
take and pay for it. Please return for your change.

This store is too small for dishonest people.

God is my security guard.

Extending Smart Trust to Employees

As well as to customers, successful organizations also lead out in extending Smart Trust to their employees. In *The Power of We,* Jack Adler, president and COO of the Loews luxury hotel chain, shared his experience in making his first presentation to the top management of Loews Corporation, including CEO Larry Tisch:

> *I described the prospects for the hotel business in some detail, and we talked about our plans a bit. Then Larry Tisch got up out of his seat at the head of the table. "Okay," he said. "Do the best you can." And he left the room. That was the end of the meeting.*
>
> *I was puzzled. . . . I was expecting a little more detailed input than that! So I went to Bob Hosman, who was my boss at the time, and said, "Larry Tisch told me to do the best I can. What does that* mean?*"*
>
> *Bob laughed and said, "It means he trusts you, and you should use your best judgment."*
>
> *That's the way we run the hotels. We trust people and ask them to use their best judgment. Usually they do—and the results prove it works.*

Those results include the fact that five of the sixteen Loews properties appeared on the 2011 *U.S. News & World Report* list of eighty-six Best Hotels in the USA.

The Chubb Group of Insurance Companies, a large property and casualty insurer, has realized significant benefits in trusting employees to work flexible hours. At first CEO John Finnegan was doubtful about the approach. He told the *Financial Times,* "To be honest, I viewed the reported benefits of flexible work hours with some skepticism. As most CEOs would, I saw it as an employee accommodation programme with a cost. I didn't know you could at the same time maintain or increase productivity."

This approach has been surprisingly beneficial for Chubb, even in the recent economic downturn. Senior Vice President Rolando Orama, who leads Chubb's Chicago operation, where 120 of his team have chosen flexible hours, reports an increase from 82 to 91 percent of customers contacted within twenty-four hours and from 90 to 100 percent of benefits paid to claimants in a timely manner. Finnegan likens it to the gains of Toyota's lean manufacturing. He says, "It's making people more responsible and accountable for what they do." Companies such as IBM, British Telecom, and AT&T extend similar trust to employees by encouraging telecommuting, resulting in reduced real estate costs and enjoying productivity increases of up to 30 percent. What qualifies these company decisions as "Smart Trust" is the setting of crystal-clear expectations with equally clear accountability to those expectations.

> *Companies should trust people to work at home more.*
> *Commuting kills so much time that could be spent creating.*
>
> RICHARD BRANSON
> CEO, VIRGIN GROUP

At Ritz-Carlton, the impact of extending trust to employees is validated by anecdotal customer reports of heroic service as well as by verifiable bottom-line results. Simon Cooper, the president of the Ritz-Carlton Hotel Company, relates the story of a team member who was looking for a guest's lost ring. When he failed to find the ring, he went through the laundry. When he still didn't find it, he proceeded to take the washing machine apart—and he finally located the ring in the catchment area of the drain. Cooper admits that as he hears of accounts like this, he realizes that even he may have stopped short of the often heroic

DILBERT © 2002 Scott Adams. Used by permission of UNIVERSAL UCLICK. All rights reserved.

efforts of his team. The bottom-line results of way-beyond-expectations service are enormous guest engagement. And Ritz-Carlton company research shows that a guest who is actively engaged with Ritz-Carlton and its staff spends 23 percent more money than one who is only moderately engaged. When employees produce a 4-percentage-point increase in customer engagement scores companywide, the Ritz-Carlton achieves an extra $40 million in incremental revenue.

Extending Smart Trust made a profound difference to employees of Procter & Gamble overseas several years ago when the area of the world in which they were operating became politically volatile and potentially dangerous. A very concerned regional manager phoned headquarters to ask what he should do and was told, in effect, "We trust you. You're on the ground. You figure this out. We will support you." The manager decided to move all employees and their families to a different country at the company's expense. When some of our colleagues worked with those employees recently, they found that the employees were still telling stories about how the manager had arranged for them and their families to be moved. The significant extension of trust to the regional manager to do what he thought best resulted in legends and lore about the company and also enormous loyalty and commitment among the employees.

> *No single set of rules can provide explicit guidance for every situation that may be faced by a complex global company such as P&G. So ultimately, P&G relies on every employee to use good judgment in everything he or she does.*
>
> A. G. LAFLEY
> FORMER CHAIRMAN AND CEO, PROCTER & GAMBLE

On a broad scale, one of the new frontiers for organizations is navigating through the issue of whether to give employees access to social networking tools and sites at work. A 2010 survey of 1,400 CIOs by Robert Half Technology showed that 54 percent of organizations blocked sites such as Facebook and Twitter altogether and only 10 percent of companies gave employees full access to such networks during the day. At the core, the reason was distrust. Organizations expressed concern that employees would waste time, be less productive, and possibly leak confidential information or speak poorly of the company (which, incidentally, they could easily do without having access to social networks during business hours). Despite those concerns, leading organizations are beginning to see this relatively new frontier as an opportunity to extend Smart Trust to employees—with clear expectations of and accountability to those expectations—believing that the trust will be reciprocated. According to a special report on social networking in *The Economist:*

> *Employees are much more trustworthy than companies think. . . . If you can't trust your employees, you have one of two problems: you are hiring the wrong people or you are not properly training the people you hire. . . . All in all, companies have more to gain than to lose by allowing employee access to social networks.*

DILBERT © 2010 Scott Adams. Used by permission of UNIVERSAL UCLICK. All rights reserved.

Extending Smart Trust to Partners

Successful companies also extend Smart Trust to their partners. Al Carey, CEO of Frito-Lay, told us of a time he attended a meeting at a hotel near Frito-Lay headquarters in Dallas. On arriving, he noticed that the placard in the lobby announced another Frito-Lay meeting in progress in the same hotel. Curious, he went to that meeting room and was surprised to find his operations team sharing the Smart Trust concepts and behaviors his company had internally embraced with their distributor partners, including

Wal-Mart, Kroger, Target, and others. Carey told us that discussing trust with those outside stakeholder partners turned out to be a huge benefit later that year, when unexpected economic conditions forced the company to change its retail pricing. During the previous twenty-plus years, price changing had been a time-consuming process, taking a minimum of sixteen weeks. But because of the new levels of internal and external trust it had built, it was able to complete the process in only five weeks!*

UPS is a standout in extending partner trust. Not only is it a delivery company, it's also a supply-chain partner that enables other companies to gain from the scale, scope, and efficiency of a global player. Since the late 1990s the company has engaged in what it calls "synchronized commerce solutions." As the UPS advertisements suggest, its supply-chain services level the playing field, especially for smaller organizations. However, larger firms embrace the services as well. The UPS model is not an old-fashioned supplier-customer model based on coordination; it is a new partnering model based on trust and collaboration. As former UPS CEO Michael Eskew explained:

> *This is no longer a vendor-customer relationship. We answer your phones, we talk to your customers, we house your inventory, and we tell you what sells and doesn't sell. We have access to your information and you have to trust us. We manage competitors, and the only way for this to work, as our founders told Gimbels and Macy's, is 'trust us.' I won't violate that. Because we are asking people to let go of part of their business, and that really requires trust.*

UPS has also been instrumental in equipping smaller entrepreneurs and midsized enterprises to have a global presence. UPS's senior vice president of sales and marketing, Kurt Kuehn, put it this way:

> *The Texas machine parts guy is worried that the customer in Malaysia is a credit risk. We step in as a trusted broker. If we have control of that*

---

*To view a brief video about the impact of our Smart Trust program at Frito-Lay as described by CEO Al Carey and his executive team, go to SmartTrustBook.com.

package, we can collect funds subject to acceptance and eliminate letters of credit. Trust can be created through personal relations or through systems and controls. If you don't have trust, you can rely on a shipper who does not turn [your package] over until he is paid. We have more ability than a bank to manage this, because we have the package and the ongoing relationship with the customer as collateral, so we have two points of leverage.

In many situations, partnership trust is either created or significantly enhanced by the personal relationships of the people involved. The collaboration of Yale University and Fudan University in Shanghai represents a significant partnership between two leading global institutions that was spawned by the trust established by Chinese professors getting their PhDs at Yale. As Yale President Richard C. Levin told Thomas Friedman, "Most of these institutional collaborations arise not from top-down directives of university administrators, but rather from long-standing personal relationships among scholars and scientists."

Extending Smart Trust in Personal Relationships and Social Networks

On a break during a presentation, a man came up to us and said, "This has been very helpful for me in my business, but I want to talk to you about my personal life. I have a teenage son, and when you talked about extending trust and how trust is reciprocal in nature, my thoughts went immediately to my son." At that point, the man became choked up. "I could hear myself saying the words that I say to him almost every day: 'I don't trust you.' 'You're not trustworthy,' 'You can't be trusted, and I'm not going to do anything for you until you prove to me that you can.' I realized that yes, he has behaved in ways that have caused me to lose trust, but I have been perpetuating it. I haven't been giving him a chance to change. I'm the leader, I'm the parent. It's my job to go first, and I haven't been doing that."

We assured this man that leading out in extending Smart Trust doesn't mean he should just ignore behavior that's taken place and caused him to lose trust. We told him that sometimes you have to look for specific situations, specific opportunities, where you might be able to express trust. It may be in just one thing or in one circumstance. We encouraged him to find some reason and some way to say to his son, "I trust you in this"—to express it, label it, call it out, and declare his intent. We again affirmed that people usually reciprocate trust in the same way they reciprocate distrust, and a leader's (or parent's) consistent actions will usually direct the cycle—either upward in trust or downward in distrust.

Clearly, trust—or the lack of it—has a powerful impact on personal relationships, We recently spoke with an entrepreneur who had sold his 50 percent interest of his business to his business partner at a significant discount, just because he wanted to get out of the relationship as fast as he could. Why? Because his partner was so distrusting of him, and of everyone and everything, that it was sapping all the joy and happiness from his life. Eliminating the negative impact distrust was having on his energy and joy was far more important to him than the economic loss he had taken to get out of the relationship. The same thing sometimes happens in divorces and in other situations where distrust has so soured the relationship that just getting out of it becomes the driving force.

As we indicated in chapter one, the connection between trust and energy and joy in social relationships is becoming more and more apparent all across the board. Cutting-edge research indicates that happiness tends to drive success, not the other way around; that the greatest predictor of happiness is relationships; and that the greatest driver of relationships is trust. As Shawn Achor wrote in *The Happiness Advantage:*

> *When we are happy—when our mindset and mood are positive—we are smarter, more motivated, and thus more successful. Happiness is the center, and success revolves around it. . . .*
>
> *In a study appropriately titled "Very Happy People," researchers sought out the characteristics of the happiest 10 percent among us. . . . Turns out, there was one—and only one—characteristic that distinguished the happiest 10 percent from everybody else: the strength of their social relationships.*

The quality of our relationships affects not only happiness but also health. A 2007 *American Journal of Public Health* survey of 24,000 workers throughout the U.S. found that those with few social relationships were two to three times more likely to suffer from depression than people who had numerous and strong social relationships.

Even modern high-tech relationships reveal a connection to trust. An interesting study released by the Pew Internet and American Life Project showed that Facebook users were 43 percent more likely than other users of the Internet to believe that "most people can be trusted." The Facebook users were also three times more likely to believe that "most people can be trusted" than people who didn't use the Internet at all. So which came first, the belief that other people can be trusted or the use of Facebook and the Internet? Although causal effects weren't examined, it's clear that even social networks both engender and help extend trust.

> If history is a trustworthy guide, state-of-the-art technology won't ever replace state-of-the-heart technology.
>
> PETER GUBER
> FORMER CEO, SONY ENTERTAINMENT

Extending Smart Trust in the Community

As you could see in the stories of the Miralles supermarket in Panama and community policing in Canada, building trust in the community pays real dividends in terms of prosperity, energy, and joy. An associate of ours shared a personal experience he'd had in creating community trust several years ago when he was working for an NGO in a European country. He and his colleagues used bicycles for transportation, but they were concerned that if they went inside an establishment and left the bikes unattended, they would be stolen by the local "hoods." They finally decided to extend trust to the local boys by treating them with respect, engaging them in friendly conversation, and answering the questions they had about American culture. They found that when they treated the boys with trust rather than distrust and suspicion, they were able to leave their bikes outside with confidence that they would still be there when they returned.

The physicians at Cleveland Clinic, a nonprofit multispecialty medical center in Cleveland, Ohio, extend Smart Trust to patients by being very transparent with them and giving them online access to their own charts and medical records, including doctors' notes. They have further increased community trust by setting up physician compensation and review in a patient-centric way. The CEO, Dr. Delos Cosgrove, a heart surgeon who has performed more than 22,000 operations, said:

> *Very few hospitals are organized the way we are. . . . First, all of us have salaries. It doesn't make any difference, if I'm a cardiac surgeon, whether I do two heart operations a day or four. I take home the same amount of money at the end of the week. So there's no incentive to do extra tests or any of that.*
>
> *Second, we all have one-year contracts, and we have annual professional reviews. So the quality of the doctors is controlled, there's no tenure, and if you don't make it, you don't get a pay raise or you may not stay. That is one of the most important things we do. It's quite different from most places, where doctors can practice for as long as they want to practice.*

The clinic is also very much physician-led. The CEO, the CIO, and the chief of staff are all doctors. When asked, "How do you get the best doctors in the world to come work for a salary?" Cosgrove replied:

> *It's the environment the doctors come to work in. They've got colleagues that they respect, and they are supported, so they can do doctor work. I mean, most of us didn't sign up to fill out insurance forms. . . . I've never sent a bill. It's all done for me. So I did doctor work, and I think that's what most doctors want to do, in an environment with equal-quality physicians.*

The Cleveland Clinic has been praised for offering the highest quality medical care at costs well below the national norm. Patients have included

King Khalid of Saudi Arabia, the Prince of Wales, Oprah Winfrey, Jack Nicklaus, and many others who could afford to go anywhere. *U.S. News & World Report* has ranked it as the number one clinic in cardiac care in its annual rankings of America's best hospitals for the past fifteen years.

Extending Smart Trust in a Country

Increasingly, individuals in progressive nations are recognizing the importance of increasing trust in their countries and are taking steps to do so. Bo Xilai, the former mayor of Dalian, introduced a movement toward the historic autonomy of city-states in China by proactively initiating trade with Japan. He built the trade up to the point where more than three thousand Japanese firms were operating in the city of Dalian independently of Bejing. When Xilai was later appointed minister of commerce of the People's Republic of China, he reciprocated the trust that had allowed him to accomplish those things by granting other city managers similar autonomy. As a result, the number of city-states with more than a million people increased from seven in the early 1990s to 150 in 2011, and the economy exploded, enabling China to make the seismic shift from a rural to an urban economic system.

Though the 2009 Edelman Trust Barometer indicates that the outside world doesn't yet have high trust in China (global respondents say they have less trust in companies based in China and Russia than in any other countries in the world), the Chinese do have a high degree of trust among themselves. In fact, in a 2007 Pew Global Attitudes Survey, China showed the highest level of societal trust among the forty-seven countries surveyed, with a remarkable 79 percent of Chinese agreeing with the statement "Most people in this society are trustworthy." In *China's Megatrends,* John and Doris Naisbitt describe China's developing vertical democracy as being based on trust, with a special emphasis on competence and results. They note that one traditional aspect of Chinese thinking is the idea that "all insight arises from practical experience." In the Naisbitts' words:

The direction of the relationship between top-down and bottom-up forces is set to create a system that is built on trust: the government trusting its people and the people trusting the government. It is a model that fits Chinese history, Chinese thinking, and the Chinese people's strong desire for a harmonious and stable society.

Indeed, in 1978 Deng Xiaoping—then the de facto leader of China as a result of the death of Mao Zedong—called for "emancipating" minds, resulting in an extension of trust to the people, which, as the Naisbitts noted, "released huge energy." Although that energy could have been destructive, it turned out instead to be constructive. As an example, in 1978 there were 165,000 college graduates in China; in 2011, the number was 6.6 million. The two of us will never forget seeing the fruits of that energy while driving between Beijing and Tianjin for the World Economic Forum in 2008 and seeing the amazing new infrastructure that had been built—including a brand-new eight-lane freeway that ran for seventy miles through completely undeveloped farmland and from the Beijing airport to Tianjin on the coast. Nor will we forget the spectacular new mega–conference center facilities that hosted the World Economic Forum meetings there.

As we discussed earlier, the Corruption Perceptions Index shows a direct correlation between trustworthiness and prosperity. A similar correlation can be seen between the propensity to trust and prosperity. As Paul Zak and Stephen Knack observed, "High trust societies produce more output than low trust societies."

> A high level of trust is the most important feature any open society can possess. Trust, in many ways, is the product of all the ingredients in America's secret sauce.
>
> THOMAS FRIEDMAN
> PULITZER PRIZE–WINNING JOURNALIST

Creating a Smart Trust Culture

The summum bonum of leaders wisely extending trust in teams and organizations is the creation of a Smart Trust culture that generates prosperity, energy, and joy. At the beginning of this book, we expressed our intent to provide convincing evidence of the power of extending Smart Trust in a low-trust world. That power is most clearly manifested in a culture of high trust.

> *Culture eats strategy for breakfast.*
>
> PETER DRUCKER

One example of a Smart Trust culture is Zappos, where management trusts employees, employees trust management, and people on every level of the organization lead out with trust. Reflective of the high-trust culture, Zappos extends trust to employees even before they begin work. Each new hire goes through a four-week training process, and at the end of the first week, Zappos offers to pay them $4,000 to quit—plus wages for the amount of time they've already worked. This is a standing offer through the end of the fourth week of training. Hsieh said, "We want to make sure that employees are here for more than just a paycheck. We want employees that believe in our long-term vision and want to be part of our culture." Zappos trusts new hires to make the decision that's right for them. "[O]n average," Hsieh says, "less than 1 percent of people end up taking the offer." He told us that in addition, Zappos trusts and encourages new managers to spend 10 to 20 percent of their paid company time outside the office with team members so that they can get to know each other better. Smart Trust? Hsieh thinks so. He tells us that although some managers initially respond, "That sounds like fun, but I've got way too much to do," they quickly find that social time together increases trust, and the team becomes "friends doing things for friends," not just coworkers. Managers report 20 to 100 percent increases in team productivity from this approach.

Other organizations we've already described such as Google, Southwest Airlines, W. L. Gore, and SAS also employ Smart Trust as a management philosophy/operating system to the extent that trust runs through the veins of the organization. Like Hsieh, Whole Foods CEO John Mackey believes that the key is to get trust flowing in all directions:

> *Trust is optimized when it flows between all levels within the organization. Many leaders make the mistake of believing that the key to increasing organizational trust is to somehow get the work force to trust the leadership more. While this is obiously very important, it is equally important that the leadership trust the workforce. To receive trust, it is usually necessary that we give trust. Organizing into small interlocking teams helps ensure that trust will flow in all directions within the organization—upwards, downwards, within the team, and across teams.*

When leaders lead out in wisely extending Smart Trust, their actions have a ripple effect that cascades throughout the team, organization, community, or family and begins to transform behavior in the entire culture. Sometimes the acts of trust-extending leaders become legendary. For example, when Gordon Bethune burned the Continental Airlines policy and procedure manuals in the parking lot and told his employees they would be trusted to use their own judgment in solving problems, that act became the symbol of Continental's new culture of trust.

One reason some leaders don't extend trust is that they think they will have greater control in a culture that depends on rules, policies, and regulations to cover every contingency. As we've pointed out, the relationship between trust and control is inverse: the greater the level of trust, the greater the actual control. The French sociologist Émile Durkheim put it this way: "When mores [cultural values] are sufficient, laws are unnecessary; when mores are insufficient, laws are unenforceable." In a low-trust culture, it's literally impossible to put enough rules and policies into place to control people's every action. In a low-trust relationship, the legal agreement can't be long enough to cover every possibility. Therefore, the best way to increase control is to create a high-trust culture.

A boss's job—a leader's job—is to facilitate, not to control.
You have to trust people to do their jobs. That's the strongest
leadership there is. Trusting your employees.

GORDON BETHUNE
FORMER CEO, CONTINENTAL AIRLINES

A Smart Trust culture is actually a culture of immense momentum, possibility, and power. The increased freedom of expression, the autonomy, the enhanced trust, and the greater speed at which things can be accomplished make an enormous tangible, measurable difference in prosperity, energy, and joy. This is one reason Smart Trust is smart. It's not built on the assumption that what we need is more rules, more regulations, and more referees; it's built on the evidence that extending trust and creating a high-trust culture in which top performance is expected bring significantly greater dividends for stakeholders on every level.

Stephen:

I learned a lot about the power of a strong, high-trust culture from (of all things) working on my lawn. I was really having a problem with weeds, and all the spraying I was doing didn't seem to work. Finally, I went over to ask my neighbor, who had a great-looking lawn, what I should do. He said, "You're kidding, right? You're the 'green and clean' guy from 7 Habits—the guy who was supposed to have learned all this from your dad when you were seven years old!" I sheepishly admitted that somehow I must have missed the part about the weeds.

My neighbor laughed, and then he said, "Well, your problem is not weeds."

"It's not?" I replied incredulously.

"No," he said, "your problem is that your lawn is not healthy. If you just keep spraying the weeds, they'll just keep coming back. What

> *you need to do is build up a healthy lawn so there won't be any room*
> *for the weeds to grow. Just starve them out."*
>
> *Well, I did—and it worked! The strong, healthy grass overtook*
> *the lawn and left no room for the scrawny weeds to grow.*
>
> *I have since realized that the same strategy works in a team or an*
> *organization. If you just "spray"—if you just hit problem behavior*
> *with more rules, regulations, policies, and procedures—the "weeds"*
> *will simply grow back or pop up in new places. On the other hand, if*
> *you create a robust, healthy, high-trust culture, the offenders will be*
> *starved out and will eventually leave. It's really a matter of watering*
> *what you want to grow.*

Mergers and Acquisitions. One key area where the Smart Trust process really becomes a game changer is in mergers and acquisitions. Research from KPMG shows that 83 percent of mergers fail to create value and more than 50 percent actually destroy value, primarily "because of the people and cultural differences." Regrettably, the first casualty of most mergers is trust. And although high trust won't necessarily rescue a poor strategy, low trust will almost always derail a good one.

The secret sauce to executing mergers is implementing a process that intentionally creates the trust necessary to ensure the successful integration of cultures. When merging entities make the creation of trust an explicit objective, they significantly increase the probability of creating a unified high-trust culture. When they act on that objective and carry out a deliberate process that generates trust, they significantly increase the probability of delivering a value-creating merger.*

> *Culture becomes a secret weapon that makes things happen.*
>
> Jon Katzenbach
> Senior partner, Booz & Company

---

*To view a short video and download a white paper on why trust is the "secret sauce" to successful mergers and acquisitions, go to SmartTrustBook.com.

For us, the poster child for leading out in creating a Smart Trust culture is Warren Buffett of Berkshire Hathaway. As of 2011, Berkshire is tied with Petrobras—Petrolio Brasiliero as the eighth largest public company in the world. The most remarkable thing about Buffett's approach is that his headquarters staff managing Berkshire's seventy-seven separate operating companies and more than 257,000 employees is a mere twenty-one people—unheard of by any measure. Stanford Business School's David F. Larcker and Brian Tayan call it "the lowest ratio of corporate overhead to investor capital among all major corporations" in the world.

When we asked Buffett All-Star Grady Rosier, who runs a $33 billion business, how Buffett is able to create trust so quickly, he replied, "You have to understand the core business philosophy at Berkshire Hathaway—the trust. Warren's ability to acquire quality companies is built around the trust. . . . Warren leaves them in charge of their businesses, and they're happy about that, and nobody wants to let Warren down. And that's the way it just cascades down the organization as to 'this is what the expectation is and this is what we're going to do.'"

How does Buffett handle a span of control that includes 77 direct reports? He operates on the premise of what he and his business partner Charlie Munger call "deserved trust"—they assume that their people deserve trust unless they prove otherwise. It's not blind trust. It's Smart Trust. It includes discerning selection of people, clear expectations, and high standards of accountability. People respond to it, they thrive on it, they're inspired by it. Munger captures this Smart Trust culture beautifully:

> *Everybody likes being appreciated and treated fairly, and dominant personalities who are capable of running a business like being trusted. A kid trusted with the key to the computer room said, "It's wonderful to be trusted."*
>
> *That's how we operate Berkshire—a seamless web of deserved trust. We get rid of the craziness, of people checking to make sure it's done right. When you get a seamless web of deserved trust, you get enormous efficiencies. . . .*
>
> *Berkshire Hathaway is always trying to create a seamless web of deserved*

trust. *Every once in a while, it doesn't work, not because someone's evil but because somebody drifts to inappropriate behavior and then rationalizes it. . . .*

How can Berkshire Hathaway work with only [21] people at headquarters? Nobody *can operate this way. But we do. . . .*

Every once in a while we get surprised by something—maybe once a decade. It's what we all want. Who in the hell would not want to be in a family without a seamless web of deserved trust? We try for the same thing in business. It's not rocket science; It's elementary. Why more people don't do it, I don't know. Perhaps because *it's elementary.*

Creating a Legacy of Smart Trust

As we've emphasized, one person's or one company's act of extending Smart Trust often inspires those on the receiving end to reach out and extend trust to others. Often those experiences become part of a "genealogy of trust." Somewhere along the line, a parent, teacher, manager, or leader extended trust to that first individual and inspired him or her with a desire to make a similar difference in the life of someone else. Over time, each act of extending trust becomes part of a legacy of trust that increases prosperity, energy, and joy in families, relationships, organizations, communities, and even countries for generations.

Stephen:

Shortly after graduating from college, I was hired by the managing partner at Trammell Crow Company and went through the process of being assigned to a local office. After interviewing with more than a dozen different partners, I was discouraged to find that no one seemed to want me. I'm sure the managing partner must have been thinking "Why did I ever hire this guy?" Then I met with another

(continued on next page)

partner, John Walsh. After our interview, he said, "I like Stephen. I
believe in him. I want him on my team."

John extended trust to me when no one else did, and it inspired
me and motivated me. I wanted to work hard for him. In fact, I
wanted to succeed for him even more than I wanted to succeed for
myself because I wanted to prove that he was right, that his faith in
me was justified. John Walsh's extension of trust brought out the best
in me. It's also caused me to repeatedly ask the question "For whom
can I be a John Walsh? Who needs someone to believe in them, to
take a risk on them, to help them succeed?" Whenever I've been on
the fence about trusting someone, my experience with John Walsh has
caused me to increase my propensity to trust and to dare to take a
risk in giving that person a leg up, similar to the way in which John
took a risk with me.

The question to ask ourselves is this: "What kind of legacy am I pass-
ing down to future generations—to my family, to my personal associates, to my community, my company, my organization, my nation? Is it
a legacy of trust that will create increasing prosperity, energy, and joy?"
This is what the renaissance of trust is all about. It's about the snowball-
ing effect of extending trust one act, one person, one team, one organization at a time.

So if you choose to be a part of this global renaissance, where might
you begin to enhance your legacy of trust? Is there a family member to
whom you could extend Smart Trust and disrupt a collusive pattern of
distrusting behavior? Is there a friend or a partner with whom you could
transform a negative relationship into a high-trust relationship of prosperity, energy, and joy? Is there a business colleague for whom or situation in which extending Smart Trust might change a vicious downward
cycle into a virtuous upward cycle? Is there an opportunity for you to lead
out in creating a culture of Smart Trust in your team or organization?

Wherever you start, your decision to lead out by extending Smart
Trust to others will be a difference maker. You may not see results immediately. And you will certainly never see the full impact as those you

trust, in turn, reach out and extend trust to others . . . who then extend trust to others . . . and so on, over time. But you will have the deep satisfaction of knowing that you are investing in something magnificently bigger than self—something that can truly affect every relationship in every team, every company, every organization, every family, and every nation throughout the world for generations. And hopefully, you will be personally enriched as well by the prosperity, energy, and joy that attend such effort.

QUESTIONS TO CONSIDER

- Think about a time when someone extended trust to you. What positive results did it produce? How did it help build your trustworthiness? Did it inspire you to trust the person who extended trust to you or to reach out and extend trust to someone else?
- Think about your family, your community, your work team, or your company. What difference would it make if you were operating with others in a culture of high trust?
- To whom might you extend trust to increase prosperity, energy, and joy?

PART III

What Can You Do?

CHAPTER NINE

Creating Your Own Renaissance of Trust

*Increase the level of trust in any group, company
or society and only good things happen.*
THOMAS FRIEDMAN
Pulitzer Prize–winning journalist

Make a dent in the universe.
STEVE JOBS

In 1999, Colombia was considered the most dangerous place on earth. Filled with anarchy and overrun by drug lords, it was the scene of 80 percent of the world's kidnappings and 55 percent of the world's terrorists' acts. Tourism had all but died, and foreign investment had dropped dramatically.

About a decade later, Colombia presented a remarkably different picture. Kidnappings had shrunk by 88 percent. Terrorist acts were down by 84 percent. Direct foreign investment was up from $500 million a year to $10 billion a year, and annual U.S. tourism was up from 5,000 to 500,000 visitors—an increase of a hundredfold. What happened during that ten-year period that created such phenomenal change?

Let's start with one of the most apparent influences. In 2002 Álvaro

Uribe was elected president. His primary platform during his eight years in office was clear and straightforward: *restaurar la confianza*—"to restore trust." This restoration was focused on improvement in three areas: security, investment, and social cohesion. The premise was that Colombia needed to restore trust in itself as a nation and that this trust needed to begin with the citizens of Colombia themselves. If the people didn't trust the country, how could the outside world trust it? Both in his speeches and in conversation with us, Uribe has repeatedly said, "In Colombia, we are working on one key word for our country: trust. Trust for people to live in Colombia, to invest in Colombia, to study in Colombia, to enjoy their lives in our country." Restoring trust became the overriding objective for the entire Uribe government.

In April 2010, at the end of Uribe's second four-year term as president (and his final term, as dictated by Colombian law), Colombia hosted the World Economic Forum meeting for Latin America. At the time, Uribe said, "Our successfully hosting this global conference with record attendance is a great measure of the success we've had in restoring and regaining trust in Colombia and on the world stage. All our efforts to focus on this are coming to fruition with this type of effort, and it's being seen and recognized by the worldwide community this way."

Although Colombia as a nation clearly is a "work in progress" and continues to have significant challenges and problems, there is no doubt that it has dramatically turned around in the last decade. Colombia's new tourism campaign highlights the turnaround with the tagline "Colombia, the only risk is wanting to stay." And although Uribe certainly has his share of detractors, as does any politician, the Colombian economist Mauricio Cárdenas of the Brookings Institution gave the consensus view of Uribe's tenure: "We were overwhelmed with our problems when he took office. Now we've regained self-esteem and, fundamentally, Colombia has become more of a nation."

> When the crisis is over, investment will be made in those
> countries where there is deepest trust.
>
> ÁLVARO URIBE

As we share the story of Colombia's transformation with people around the world, a common reaction, especially among people from developing nations, is "Wow! I wish we could have a leader like Álvaro Uribe." We would have to agree that such a leader, operating from a position of formal authority, can make an enormous difference. However, unknown to many, Uribe's efforts were preceded by those of others—in particular, one individual citizen who had a vision for Colombia but was not in a comparable position of power or clout. Yet that man's efforts paved the way for Uribe's success. His name was Pedro Medina.

Yo Creo en Colombia

In 1999 Pedro Medina was busy overseeing the McDonald's operations for all of Colombia and teaching strategy classes at a university in Bogotá. But in the midst of the devastating chaos that year, he realized that the Colombia he was seeing was drastically different from the country he envisioned and loved. In the classroom one day, he asked his students, "How many of you intend to be here in Colombia in five years?" Only twelve of thirty-nine students raised their hands. "Let me ask the twenty-seven of you who didn't raise your hands: Why not?" They replied, "Tell us why we should. What is there to compel us to stay here in Colombia? Everything is lost. There is no security. There is no hope for this country." Sadly, Medina realized that he couldn't provide compelling answers for these students, for he, too, had begun to lose faith and hope in his country.

As a result of this experience, Medina began to develop a presentation he called "Why One Should Believe in Colombia." During the preparation process, it became clear to him that Colombia had lost its trust in itself and its trustworthiness as a nation and that without those two things it would not survive. Trust needed to be restored, but Medina concluded that it wasn't going to just happen in the midst of the chaos; it would take deliberate focus and the creation of a critical mass of like-minded people.

Medina began to give his presentation. It wasn't just rhetoric filled with nice platitudes; it was a thoughtful, passionate plea deeply rooted in analysis based on comparative advantages of nations. He outlined the natural strengths of Colombia and affirmed its greatness. He explained that the current situation did not have to define the country and told his listeners how they could take back control from the inside out, starting with themselves. People overwhelmingly resonated with the speech. He received requests to give it again and again and again because it provided such enormous hope at a time when there was no hope. Over a period of eight months, he gave the speech 256 times. His listeners became engaged. They wanted to hope. They wanted to believe. They wanted something to believe in.

Medina created a foundation called Yo Creo en Colombia (I Believe in Colombia), whose sole purpose was (and still is) to increase trust and confidence in Colombia, first at home and then abroad. He courageously quit his work for McDonald's and focused full-time on this effort because he felt it would do more good for his country than anything else he could possibly do. As a result of his efforts, a critical mass of people began to embrace the message that restoring trust and confidence would lift the country out of the chaos it was in.

So although it is true that when Álvaro Uribe and his government came into power in 2002 they did much to transform Colombia, it is also true that they were building on the strong foundation of the hope and belief of a critical mass that had been created by an individual citizen: Pedro Medina. As one individual, Medina literally helped change the course of an entire nation.

In September 2004 President Uribe and the newspaper *El Colombiano* awarded Medina the Exemplary Colombian Award. To date, Medina's foundation has held programs in more than 157 cities and 26 nations in helping to build trust and confidence in Colombia.

Un Millón de Voces Contra Las FARC

Another individual who made a significant contribution to the Colombian transformation and the cause of freedom throughout the world was a thirty-three-year-old electrician named Oscar Morales. Like many other Colombians, in January 2008 Morales was incensed by the unfolding news story of the discovery of Emmanuel, a four-year-old child who had been abandoned two years previously by an extremist group, FARC, that had been terrorizing Colombia for more than forty years. FARC had kidnapped Manuel's mother in 2002, and the boy had been born in the jungle in captivity. FARC had announced the release of mother and son in 2007, but Colombians soon discovered that FARC had lied about the boy. With an injured shoulder and diseases incident to jungle life, Emmanuel had been taken from his mother and left at a clinic when he was just two years old. His mother did not see him again until she was released, and the boy was finally found in an orphanage under another name.

Disgusted by the repeated kidnappings, bombings, and other atrocities committed by FARC, Morales decided it was time to fight back. On January 4, 2008, he started a Facebook campaign, Un Millón de Voces Contra las FARC (One Million Voices Against the FARC)—to gather people to protest against the cruelty of the terrorist organization. This decision was extremely courageous because by using Facebook, Morales knew that he and all who joined him would be putting their lives in danger by revealing their actual names and faces. Though FARC's guerrilla activities had diminished somewhat under Uribe's regime, there was still widespread fear induced by its violent history and the organization still held hundreds of hostages. Nevertheless, Morales sent out the message "No more kidnappings. No more lies. No more FARC." By the next morning, 1,500 people had already joined his Facebook website, increasing to 4,000 by the end of the day. The following day, the number increased to 8,000, and the figures continued to increase rapidly. Encouraged by the momentum, Morales decided to take the protest to the streets. He found volunteers to organize demonstrations, and just a month after his Facebook launch, streets in more than two hundred cities and forty different countries around the globe were flooded with more than 12 million protestors, creating the largest antiterrorism demonstration in history. Hostages who were subsequently freed said they had heard about the protest on the radio and it had given them hope that they might survive. The demonstration also caused many FARC members to realize that they were not supported by the people, and they began to desert in large numbers. According to Morales, as of early 2010, FARC membership had dropped from 40,000 to 7,000, and the remaining forces had been driven back into the jungle.

Morales went on to establish the One Million Voices Foundation, which works to give Colombian youths a way to engage in civil society so they aren't enticed to take up arms and join the FARC. Once again, President Uribe's formal efforts were powerfully enhanced by the courageous efforts of a single individual.

The Power of One

The reason we share these stories is to point out the power of one individual such as Pedro Medina or Oscar Morales in helping to fuel this renaissance of trust. And sometimes it's not just one individual but a small group of people who create dramatic social change.

Some thirty years ago, in the remote village of Xiaogang, China, a group of eighteen impoverished farmers secretly met and "dipped their fingers in red ink," covenanting to split up the communal land into individual plots so that individual households could be rewarded for their own efforts and success instead of sharing equally across the village what always ended up being far too little. As John and Doris Naisbitt tell the story in *China's Megatrends,* this secret agreement was both revolutionary and dangerous. It was in defiance of decades of rules and communal culture, and the participants were at risk of being "persecuted, dispossessed, or even killed as bourgeois 'landlords.'" Yet the search for a better life led this small group to sign an oath stating "If we are successful we will not ask the country for any money or grain. If we are not [successful] we cadres are willing to risk imprisonment or the death penalty." Not only did this bold action of a small group succeed enormously, but its success came to the attention of Communist Party leader Deng Xiaoping. His subsequent economic reforms resulted in restoring family farms and allowed for market distribution, the cumulative effect of which "changed the course of Chinese history."

Never doubt that a small group of thoughtful, committed citizens can change the world. Indeed, it is the only thing that ever has.

MARGARET MEAD
CULTURAL ANTHROPOLOGIST

The point is that the acts of one person or one small group of people can change history. Those who are involved may not fully realize it at the time. It may take years for the effects of their choices to manifest themselves in the destiny of people, families, companies, and nations. But no one can deny that there is power in "one" to effect change.

As we've noted with the other stories we've shared, what happened in Colombia and China is merely a snapshot. It is the current result of the choices of the leaders and individuals involved. As different leaders and other individuals make other choices, things may change. Back in 1999, when Colombia was in such dire straits, Venezuela had been prospering in comparison and was widely viewed by most observers as the stronger of the two nations. But today, as a result of the choices of the leaders of both nations, the two countries have almost switched places: Colombia has gained the vibrancy of a nation on the rise, with its expatriates returning enthusiastically, while Venezuela, under Hugo Chávez, has been in the midst of decline despite its natural resources and has experienced a "brain drain" emigration of more than 1 million creative citizens during Chávez's reign. This reversal is yet another manifestation of the Great Paradox—the juxtaposition of the renaissance of trust with the crisis of trust in worldwide society—and the impact of personal choice.

The potential of the renaissance of trust has dramatically increased in today's flat, global, transparent, interdependent, connected, networked world of instantaneous communication. As Facebook founder Mark Zuckerberg presciently commented in 2008:

> *The Colombia thing is a very early indicator that governance is changing—[and of how] powerful political organizations can form. These*

things can really affect people's lives, liberties and freedom, which is kind of the point of government. . . . In fifteen years maybe there will be things like what happened in Colombia almost every day. . . .

[Openness] puts the onus on companies and organizations to be more good, and more trustworthy. . . . It's really changing the way that governments work. A more transparent world creates a better-governed world and a fairer world.

Today's technology is creating a profound shift, a veritable sea change in how the world operates by dramatically enhancing engagement and empowerment, particularly among youth. Consider what is happening in Egypt, Tunisia, Syria, Yemen, Libya, and elsewhere in the so-called Arab spring, with its uprisings inspired by freedom and autonomy and enabled by social media. Although the final outcomes are unclear, the process of social change has been altered forever. The Internet not only democratizes information, it also facilitates a different-in-kind level of transparency. The result is the creation of conditions in which people, organizations, and even governments are held accountable in a way that they haven't been, and couldn't be, before.

In today's society, where collaboration reigns and our reputations precede us, everything centers around the primacy of trust. As we've said, it's the new currency, the new money. It's what enables the markets to work. In *Jump Point*, Tom Hayes astutely poses the key question "Will the global Web after the Jump Point [the point at which there will be 3 billion people on the Web] be characterized by trust or mistrust?" According to Hayes, "In a global network economy where billions of impersonal and anonymous interactions take place daily, trust is everything: every breach is a crisis."

> *Historically there have been only two basic ways to aggregate and amplify human capabilities. They were bureaucracy and markets. Then in the last ten years we have added a third— networks.*
>
> GARY HAMEL
> AUTHOR AND PROFESSOR, LONDON BUSINESS SCHOOL

"Lift Where You Stand"

Though we may not be a Pedro Medina, an Oscar Morales, or part of a small, courageous group of farmers in China, each of us can act within our own sphere of influence to establish, extend, and restore trust and increase the benefits of trust in the world. And in today's remarkably interdependent, interconnected, and socially responsible world, our circle of influence may be much larger than we think.

So how can we do it? The basic idea is captured beautifully in an experience shared by Dieter Uchtdorf, a religious leader, former chairman of the flight operations committee of the International Air Transport Association, and former chief pilot of Lufthansa German Airlines:

> *Some years ago in our meetinghouse in Darmstadt, Germany, a group was asked to move a grand piano from the chapel to the adjoining cultural hall, where it was needed for a musical event. None were professional movers, and the task of getting that gravity-friendly instrument through the chapel and into the cultural hall seemed nearly impossible. Everybody knew that this task required not only physical strength but also careful coordination. There were plenty of ideas, but not one could keep the piano balanced correctly. They repositioned by strength, height, and age over and over again— nothing worked.*
>
> *As they stood around the piano, uncertain of what to do next, a good friend of mine . . . spoke up. He said, "Stand close together and lift where you stand."*
>
> *It seemed too simple. Nevertheless, each lifted where he stood, and the piano rose from the ground and moved into the cultural hall as if on its own power. That was the answer to the challenge. They merely needed to stand close together and lift where they stood.*

> Few will have the greatness to bend history itself. But each of us can work to change a small portion of events, and in the total of all these acts will be written the history of this generation.
>
> ROBERT F. KENNEDY

This is how we each can become part of the renaissance of trust. Wherever we stand—in our personal lives, our teams, our organizations, our communities, our relationships, our families, our nations—we can "lift" by taking the five actions of smart trust:

We can choose to believe in trust. We can draw inspiration from what Isadore Sharp learned from his father, who believed in being worthy of trust at any cost; from Muhammad Yunus, who created a new industry out of his belief that most people can be trusted, even the poorest; and from Pierre Omidyar, Tony Hsieh, and countless others whose actions grow out of a deep conviction that most people are trustworthy and that growing trust brings prosperity, energy, and joy. And we can make the choice to believe in trust.

We can start with ourselves. We can think of the self-confidence of Magic Johnson, the boldness of Peter Aceto, and the integrity of Frances Hesselbein, all of whom have given their stakeholders leaders they can trust. We can think of companies such as SAS, W. L. Gore, Wipro, the Cleveland Clinic, and others that create remarkably high-trust cultures and give employees and customers a company they can trust. And we can choose to give ourselves and others a person, a leader, a company, a spouse, a parent, a friend who is worthy of trust.

We can declare our intent and assume positive intent in others. We can think of the extraordinary declaration of intent of Warren Buffett and Bill Gates in creating the Giving Pledge, inspiring sixty-nine billionaires to commit to giving at least half their fortunes to charity. We can think of the impact of the caring intent declared by John Mackey, who declines his salary yet continues to lead because he loves Whole Foods Market and its people. We can think of the courageous declaration of Indra Nooyi and PepsiCo through Performance with Purpose, including voluntary commitments that demonstrate that *how we do what we do* truly matters. We can recognize the importance of the hope created by such declarations. And we can choose to examine and refine our own intent, to declare it with straightforwardness and transparency, and always to assume the best intent in others, unless they prove otherwise.

We can do what we say we're going to do. We can think of Grady Rosier, whose highly credible "do what you say" reputation gave Warren

Buffett the confidence to make a deal to acquire his $23 billion food services company in less than a month, on a handshake. We can think of Firoz "King" Husein, whose commitment to do what he said he would do in both his personal and professional life earned the trust and business of Costco for two decades. We can think of FedEx, LEGO, Apple, BMW, and other companies that have strong brand promises—and consistently deliver on those promises. We can choose to make our own word our bond—to deliver or overdeliver on every promise we make. And we can realize that each time we do, no matter how large or how small the promise, we are building accounts of trust that will pay rich dividends over time.

We can lead out in extending Smart Trust to others. We can think of people such as Dr. Mimi Silbert of the Delancy Street Foundation, Isabel Blanco of the Georgia Division of Family and Children Services, and Pepe Miralles's mother, all of whom have made an enormous difference in the quality of life for generations to come by extending trust. We can think of companies such as Whole Foods, Zane's Cycles, and Cleveland Clinic, whose abundant extension of trust to customers, employees, and partners is reciprocated, creating a virtuous upward cycle. We can look for opportunities to extend trust in our personal relationships, on our teams, in our families, in our organizations—and we can choose to act on those opportunities.

As we make choices to take these 5 Smart Trust Actions and lift where we stand, we can do a great deal to increase and restore trust, and we, our families, our communities, our teams, our organizations—even our countries—will reap the dividends of increased prosperity, energy, and joy.

> *How wonderful it is that nobody need wait a single moment before starting to improve the world.*
>
> ANNE FRANK

The Smart Trust Choice Takes Courage

There's no doubt that making the Smart Trust choice takes courage. For some of us, it's much easier in the short run to choose blind trust—to simply go with our propensity to trust without having to worry about developing excellence in our analytical skill. For others, it's easier to choose distrust—to simply go with our scripting or tendency to analyze things and not have to worry about changing a deep-set paradigm or gaining the strength to take a leap of trust. For many, the fear sometimes associated with extending trust can be a significant deterrent. As NeuroLeadership Institute founder, David Rock, says, "The limbic system fires up far more intensely when it perceives a danger compared to when it senses a reward. . . . Human beings *walk* toward, but *run* away."

Nevertheless, the unique opportunity we've had over the past twenty years to grapple with critical trust issues with leaders and influencers around the world has unequivocally convinced us that those who make the choice to master Smart Trust are the ones who are experiencing increased prosperity, elevated energy and enhanced joy. We are inspired by—and take courage from—the words of Helen Keller, "I am only one, but still I am one. I cannot do everything, but still I can do something; and because I cannot do everything, I will not refuse to do something that I can do."

George Bernard Shaw once said that to him, life was no "brief candle" but rather a "splendid torch" that he wanted to make "burn as brightly as possible before handing it on to future generations." To us, Smart Trust is a splendid torch that we want to make burn as brightly as possible, not only in handing it on to future generations, but also in engaging the current generation to achieve better results, feel stronger passion, and experience greater happiness—in other words, to create prosperity, energy, and joy. It is our desire and hope that you will join us as co-catalysts, along with countless others, in seeking to bring about a global renaissance of trust for the benefit of people everywhere.

About the Authors

Stephen M. R. Covey

Stephen M. R. Covey is a cofounder of CoveyLink and the FranklinCovey Global Speed of Trust Practice. A sought-after and compelling keynote speaker and adviser on trust, leadership, ethics, sales, and high performance, he speaks to audiences around the world. He is the *New York Times* and number one *Wall Street Journal* best-selling author of *The Speed of Trust,* a groundbreaking, paradigm-shifting book that challenges our age-old assumption that trust is merely a soft social virtue and instead demonstrates that it is a hard-edged economic driver—a learnable, measurable skill that makes organizations more profitable, people more promotable, and relationships more energizing. He advocates that nothing is as fast as the speed of trust and that the ability to establish, grow, extend, and restore trust with all stakeholders is *the* critical leadership competency of the new global economy. Covey passionately delivers that message and is skilled in enabling leaders and organizations to experience the dividends of high trust. Audiences and organizations alike resonate with his insightful, relevant approach to real-time issues that affect their immediate and long-term performance.

He is the former CEO of Covey Leadership Center, which, under his stewardship, became the largest leadership development company in the world. Covey, with Greg Link, led the strategy that propelled his father's book,

Dr. Stephen R. Covey's *The 7 Habits of Highly Effective People,* to be one of the two most influential business books of the twentieth century, according to *CEO Magazine.* A Harvard MBA, he joined Covey Leadership Center as a Client Developer and later became National Sales Manager and then President and CEO. Under Covey's direction, the company grew rapidly and profitably, achieving *Inc.* 500 status. As President and CEO, he nearly doubled revenues to over $110 million while increasing profits twelvefold. During that period, both customer and employee trust reached new highs and the company expanded throughout the world into more than forty countries. This greatly increased the value of the brand and company. The company was valued at only $2.4 million when Covey was named CEO, and, within three years, he grew shareholder value to $160 million in a merger he orchestrated with Franklin Quest to form FranklinCovey.

Over the years, Covey has gained considerable respect and influence with executives and leaders of Fortune 500 companies as well as with mid- and small-sized private-sector and public-sector organizations he has consulted with. Clients recognize his unique perspective on real-world organizational issues based on his practical experience as a former CEO.

Covey currently serves on the board or advisory board of several entities. He resides with his wife and children in the shadows of the Rocky Mountains.

Greg Link

Greg Link is a cofounder of the former Covey Leadership Center, CoveyLink, and the FranklinCovey Global Speed of Trust Practice, a fast-growing global consultancy committed to influencing influencers to grow their careers and their organizations at the Speed of Trust.

A recognized authority on leadership, trust, sales, marketing, and high performance, Link is a sought-after adviser and speaker. His authentic, engaging style endears him to audiences at all levels, from senior executives to the front lines. He is a "business expert who speaks," not a "speaker who theorizes."

Link, his business partner Stephen M. R. Covey, and the team at the Speed of Trust Practice equip people and organizations to transform toxic relationships, teams, and organizational cultures and to harness high trust as a performance multiplier. Link convincingly challenges the age-old assumption that trust is merely a soft social virtue and demonstrates that it is a hard-edged economic driver—a learnable, measurable skill that makes organizations more profitable, people more promotable, and relationships more energizing.

As a cofounder of the Covey Leadership Center, he and Stephen M. R. Covey orchestrated the strategy that led Dr. Stephen R. Covey's book *The 7 Habits of Highly Effective People,* to become one of the two best-selling business books of the twentieth century, according to *CEO Magazine,* selling more than 20 million copies in thirty-eight languages. He created the marketing momentum that helped propel Covey Leadership Center from a start-up company to a $110-plus-million-dollar enterprise with offices in forty countries before merging with Franklin Quest to form FranklinCovey.

He also led the center's international publishing success, resulting in partnerships with more than thirty publishers worldwide. This included making publishing history in Japan, leading the strategy that sold more than 1 million copies of a foreign-language translation nonfiction business book, *The 7 Habits of Highly Effective People,* in Japanese. He was also instrumental in formulating and executing one of the world's largest international business satellite broadcasts with partners Lessons in Leadership and *Fortune* magazine.

Link has taught The Seven Habits, Principle Centered Leadership, and The Speed of Trust and advised executives at numerous leading enterprises, including Hewlett-Packard, the U.S. Navy, Sony, Chevron, IBM, Microsoft, Boeing, and many other well-known organizations. He is a trusted confidant to CEOs and other senior executives.

His business acumen and experience as a successful real-world executive inform his presentations and make them uniquely relevant to clients and convention audiences alike.

Link resides with his wife, Annie, on a quiet stream in the shadows of the Utah Rockies in Alpine, Utah. He can be reached at Link@CoveyLink.com.

Rebecca R. Merrill

Rebecca R. Merrill is a gifted writer. In addition to her primary focus on home and family over the years, she has been a writing partner on some of the most significant leadership books written in the last several years, including *The Speed of Trust* by Stephen M. R. Covey and *You Already Know How to Be Great* by Alan Fine. She also coauthored the *New York Times* best seller *First Things First* with Dr. Stephen R. Covey and Roger Merrill and *Life Matters* and *Connections* with Roger Merrill. In addition, she provided assistance to Dr. Covey on *The 7 Habits of Highly Effective People, The 7 Habits of Highly Effective Families,* and *The Nature of Leadership.*

About CoveyLink and the FranklinCovey Global Speed of Trust Practice

The FranklinCovey Speed of Trust Practice is a global trust practice focused on measurably increasing the performance and influence of people and organizations worldwide by enabling them to lead in a way that inspires trust, thus increasing speed and lowering cost.

We believe that a powerful global renaissance of trust has begun. Sparked by recent world events, business ethics, and the transparency of conversations enabled by the World Wide Web, as this book reinforces, this call for a renaissance of high-trust leadership is reverberating around the globe.

At the Global Speed of Trust Practice, we define leadership as producing results in a way that inspires trust. Doing so consistently amplifies the speed with which you are able to influence and get results the next time—and there is always a next time. Simply put, trusted people have greater influence and get better outcomes.

Our intent is to amplify the global ripple effect of Smart Trust leadership. By influencing influencers, we mean that we inspire and activate people and organizations throughout the world to be high trust and high performers and to make a difference in the lives of others. In doing so, we inspire our clients, as George Bernard Shaw expressed it, "to be used for a purpose recognized by themselves as a mighty one."

We have become passionately convinced that *trust* is the one thing that changes everything—and is the root of all leadership influence.

We take a highly pragmatic approach to leadership and trust by focusing on practical actions and behaviors. Our Speed of Trust Transformation Process institutionalizes new language and new behavior in a profoundly simple, repeatable process in the context of real work. This equips leaders and individual contributors to be more energized and engaged as well as more accountable for performance. Rather than displacing programs and strategies in which organizations are presently investing, we help implement Smart Trust as a performance multiplier to amplify existing programs and significantly increase their ability to execute existing strategies. We teach leaders and organizations to create high-trust, high-performance cultures by developing trusted influencers, who in turn influence others. The ripple effect of installing Smart Trust as an organizational operating system manifests itself in measurable, sustainable organizational growth and momentum.

Enhancing the ability of organizations to establish, grow, extend, and restore trust with all stakeholders will significantly increase the opportunities and influence people have, whether as leaders, workers, business partners, customers, parents, or in any other role in life.

Through a license with CoveyLink, the FranklinCovey Global Speed of Trust Practice provides access to additional resources for individuals and organizations in over 100 countries worldwide to increase Smart Trust, including open enrollment Leading at the Speed of Trust and Smart Trust workshops, keynote speeches, on-site programs, train the trainer certification, webinars, online learning, individual and organizational assessments, application tools, advisory services, and custom consulting.

To inquire about speaking by the authors or others from the Global Speed of Trust practice or beginning the Speed of Trust Transformation Process in your team or organization, e-mail us at info@SmartTrustBook.com or go to our website at SmartTrustBook.com.

Notes

Our Intent

P. xxii   **"There are no excellent companies":** Tom Peters, *Thriving on Chaos: Handbook for a Management Revolution* (New York: Knopf, 1987), 3.

P. xxii   **"Somebody is doing something":** "Full Text of Warren Buffett's Memorandum," *Financial Times,* October 9, 2006, www.ft.com/cms/s/0/48312832 -57d4-11db-be9f-0000779e2340.html#axzz1bBGEo1em.

Chapter One: The Great Paradox

P. 6   **"All this misery":** Muhammad Yunus, *Banker to the Poor: Micro-Lending and the Battle Against World Poverty* (New York: Public Affairs, 2003), 50.

P. 6   **"He fell from the sky!":** Muhammed Yunus, "Fighting Poverty From the Bottom Up," speech by Mohammed Yunus, December 1996, Grameen-info.org.

P. 7   **"All her life":** Yunus, *Banker to the Poor,* 65.

P. 7   **an amazing 98 percent:** Grameen Bank, "Grameen Bank at a Glance," August 2011,www.grameen-info.org/index.php?option=com_content&task=view&id= 26&Itemid=175.

P. 8   **more than $6 billion in loans:** Alison Benjamin, "Money Well Lent," *The Guardian,* June 3, 2009.

P. 8   **Presidential Medal of Freedom:** "President Obama Names Medal of Freedom Recipients," press release, Office of the Press Secretary, White House, July 30, 2009.

P. 9   **"If Grameen was to work":** Yunus, *Banker to the Poor,* 65.

P. 9   **Numerous global businesses:** Penelope Patsuris, "The Corporate Scandal Sheet," August 26, 2002, www.forbes.com/2002/07/25/accountingtracker .html.

P. 10   **more than two hundred public companies:** Bill George, *7 Lessons for Leading in Crisis* (San Francisco: Jossey-Bass, 2009), 7.

P. 10   **some two hundred airline pilots:** "Many Airline Pilots Have Fake Credentials," September 7, 2010, www.chinadaily.com.cn/2010-09/07/content_1127 3606.htm.

P. 10 **Ramalinga Raju:** Manjeet Kripalani, "India's Madoff? Satyam Scandal Rocks Outsourcing Industry," Bloomberg Businessweek, January 7, 2009, www.business week.com/globalbiz/content/jan2009/gb2009017_807784.htm.

P. 10 **In the United States:** Trip Gabriel, "Under Pressure, Teachers Tamper with Tests," *The New York Times,* June 11, 2010.

P. 10 **Thousands of investors:** Adam LeBor, *The Believers: How America Fell for Bernard Madoff's $65 Billion Investment Scam* (London: Orion Publishing Group, 2009).

P. 10 **A British tabloid newspaper:** Michel Anteby, "Rupert Murdoch and the Seeds of Moral Hazard," Harvard Business School, July 19, 2011, http:/hbswk .hbs.edu/item/6777.html.

P. 11 **The U.S. finds itself:** "Emerging Markets Dominate as 'Business Trusters,' U.S. Drops to Within 5 Points of Russia," Edelman Trust Barometer Annual Global Opinion Leaders Study, 2011.

P. 11 **Trust in media:** Lymari Morales, "Distrust in U.S. Media Edges Up to Record High," September 29, 2010, www.gallup.com/poll/143267/distrust-media-edges -record-high.aspx.

P. 11 **Only 46 percent of informed respondents:** "Emerging Markets Dominate as 'Business Trusters,' " Edelman Trust Barometer, 2011.

P. 11 **Only 40 percent of informed respondents:** Ibid.

P. 11 **Only 33 percent of Americans:** Harris Interactive, "Confidence in Congress and Supreme Court Drops to Lowest Level in many Years," May 11, 2011, www.harrisinteractive.com/NewsRoom/HarrisPolls/tabid/447/ctl/Read Custom%20Default/mid/1508/ArticleId/780/Default.aspx.

P. 11 **53 percent of U.S. employees:** Boss Day study, American Workplace Insights Survey, Adecco Group North America, October 15, 2009.

P. 11 **69 percent of Americans:** Jeffrey M. Jones, "U.S. Satisfaction with Gov't, Morality, Economy Down Since '08," January 24, 2011, www.gallup.com/ poll/145760/satisfaction-gov-morality-economy-down.aspx.

P. 11 **only 20 percent of Americans:** Financial Trust Index, Chicago Booth/Kellogg School, May 2011.

P. 11 **national credit downgrade:** Zachary Goldfarb, "S&P Downgrades U.S. Credit Rating for First Time," *The Washington Post,* August 5, 2011.

P. 11 **"2011 will be the year of distrust":** Albert O. Hirschman, Ivan Krastev, and Richard Edelman, "Losing Faith in the Government," August 5, 2011, http:// bermudaisanotherworld.org/forum/index.php?topic=3874.0.

P. 12 **only 13 percent of Chileans:** Catherine Rampell, "Trust Me, We're Rich," *The New York Times,* April 18, 2011. Data from Organization for Economic Cooperation and Development (OECD).

P. 12 **"Trust is like the air":** Del Galloway, "In Today's Absence of Trust and Truth, PR Is Paramount," *PR Week,* March 15, 2004, 6.

P. 13 **"One day, a company":** Adam L. Penenberg, "Social Networking Affects Brains like Falling in Love," July 1, 2010, www.fastcompany.com/magazine/ 147/doctor-love.html.

P. 13 **"The world's financial markets":** Dov Seidman, "Building Trust in Business by Trusting," *BusinessWeek,* September 7, 2009.

P. 14 **"It's about who has":** Richard McGill Murphy, "Why Doing Good Is Good for Business," *Fortune,* February 2, 2010.

P. 15   **Trustworthiness and Prosperity of Nations graph:** Data from Transparency International's Corruption Perceptions Index, Transparency International, and GDP data from International Monetary Fund.

P. 15   **"It can be plausibly argued":** Kenneth J. Arrow, "Gifts and Exchanges," *Philosophy & Public Affairs* 1, no. 4 (Summer 1972), 343–362.

P. 16   **which lost 78 percent:** "Rs 8,000 Cr Fraud Hits Satyam; Raju May Get 7-Yr Jail," January 7, 2009, www.indianexpress.com/news/rs-8-000-cr-fraud-hits-satyam;-raju-may-get-7yr-jail/407821/0.

P. 16   **According to a Watson Wyatt study:** Watson Wyatt, WorkUSA study, 2002.

P. 17   **"Our approach is based":** Great Place to Work Institute, www.gptw-events .com/index.php?option=com_content&view=article&id=10&Itemid=30.

P. 17   **"investment and growth improve":** Paul Zak and Stephen Knack, "Trust and Growth," *The Economic Journal* 111, no. 470 (April 2001), 317.

P. 17   **"Because trust reduces":** Ibid., 296.

P. 20   **A 2008 Dublin City University:** Aamir Ali Chughtai and Finian Buckley, "Work Engagement and its Relationship with State and Trait Trust: A Conceptual Analysis," Dublin City University Business School, Ireland, 2008.

P. 20   **"We have what we call":** Jennifer Robison, interview with Doug Conant, "Saving Campbell Soup Company," *Gallup Management Journal,* February 11, 2010.

P. 20   **"The greater the contrast":** Ard-Pieter de Man, Geert Duysters, and Ash Vasudevan, *The Allianced Enterprise: Global Strategies for Corporate Collaboration* (London: Imperial College Press, 2001), 84.

P. 21   **"Trust between people":** Innovation Survey (London: Pricewaterhouse-Coopers, 1999).

P. 21   **"[T]he existence of trust":** Tom Hayes, *Jump Point: How Network Culture Is Revolutionizing Business* (New York: McGraw-Hill, 2008), 145.

P. 21   **"All innovation comes":** Charles H. Green, "Robert Porter Lynch on Trust, Innovation and Performance," March 3, 2010, http://trustedadvisor.com/trustmatters/robert-porter-lynch-on-trust-innovation-and-performance-trust-quotes-2.

P. 21   **"No low trust society":** Thomas L. Friedman, *The World Is Flat 3.0: A Brief History of the Twenty-First Century* (New York: Picador, 2007), 334.

P. 22   **a study of 97,000 women:** NHLBI Women's Health Initiative, U.S. Department of Health and Human Services; see also January W. Payne, "Health Buzz: Importance of a Positive Attitude and Other Health News," *US News & World Report,* March 9, 2009; see also Salynn Boyles, "Pessimism, Cynicism Can Hurt Your Heart," August 10, 2009, www.webmd.com/heart-disease/news/20090810/pessimism-cynicism-can-hurt-your-heart.

P. 22   **"[A] nation's well-being":** Francis Fukuyama, *Trust: The Social Virtues and the Creation of Prosperity* (New York: Free Press, 1995), 7.

P. 22   **"flourishing":** Martin Seligman, *Flourish: A Visionary New Understanding of Happiness and Well-being* (New York: Free Press, 2011), front jacket flap.

P. 23   **"More than any other element":** Richard Branson, *Losing My Virginity: How I Survived, Had Fun, and Made a Fortune Doing Business My Way* (New York: Crown Business, 2011), 398.

P. 23   **"gross national happiness":** Nadia Mustafa, "What About Gross National Happiness?," *Time,* January 2005.

P. 23   **According to a BBC survey:** "Denmark 'Happiest Place on Earth,'" BBC News, July 28, 2006, http://news.bbc.co.uk/2/hi/5224306.stm.

P. 23   **relationships of trust:** Karen Gram, "Happiness—We All Just Need a Little Faith and a Point of View," *Vancouver Sun,* October 28, 2006.

P. 23   **"social relationships are":** Shawn Achor, *The Happiness Advantage: The Seven Principles of Positive Psychology That Fuel Success and Performance at Work* (New York: Crown Business, 2010), 14.

P. 23   **Harvard Study of Adult Development:** Ibid., 176.

P. 24   **the happiest nation on Earth:** Michael B. Sauter, Charles B. Stockdale, and Douglas A. McIntyre, "US Doesn't Make Cut for Happiest Nations List," June 6, 2011, www.msnbc.msn.com/id/43287918/ns/business-world_business/t/us-doesnt-make-cut-happiest-nations-list/#.Tp4pH2FbySo; see also Francesca Levy, "The World's Happiest Countries," July 14, 2010, www.forbes.com/2010/07/14/world-happiest-countries-lifestyle-realestate-gallup.html.

P. 24   **Trust and Happiness of Nations graph:** Data from World Values Survey and Gallup World Poll survey.

P. 25   **a 2008 study:** John F. Helliwell and Haifang Huang, "Well-Being and Trust in the Workplace," Working Paper 14589, National Bureau of Economic Research, December 2008.

P. 25   **"The advantage to mankind":** John Stuart Mill, *Principles of Political Economy* (London: John W. Parker, 1848).

P. 26   **"The more open societies":** Friedman, *The World Is Flat 3.0,* 558.

P. 27   **"The incentives for participation":** Hayes, *Jump Point,* 144.

P. 27   **One example is Azim Premji:** S. H. Venkatramani, "Morals in Management," June 1999, www.lifepositive.com/mind/work/corporate-management/business-ethics.asp.

P. 28   **"Go ahead and plead":** Suresh Kant Sharma, *Encyclopedia of Higher Education: Scientific and Technical Education* (New Delhi, India: Mittell Publications, 2005), 344.

P. 28   **hundred most influential people:** *Time,* April 2004.

P. 28   **one of twenty-five people worldwide:** *Financial Times,* October 2005.

P. 29   **"Nobody can enjoy":** Sharma, *Encyclopedia of Higher Education,* 344.

P. 29   **"When it was just":** Tony Hsieh, *Delivering Happiness* (New York: Business Plus, 2010), 48.

P. 29   **"dreaded getting out of bed":** Greg Link, interview with Tony Hsieh, February 7, 2011.

P. 29   **"We don't have scripts":** Hsieh, *Delivering Happiness,* 147.

P. 30   **a pricing error resulted:** Dan Nosowitz, "Zappos Loses $1.6 Million in Six-Hour Pricing Screw-Up," *Fast Company,* May 2010.

P. 30   **To Hsieh:** Ibid.

P. 30   **"An enormous pleasure":** Charlie Munger, Wesco Annual Meeting, May 9, 2007 (Whitney Tilson's notes).

P. 31   **"If you do build":** Omar Zaibak, "101 Inspirational Customer Service Quotes," www.customerservicemanager.com/101-inspirational-customer-service-quotes.htm.

P. 31   **"surgery with a warranty":** www.geisinger.org/provencare/faq.html.

P. 31   **highest customer satisfaction ratings:** ISI Wissing, www.max.se.

P. 31   **"values jam":** Samuel J. Palmisano, "Our Values at Work on Being an IBMer," www.ibm.com/ibm/values/us/.

P. 32   **100 percent approval rating:** www.Glassdoor.com.

P. 32   **"alternative approach to building":** Michael Bassett, "The Dalton Company Ltd.: Building on a Foundation of Trust," Conference Board of Canada, September 2009, www.conferenceboard.ca/documents.aspx?did=3182; also "Canadian Company Defies Current Trend of Declining Trust in Business," September 3, 2009, www.daltonbuild.com/news-details.php?id=44.

P. 32   **"Physician's Compact":** "Virginia Mason Medical Center Physician Compact," www.virginiamason.org/workfiles/HR/PhysicianCompact.pdf.

P. 32   **According to a *New York Times* article:** Kemal Jufri, "Making Honesty a Policy in Indonesia Cafes," *The New York Times,* June 17, 2009.

P. 33   **"Performance with Purpose":** Indra K. Nooyi, "Letter from Indra Nooyi," www.pepsico.com/Purpose/Performance-with-Purpose/Letter-from-Indra-Nooyi.html.

P. 33   **"A company is granted":** "The CEO of the Future," Indra Nooyi, speech to the Economic Club of Washington, May 12, 2009.

P. 34   **The plan grew out:** Muhammed Yunus, *Creating a World Without Poverty: Social Business and the Future of Capitalism* (New York: Public Affairs, 2009), xv.

P. 34   **Grameen Danone built:** "Grameen Danone Foods Opens Wednesday," *The Daily Star,* November 6, 2006.

P. 34   **Grameen has since formed:** Muhammad Yunus, *Building Social Business* (New York: Public Affairs [reprint], 2011), Introduction.

P. 34   **"We can make market forces":** "Remarks of Bill Gates, Harvard Commencement 2007," *Harvard Gazette,* June 7, 2007.

P. 35   **"If you don't have the trust":** "Open Labs, Open Minds," Andrew Witty, speech at the Council on Foreign Relations in New York, January 20, 2010.

Chapter Two: Blind Trust or Distrust: Which Glasses Are You Wearing?

P. 39   **"We may not be born":** Eric Uslaner, *The Moral Foundations of Trust* (Cambridge, England: Cambridge University Press, 2002), 76.

P. 39   **"No question children are":** "Innovation: The Critical Link to Trust," February 4, 2010, http://trustedadvisor.com/trustmatters/innovation-the-critical-link-to-trust.

P. 40   **"If it seems too good":** Mark Twain, *The Prince and the Pauper* (Clayton, Del.: Prestwick House, 2007).

P. 40   **Nick Leeson:** Helga Drummond, *The Dynamics of Organizational Collapse: The Case of Barings Bank* (New York: Routledge, 2008).

P. 41   **$2.9 *trillion* a year:** Association of Certified Fraud Examiners, "Report to the Nations on Occupational Fraud and Abuse," 2010, www.acfe.com/rttn/.

P. 41   **88 percent of enterprises:** Kroll, "Global Fraud Report," October 2010, www.krollconsulting.com/media/pdfs/FraudReport_English-US_Oct10.pdf.

P. 41   **"It's only when the tide goes out":** "Indecent exposure: Markets Reveal the Good, the Bad and the Ugly," *The Economist,* August 5, 2007.

P. 41   ***New York Post* articles:** Kevin Fasick and Todd Venezia, "A Bum You Can Trust—Honest!," *New York Post,* August 13, 2010.

P. 44   **"The cost of trust":** Robert Solomon and Fernando Flores, *Building Trust: In Business, Politics, Relationships, and Life* (New York, Oxford University Press, 2003), 43.

P. 45   **people's lack of trust:** "U.S. Financial Services Trust Barometer," 2010, www .edelman.com/trust/2010/docs/2010_Financial_Services_US_Trust_Results _Deck.pdf.

P. 46   **the compliance cost:** James Freeman, "The Supreme Case Against Sarbanes-Oxley," *The Wall Street Journal,* December 15, 2009.

P. 47   **average turnover rate:** "Turnover in Supermarkets," *Workforce Management,* Food Marketing Institute charts.

P. 47   **The cost of turnover:** Scott Allen, "The High Cost of Employee Turnover," American Express Open Forum, April 7, 2010.

P. 47   **3 percent or less:** Rodd Wagner and Gale Muller, *Power of 2: How to Make the Most of Your Partnerships at Work and in Life* (New York: Gallup Press, 2009), 77.

P. 47   **"Trust is the linchpin":** Ibid., 77.

P. 51   **"To trust is to take a risk":** Solomon and Flores, *Building Trust,* 43.

Chapter Three: The Third Alternative: "Smart Trust"

P. 54   **"blown away":** Meg Whitman, *The Power of Many: Values for Success in Business and in Life* (New York: Crown, 2010), 14.

P. 54   **"most people are basically good":** Pam and Pierre Omidyar, "From Self to Society: Citizenship to Community for a World of Change," Commencement address, Tufts University, May 19, 2002.

P. 54   **"More than a decade later":** Whitman, *The Power of Many,* 27.

P. 54   **"Pierre's premise was":** Ibid.

P. 55   **"If we believed":** Tom Hayes, *Jump Point: How Network Culture is Revolutionizing Business* (New York: McGraw-Hill, 2008), 148.

P. 55   **"Many participants report":** Peter Kollock, "The Production of Trust in Online Markets," 1999, www.connectedaction.net/wp-content/uploads/ 2009/05/1999-peter-kollock-the-production-of-trust-in-online-markets .htm.

P. 56   **of the 2 million auctions:** "eBay Inc.—Company Profile, Business Description, History, Background Information on eBay Inc.," www.referenceforbusiness .com/history2/44/eBay-Inc.html.

P. 56   **"The remarkable fact":** Kevin Maney, "10 Years Ago, eBay Changed the World, Sort of by Accident," *USA Today,* March 22, 2005.

P. 56   **more than 20 million subscribers:** Andy Fixmer, "Netflix Gains as Movie-Rental Customers Top 20 Million," January 27, 2011, www.bloomberg .com/news/2011-01-26/netflix-says-profit-beat-estimates-as-users-surpass-20 -million.html.

P. 56   **ranked number three:** Kathy Grannis, "Zappos.com Tops in Customer Service, According to NRF Foundation/American Express Survey," January 11, 2011, www.nrf.com/modules.php?name=News&op=viewlive&sp_id=1067.

P. 57   **"Our products are guaranteed":** www.llbean.com/customerService/about LLBean/guarantee.html?feat=ln&nav=ln.

P. 57   **"If we expected customers":** Leon A. Gorman, *L.L.Bean: The Making of an American Icon* (Boston: Harvard Business School Press, 2006), 73.

P. 57   **An L.L.Bean executive told us:** Greg Link, interview, June 3, 2011.

P. 61   **"Civility has two parts":** Stephen L. Carter, *Civility: Manners, Morals, and the Etiquette of Democracy* (New York: HarperCollins, 1998), 62.

P. 62   **"We are witnessing the growth":** Jeff Jarvis, *What Would Google Do?* (New York: HarperCollins, 2009), p.152.

P. 63   **at one time he was involved:** Jon M. Huntsman, *Winners Never Cheat—Even in Difficult Times* (New York: Pearson Prentice Hall, 2008), 49–50.

P. 64   **"I said we had no intention":** Ibid., 43–44.

P. 64   **"I have never had anyone":** Ibid., 45.

P. 67   **"Now, I want you":** Tom Schulman, *Dead Poets Society* movie script, 1989.

P. 67   **"We don't read and write":** Ibid.

P. 68   **"Good judgment comes":** Rita Mae Brown, *Alma Mater* (New York: Ballantine, 2001), 108.

P. 69   **"We can afford to lose":** Patricia Sellers, "How Warren Buffett Manages His Managers," *Fortune,* October 12, 2009.

P. 69   **"Somebody is doing something":** "Full Text of Warren Buffett's Memorandum," *Financial Times,* October 9, 2006, www.ft.com/cms/s/0/48312832-57 d4-11db-be9f-0000779e2340.html#axzz1bBGEo1em.

P. 69   **"But we can have":** Ibid.

P. 70   **"Warren makes us feel":** Sellers, "How Warren Buffett Manages His Managers."

P. 70   **third richest man in the world:** "The Richest People in America 2011," *Forbes,* September 23, 2011.

P. 70   **donate 99 percent:** http://givingpledge.org/#warren_buffett.

P. 70   **"The five most dangerous words":** "Full Text of Warren Buffett's Memorandum," *Financial Times,* October 9, 2006.

P. 73   **"The effort has borne":** Charo Quesada, "The People's Police: Why the Residents of Bogotá Have Come to Love Their Police Force, After Years of Suspicion and Resentment," June 2004, www.iadb.org/idbamerica/index.cfm? thisid=2817.

P. 73   **The impact of this approach:** Ward Clapham, "'Positive Tickets' from the Police in Canada," Center for Advanced Research, FranklinCovey study, February 2011; see also "Positive Ticketing for Youth," www.strategiesforyouth .org/archives/positive_ticketing.htm.

P. 74   **"It's not about":** "Positive Ticketing for Youth."

P. 74   **"When you build relationships":** Ward Clapham, *Breaking with the Law: The Story of Positive Tickets* (available at www.positivetickets.com/discover_the_ book.html).

P. 74   **One such study:** Paul J. Zak, Robert Kurzban, and William T. Matzner, "The Neurobiology of Trust," Center for Neuroeconomics Studies, Claremont Graduate University, 2004; see also Paul J. Zak, Robert Kurzban, and William T. Matzner, "Oxytocin Is Associated with Human Trustworthiness," *Hormones and Behavior* 48 (2005), 522–527.

P. 76   **The company extends trust:** Ben Casnocha, "Success on the Side," *The American Magazine,* April 24, 2009.

P. 76   **"We let engineers":** Chuck Salter, "Marissa Mayer's 9 Principles of Innovation," *Fast Company,* February 19, 2008.

P. 76   **(at one point 50 percent):** Ibid.

P. 76   **"When you're passionate":** Erin Hayes, "Google's 20 Percent Factor," May 12, 2008, http://abcnews.go.com/Technologystory?id=4839327&page=1.

P. 77   **increased by 35 percent:** "Working 24/7," *60 Minutes,* April 2, 2006.

P. 77   **"The ironic thing":** Ibid.

P. 77   **"I am a happier employee":** Ibid.

P. 77   **The Nordstrom Handbook:** Greg Link, interview with Nordstrom Human Resources, May 2006.

Chapter Four: Smart Trust Action 1: Choose to Believe in Trust

P. 85   **"So much of long-term success":** Isadore Sharp, *Four Seasons: The Story of a Business Philosophy* (New York: Portfolio, 2009), Introduction.

P. 86   **The Empty Pot:** Demi, *The Empty Pot* (New York: Henry Holt and Company, 1990).

P. 87   **"[B]eliefs control behavior":** Bruce H. Lipton, *The Biology of Belief* (Carlsbad, Calif.: Hay House, 2008), 257.

P. 91   **"On his first job":** Sharp, *Four Seasons,* 8.

P. 92   **"Grameen assumes":** Muhammad Yunus, *Banker to the Poor: Micro-Lending and the Battle Against World Poverty* (New York: Public Affairs, 2003), 70.

P. 92   **more than a million:** Scott Wingo, "Fun eBay Math—What Does 1.4 Million Cyber Monday Transactions Mean?," December 7, 2009, http://ebay strategies.blogs.com/ebay_strategies/2009/12/fun-ebay-math-what-does-14 -million-cyber-monday-transactions-mean.html.

P. 92   **"Pierre showed me":** Meg Whitman, *The Power of Many: Values for Success in Business and in Life* (New York: Three Rivers Press, 2010), 31.

P. 92   **"20 percent time":** Ben Casnocha, "Success on the Side," *The American Magazine,* April 24, 2009.

P. 92   **"When I arrived":** Alan Deutschman, *Change or Die: The Three Keys to Change at Work and in Life* (New York: ReganBooks, 2007), 113.

P. 93   **As one associate explained:** Gary Hamel with Shirley Spence, "Innovation Democracy: W. L. Gore's Original Management Model," December 29, 2010, www.managementexchange.com/story/innovation-democracy-wl-gores -original-management-model.

P. 93   **"the world's most innovative":** Gary Hamel, *The Future of Management* (Boston: Harvard Business School Press, 2007), 65.

P. 93   **"Like fish that can't conceive":** Ibid., 128.

P. 94   **"There is an inverse correlation":** Jeff Jarvis, *What Would Google Do?* (New York: HarperCollins, 2009), 82.

P. 94   **"The more you control":** Ibid.

P. 94   **"We felt that a lot":** Gordon Forward, "Conversation with Gordon Forward," *Organizational Dynamics* 20, no. 1, 63–72.

P. 96   **"We knew we couldn't":** Ross Smith, "Organizational Trust 2.0: 42projects," April 11, 2010, www.managementexchange.com/story/organizational-trust -20-42projects.

P. 96   **a 20 to 50 percent increase:** Ibid.

P. 96   **a 10 to 60 percent increase:** Ibid.

P. 96   **"Talented, happy people":** Ibid.

P. 96 **"42Projects tries":** Julian Birkinshaw and Stuart Crainer, "Game On: Theory Y meets Generation Y," *Business Strategy Review,* Winter 2008, 4–10.

P. 97 **"Inside the beloved companies":** Jeanne Bliss, *I Love You More than My Dog: Five Decisions That Drive Extreme Customer Loyalty in Good Times and Bad* (New York: Portfolio, 2011), 27.

P. 97 **"When I was about twelve years old":** Email from Jose Gabriel "Pepe" Miralles to Stephen M. R. Covey, July 8, 2011.

P. 98 **"If you give respect":** "John Wooden's Leadership Lessons That Work on and off the Court," June 7, 2010, http://hr.blr.com/whitepapers/Staffing-Training/Leadership/Acclaimed-Coach-Offers-Leadership-Lessons-That-Wor/.

P. 98 **"Youth + freedom":** Dan Farber, "Kai Fu Lee: I Need to Follow My Heart," August 9, 2005, www.zdnet.com/blog/btl/kai-fu-lee-i-need-to-follow-my-heart/1697.

P. 99 **"Trust was the emotional capital":** Sharp, *Four Seasons,* 262.

P. 99 **"Our team trusts each other":** Video transcript of interview with Dean W. Collinwood and Al Carey, FranklinCovey, 2009.

P. 99 **"Our entire model":** Hollie Shaw and Jonathon Gatehouse, "Avon to Peddle Lawyers, Roofers, Doctors and More in Canadian Test," *National Post,* August 3, 2001.

P. 100 **"Our model is a seamless web":** Liz Claman, "Berkshire Weekend: Buffett, Munger on Contracts Versus Understandings," May 2, 2009, http://seekingalpha.com/instablog/315877-the-manual-of-ideas/2654-berkshire-weekend-buffett-munger-on-contracts-versus-understandings; also Charlie Munger, commencement address, USC Law School, May 13, 2007.

P. 100 **"More than a decade later":** Whitman, *The Power of Many,* 27; see also Adam Cohen, *The Perfect Store: Inside eBay* (Boston: Little, Brown and Company, 2002), 310.

P. 100 **"We were convinced":** Yunus, *Banker to the Poor,* 70.

P. 100 **"People everywhere prefer":** www.grameen-info.org/index.php?option=com_content&task=view&id=215&Itemid=541&limit=1&limitstart=7.

P. 100 **"I believe management must trust":** Jason Chow, "For SAS, Asia Presents Risks and Potential," November 21, 2010, http://online.wsj.com/article/SB10001424052748704170404575623952475539676.html.

P. 100 **"When you trust people":** "SAS CEO Jim Goodnight Will Participate in The Economist's Ideas Economy," August 25, 2010, www.sas.com/news/preleases/the-economists-ideas-goodnight.html.

P. 100 **"Values are a matter of trust":** Azim Premji, convocation address delivered at the Indian Institute of Technology, Chennai, 2002.

P. 100 **"[T]here are some fundamental things":** Gary Hamel, "W. L. Gore: Lessons from a Management Revolutionary, Part 2," April 2, 2010, http://blogs.wsj.com/management/2010/04/02/wl-gore-lessons-from-a-management-revolutionary-part-2/.

P. 100 **"We trust our employees":** Tony Hsieh, *Delivering Happiness* (New York: Business Plus, 2010), 145.

P. 101 **"The competitive advantage of trust":** Sarah Chong, "50 Most Admired Brands in the World," *Fortune,* March 26, 2010.

P. 101 **"I believe the following":** "John Wooden's Leadership Lessons That Work on and off the Court," June 7, 2010, http://hr.blr.com/whitepapers/Staffing-Training/Leadership/Acclaimed-Coach-Offers-Leadership-Lessons-That-Wor/.

P. 101   **"Too many companies"**: Jarvis, *What Would Google Do?*, 87.

P. 101   **"Only in the leap"**: "Memorable Quotes for Indiana Jones and the Last Crusade," www.imdb.com/title/tt0097576/quotes.

P. 102   **in 2007 Ted Morgan**: Stephen M. R. Covey, interviews with Ted Morgan, February 8, 2010, and August 23, 2011.

P. 102   **"I know that"**: Jefferson Graham, "Jobs, iPhone Have Skyhook Pointed in Right Direction," January 23, 2008, www.usatoday.com/tech/products/2008-01-22-skyhook_N.htm.

P. 103   **"This relationship is very sacred"**: "25 Top Women Business Builders," *Fast Company,* May 1, 2005.

P. 104   **"When a handshake is given"**: Jon M. Huntsman, *Winners Never Cheat: Everyday Values We Learned as Children* (New York: Pearson Education, 2005), 37.

P. 104   **"Get yourself a banker"**: Ike Wilson, "Speaker Stresses Dreams in Spite of Recession," November 21, 2009, www.fredericknewspost.com/sections/story Tools/print_story.htm?storyID=98054&cameFromSection=bus.

P. 104   **"Look at the big picture"**: Dexter Roberts, "Novartis Unveils $1.25 Billion China Investment," Bloomberg Businessweek, November 3, 2009, www.business week.com/globalbiz/content/nov2009/gb2009113_520982.htm.

P. 105   **"Ultimately, locating"**: Andrew O'Connell, "Novartis's Great Leap of Trust," *Harvard Business Review,* March 2007.

Chapter Five: Smart Trust Action 2: Start with Self

P. 109   **"During my growing-up years"**: Greg Link and Stephen M. R. Covey, interview with Roger Merrill, April 2011.

P. 112   **"We need new leadership"**: William W. George, *Authentic Leadership: Rediscovering the Secrets to Creating Lasting Value* (San Francisco: Jossey-Bass, 2003), 5.

P. 113   **"Distrust is often a projection"**: Robert Solomon and Fernando Flores, *Building Trust: In Business, Politics, Relationships, and Life* (New York: Oxford University Press, 2003), 15.

P. 114   **"I know what the problem is"**: Peter Guber, *Tell to Win: Connect, Persuade, and Triumph with the Hidden Power* (New York: Crown Business, 2011), 125.

P. 114   **"Johnson's confidence lifted"**: "Magic Fills In at Center," *NBA Encyclopedia, Playoff Edition.*

P. 114   **"The irony is"**: Guber, *Tell to Win,* 126.

P. 115   **"Magic Johnson gained"**: Ira Berkow, "Sports of The Times; Magic Johnson's Legacy," *The New York Times,* November 8, 1991.

P. 115   **"When people ask me"**: Marshall Goldsmith, *What Got You Here Won't Get You There: How Successful People Become Even More Successful* (New York: Hyperion, 2007), 44.

P. 116   **"In the end"**: Rodd Wagner and Gale Muller, *Power of 2: How to Make the Most of Your Partnerships at Work and in Life* (New York: Gallup Press, 2009), 76.

P. 117   **"Dear Teammates"**: Stephen M. R. Covey, interview with Peter Aceto, August 25, 2009. Email is dated May 5, 2009.

P. 118   **"one-fifth of the people"**: Robert F. Kennedy, speech to law students at the University of Pennsylvania, Associated Press, May 7, 1964.

P. 118 **"If you or your business":** Empire Club of Canada, "Social Media and Corporate Trust," May 7, 2009, http://speeches.empireclub.org/69578/data.

P. 120 **he never earned more than $35,000:** "John Wooden, Former UCLA Coach, Dies at 99," *The Press-Enterprise,* June 4, 2010.

P. 120 **"Many have called Coach Wooden":** David Wharton and Chris Foster, "John Wooden's Words Live On in the Hearts of His Admirers," June 6, 2010, http://articles.latimes.com/2010/jun/06/sports/la-sp-0606-john-wooden -20100606.

P. 120 **"At 89, John Wooden is happier":** "John Wooden, like UCLA, Simply the Best," www.billwalton.com/component/content/article/47;Itemid=55.

P. 120 **"Ability may get you":** "Wooden on Leadership," www.johnlutz.com/uplifting -quotes/john-wooden.htm.

P. 121 **"It's exciting to . . . see":** "Fiona Wood," *George Negus Tonight,* June 25, 2003.

P. 121 **"I firmly believe":** FranklinCovey video case study, 2006.

P. 122 **In 1990, Canada became president:** "About Geoffrey Canada," www.hcz.org/ about-us/about-geoffrey-canada/144.

P. 122 **(now almost a hundred):** Ibid.

P. 122 **"If your child comes":** Daniel Schorn, "The Harlem Children's Zone," *60 Minutes,* February 11, 2009, www.cbsnews.com/stories/2006/05/11/60minutes/ main1611936.shtml.

P. 122 **"Canada's new program combines":** "About Geoffrey Canada," www.hcz .org/about-us/about-geoffrey-canada/144.

P. 122 **"one of the most ambitious":** Rosetta Thurman, "28 Days of Black Nonprofit Leaders: Geoffrey Canada," February 7, 2010, www.rosettathurman .com/2010/02/28-days-of-black-nonprofit-leaders-geoffrey-canada/; also "About Geoffrey Canada," www.hcz.org/about-us/about-geoffrey-canada/144.

P. 123 **one of America's Best Leaders:** Ibid.

P. 123 **"There are enough children":** Geoffrey Canada, *Reaching Up for Manhood: Transforming the Lives of Boys in America,* 156.

P. 123 **"We do not believe":** William Watson Purkey and Betty L. Siegel, *Becoming an Invitational Leader* (Atlanta, Ga.: Humanic Trade Group Publishing, 2003), 152.

P. 124 **"My defining moment":** Bill George, "Values-Centered Leadership: The Key to Success in the 21st Century," commencement address, Opus College of Business, University of St. Thomas, May 21, 2011, www.stthomas.edu/Business/ events/commencement/speakerinfo/commencementAddress_George.html.

P. 124 **grew from $1.1 billion:** "National Magazine Selects 10 Manufacturing Leaders into the IW Manufacturing Hall of Fame," November 18, 2009, www .prnewswire.com/news-releases/national-magazine-selects-10-manufacturing -leaders-into-the-iw-manufacturing-hall-of-fame-70359252.html.

P. 125 **"We have also learned":** Bill George, "Values-Centered Leadership: The Key to Success in the 21st Century."

P. 125 **"total transformation":** Frances Hesselbein, *My Life in Leadership: The Journey and Lessons Learned Along the Way* (San Francisco: Jossey-Bass, 2011), 72.

P. 125 **"a Navajo girl":** Ibid., 79.

P. 125 **"They trusted me":** Greg Link, interview with Frances Hesselbein, April 2011.

P. 126   **"How can we . . . regain":** Frances Hesselbein and Marshall Goldsmith, eds., *Leader of the Future 2: Visions, Strategies and Practices for the New Era* (San Francisco: Jossey-Bass, 2006), 154.

P. 126   **"Will it be the leader":** Frances Hesselbein, *Hesselbein on Leadership* (New York: Jossey-Bass, 2002), 10, 34.

P. 127   **On May 7, 2010:** "Almaz Gebremedhin Worked 3 Jobs to Support 5 Kids," *Good Morning America,* May 7, 2010.

P. 128   **one of the top two:** Nick Bilton, "Apple Is the Most Valuable Company," *The New York Times,* August 9, 2011.

P. 128   **number one brand in the world:** Tom Brewster, "Apple Topples Google in Brand Value Rankings," www.itpro.co.uk, May 9, 2011, www.itpro.co .uk/633319/apple-topples-google-in-brand-value-rankings; see also Randy, "Apple No. 1 in the 2011 BrandZ Top Brands Ranking," May 13, 2011; see also "BrandZ Top 100 Most Valuable Global Brands 2011," www.millwardbrown .com/libraries/optimor_brandz_files/2011_brandz_top100_chart.sflb.ashx.

P. 128   **"What makes Apple so admired?":** "World's Most Admired Companies," *Fortune,* 2010.

P. 129   **highest sales per square foot:** Yukari Iwatani Kane and Ian Sherr, "Secrets from Apple's Genius Bar: Full Loyalty, No Negativity," *The Wall Street Journal,* June 15, 2011.

P. 129   **U.S. mall average of $386 per square foot:** Linda Humphers, "U.S. Outlet Center and Owners Report," *Value Retail News,* November 2009, www .valueretail news.com/pdfs/09State_of_Industry_Part2.pdf.

P. 129   **$35,000 in sales per square foot:** Allison Schwartz and Oshrat Carmiel, "Apple May Be Highest Grossing Fifth Avenue Retailer (Update2)," August 24, 2009, www.bloomberg.com/apps/news?pid=newsarchive&sid=aK4TfewPa37M.

P. 129   **"pretty cool":** Betsy Morris, "What Makes Apple Golden," *Fortune,* March 3, 2008.

P. 129   **"You have to disconnect":** FranklinCovey training video, 2006.

P. 130   **"What was happening":** Ibid.

P. 130   **decreased by 42 percent:** Ibid.

P. 130   **reduced by 49 percent:** Ibid.

P. 130   **"I think that trust is critical":** Ibid.

P. 130   **"Tim Rose":** Steven Greenhouse, "How Costco Became the Anti-Wal-Mart," *The New York Times,* July 17, 2005.

P. 131   **"That's easy. It's Costco.":** Morgan Housel, "Charlie Munger's Love Affair with Costco," July 7, 2011, http://money.msn.com/investment-advice/article .aspx?post=7f0e084a-3473-41cc-b7e9-f4353e0deeb3&ucsort=2.

P. 131   **"It all starts with":** Joseph A. Michelli, *The New Gold Standard: 5 Leadership Principles for Creating a Legendary Customer Experience* (New York: McGraw-Hill, 2008), 106.

P. 132   **"My chief assets drive out":** Maureen Bridget Rabotin, *Culture Savvy: Working and Collaborating Across the Globe* (Washington, D.C.: ASTD Press, 2011), 161.

P. 132   **"There will be no layoffs":** Rick Smith, "Having Pledged No Layoffs, Good-night Still Sees Record Year for SAS," October 27, 2009, http://wraltechwire .com/business/tech_wire/news/blogpost/6290817/.

P. 132   **"The difference at SAS":** David A. Kaplan, "SAS: A New No. 1 Best Employer," *Fortune,* January 21, 2010.

P. 133   **"The highest form a civilization":** Charlie Munger, commencement address to USC Law School, May 14, 2007.

P. 133   **number two hospital overall:** Paul Walsh and Maura Lerner, "Mayo Clinic Slips to 3rd in U.S. News Rankings," [Minneapolis] *StarTribune,* July 19, 2011.

P. 133   **ranked number three:** "Harris Poll Finds: St. Jude's Research Hospital and Susan G. Komen for the Cure Are Among Most Trusted Non-Profits," www .harrisinteractive.com/NewsRoom/PressReleases/tabid/446/ctl/ReadCustom Default/mid/1506/ArticleId/52/Default.aspx.

P. 134   **"If you have a workforce":** Geoff Colvin, "United Continental's King of the Skies," *Fortune,* April 21, 2011.

P. 134   **"If the letter is full":** David Robinson, "Shareholder Letter: Annual Reports Can Tell a Lot About a Company," *Buffalo News Business,* May 25, 2002.

P. 134   **CEO Candor Surveys:** "Rittenhouse Rankings CEO Candor Survey Reports Top-Ranked Companies Outperform Bottom-Ranked Companies for Fifth Consecutive Year," April 29, 2011, http://newyork.citybizlist.com/18/2011/4/29/ Rittenhouse-Rankings-CEO-Candor-Survey-Reports-TopRanked-Companies -Outperform-BottomRanked-Companies-for-Fifth-Consecutive-Year.aspx; see also Stephen Dandrow, "Rittenhouse Rankings CEO Candor Survey Reports Top-Ranked Companies Outperform Bottom-Ranked Companies for Fifth Consecutive Year," April 28, 2011, www.rittenhouserankings.com/2010_Ritten house_Rankings_CEO_Candor_Survey_Release.pdf.

P. 134   **by 18 percent on average:** Ibid.

P. 134   **by 31 percent:** Ibid.

P. 135   **88.8 percent of Danes:** Mike Alberti, "Being a Citizen, Danish style," September 21, 2011, www.remappingdebate.org/article/being-citizen-danish -style. Data from OECD.

P. 135   **IMD ranked the country number one:** IMD World Competitiveness Yearbook.

P. 136   **"executives forgot to read":** "Our View on Drug Safety: J&J Loses Its Way with Secret Buy-up of Defective Drug," *USA Today,* October 4, 2010.

P. 136   **recall of 130 million bottlers:** Ibid.

P. 136   **"I know that we let":** "Opposing View on Drug Safety: 'We Let the Public Down,' " *USA Today,* October 4, 2010.

P. 137   **"One company to carefully monitor":** "Harris Poll Finds That Consumers Love Kisses: Hershey's Ranks," February 24, 2010, www.bloomberg.com/ apps/news?pid=newsarchive&sid=a1jqU1tq2Xo8.

P. 137   **"We will be closely monitoring":** "Hyundai and Subaru Mark Significant Growth in Brand Equity and Sales. Coincidence?" March 16, 2010, www .bloomberg.co.jp/apps/news?pid=90970900&sid=apjCJVMWRNuM.

P. 137   **"I am deeply sorry":** Brian Ross, "Toyota CEO Apologizes to His Customers: 'I Am Deeply Sorry,' " January 29, 2010, http://abcnews.go.com/Blotter/toy ota-ceo-apologizes-deeply/story?id=9700622.

P. 138   **"We all grow up":** Harvey A. Hook, *The Power of an Ordinary Life: Discover the Extraordinary Possibilities Within* (New York: Tyndale Press, 2007), 165.

P. 139   **"a bumpy original response":** "Corporate Responsibility Report," 2004, www .nikebiz.com/responsibility/documents/Nike_FY04_CR_report.pdf, 9.

P. 139   **ranked number ten:** "Corporate Responsibility Magazine's '100 Best Corporate Citizens List,' " *CR Magazine,* 2011.

P. 140   **"Cohler [one of the first executives]":** David Kirkpatrick, *The Facebook Effect: The Inside Story of the Company That Is Connecting the World* (New York: Simon & Schuster, 2011), 123.

P. 140   **more than 800 million:** Vittorio Hernandez, "Facebook Members Exceed 800 Million Mark," *International Business Times,* October 5, 2011.

P. 140   **more than $80 billion:** Dave Manuel, "Facebook Continues to Surge in Value," March 12, 2011, www.davemanuel.com/2011/03/12/facebook-now-valued-at-around-79-billion/.

Chapter Six: Smart Trust Action 3:
Declare Your Intent . . . and Assume Positive Intent in Others

P. 142   **"What is the quality of your intent?":** Merry Gordon, "Four Life Lessons from the Civil Rights Movement," www.education.com/magazine/article/life-lessons-civil-rights-movement/.

P. 145   **"Our school district had made":** Stephen M. R. Covey and Rebecca Merrill, interview with Doug Whitaker, July 2005.

P. 147   **"I, for one":** John O. Edwards, "Gen. Franks Doubts Constitution Will Survive WMD Attack," November 21, 2003, http://archive.newsmax.com/archives/articles/2003/11/20/185048.shtml.

P. 147   **$729 million systemwide conversion:** Mike Folta, "Open Road Tolling Spells Instant Relief for Chicago and Suburbs," October 29, 2006, www.burnsmcd.com/Resource_/PageResource/Open-Road-Tolling-Plazas/article-OpenRoadTolling-Folta.pdf.

P. 148   **in an unprecedented twenty-two months:** "Project Achievement Awards 2007," CMAA, cmaanet.org/project-achievement-awards-2007.

P. 148   **"People need to find":** Peter Senge, *The Fifth Discipline* (New York: Currency/Doubleday, 2006), 316.

P. 149   **"I believe this nation":** John F. Kennedy, speech to U. S. Congress, May 25, 1961.

P. 149   **"We choose to go":** John F. Kennedy, speech at Rice University, September 12, 1962.

P. 150   **"to develop leaders":** A. B. Combs website; also Greg Link, interview with Muriel Summers, May 2011.

P. 150   **give away at least half:** Gregory Lamb, "Giving Pledge: A Big-Hearted Billionaires Club, Led by Bill Gates and Warren Buffett, Keeps Growing," *The Christian Science Monitor,* May 11, 2011.

P. 150   **"Giving Pledge":** Ibid.

P. 151   **"I think it is fitting":** http://givingpledge.org/#warren_buffett.

P. 152   **"We've learned that the best way":** "Lilly Set to Become First Pharmaceutical Research Company to Disclose Physician Payments," September 24, 2008, http://newsroom.lilly.com/releasedetail.cfm?ReleaseID=336444.

P. 153   **a translator for CNN mistranslated:** "CNN in Trouble with Iran over Mistranslation," Canadian Broadcasting Association, January 17, 2006.

P. 153   ***"The distortion was deliberate":*** Ibid.

P. 153   **a Danish woman was arrested:** Tony Marcano, "Toddler, Left Outside Restaurant, Is Returned to Her Mother," *The New York Times,* May 14, 1997; see also, David Rohde, "Court Ruling Favors 2 Who Left Baby Outside," *The New*

York Times, July 23, 1999; see also, Benjamin Weiser, "Danish Mother's Claim of False Arrest Is Rejected," *The New York Times,* December 15, 1999.

P. 154   **as was the custom:** Anastasya Partan, "Let Your Baby Sleep Outside? Surprising Parenting Wisdom from Scandinavia," December 27, 2010, www.babble .com/baby/baby-health-and-safety/baby-sleep-parenting-wisdom-scandinavia/.

P. 154   **"I'm out talking":** "Jeff Immelt, CEO," www.ge.com/company/leadership/ ceo.html.

P. 155   **"There are three people":** Pam McGee, "Trust: A Competitive Advantage," *The Partner Channel Magazine,* February 22, 2010.

P. 156   **nurses are typically ranked:** "Nurses and Pharmacists More Trusted than Doctors," April 17, 2009.

P. 156   **most trusted profession:** Mark Hofmans, "Trust in Charities and Judges Rising Internationally," June 17, 2011, www.gfk.com/group/press_information/ press_releases/008190/index.en.html.

P. 156   **"Being roped together":** Stephen M. R. Covey, *The Speed of Trust: The One Thing That Changes Everything* (New York: Free Press, 2006).

P. 156   **"What I find":** "Interview with Michael Brown, Farther than the Eye Can See," May 7, 2009, www.hulu.com/farther-than-the-eye-can-see?forums=1 &post_id=216408&topic_id=54961.

P. 157   **"I want GSK to be":** Donald McNeil Jr., "Ally for the Poor in an Unlikely Corner," *The New York Times,* February 8, 2010.

P. 158   **"The tremendous success":** John Mackey, "I No Longer Want to Work for Money," *Fast Company,* February 1, 2007.

P. 158   **"Declaration of Interdependence":** www.wholefoodsmarket.com/company/ declaration.php.

P. 158   **"Ultimately we cannot create":** John Mackey, "Creating a High Trust Organization," March 14, 2010, www.huffingtonpost.com/john-mackey/creating -the-high-trust-o_b_497589.html.

P. 158   **"The leadership must embody":** Ibid.

P. 159   **"Zappos is about delivering":** Tony Hsieh, *Delivering Happiness* (New York: Business Plus, 2010), Introduction.

P. 159   **"quirky, happy culture":** Fredric Paul, "A Business Is Not a Family," *InformationWeek,* December 17, 2008.

P. 161   **"Whether you're a CEO":** Peter Guber, *Tell to Win: Connect, Persuade, and Triumph with the Hidden Power* (New York: Crown Business, 2011), 96.

P. 162   **"five whys" process:** Taiichi Ohno, *Toyota Production System: Beyond Large-Scale Production* (New York: Productivity Press, 1988), 123.

P. 163   **$30 billion by 2020:** J. Mangalindan, interview with Indra Nooyi, "PepsiCo CEO: If All Consumers Exercised . . . Obesity Wouldn't Exist," *Fortune,* April 27, 2010.

P. 163   **"The Promise of PepsiCo":** "Performance with Purpose: The Promise of PepsiCo," Annual Report, 2009, www.pepsico.com/Download/PEPSICO_ AR.pdf.

P. 165   **number one most powerful woman:** "50 Most Powerful Women in Business," October 18, 2010, http://money.cnn.com/magazines/fortune/most powerfulwomen/2010/full_list/.

P. 165   **"While we value and expect":** "Linking Opportunity with Responsibility," *Procter & Gamble Sustainability Report—Executive Summary,* 2004.

P. 165 **Children's Safe Drinking Water Program:** "Children's Safe Drinking Water," www.purwater.com/childrens-safe-drinking-water.html.

P. 166 **nearly 4 billion liters:** "PUR Packets at Work," June 17, 2011, www.csdw .com/csdw/pur_packet_at_work.shtml.

P. 166 **"improve the lives":** Ibid.

P. 166 **thirty-eight straight years of profitability:** "2010 Southwest Airlines One Report," www.southwestonereport.com/_pdfs/SouthwestOneReport2011.pdf.

P. 166 **"It used to be regarded":** J. B. Bird, interview with Herb Kelleher, July 9, 2002.

P. 166 **Southwest recently updated:** "The Mission of Southwest Airlines," www .southwest.com/html/about-southwest/index.html.

P. 166 **"We credit our success":** "2010 Southwest Airlines One Report," www.south westonereport.com/_pdfs/SouthwestOneReport2011.pdf.

P. 167 **The president of Coca-Cola Philippines:** Stephen M. R. Covey, discussions with William Schultz, February 23, 2011, and April 1, 2011.

P. 168 **by up to 40 percent:** LogicaCMG and Warwick Business School outsourcing study.

P. 168 **"Declare yourself!":** Stephen M. R. Covey, interview with Doug Conant, July 12, 2011.

P. 168 **"So, here's what":** Douglas R. Conant and Mette Norgaard, *TouchPoints: Creating Powerful Leadership Connections in the Smallest of Moments* (San Francisco: Jossey-Bass, 2011), 157; also Stephen M. R. Covey, interview with Doug Conant, July 12, 2011.

P. 169 **"Never is the truth":** Barry Salzberg, "Trusting a CEO in the Twitter Age," Bloomberg Businessweek, August 7, 2009, www.businessweek.com/managing/content/aug2009/ca2009087_680028.htm.

P. 171 **"Commander's Intent":** Robert Kreitner, *Management* (New York: Houghton Mifflin, 2009), 192.

P. 171 **"The competitive advantage is nullified":** *Harvard Business Review on Turnarounds*, 1999, 73.

P. 172 **"My father was":** Indra Nooyi, "The Best Advice I Ever Got," *Fortune*, April 30, 2008.

P. 173 **"I have an amazing":** Stephen M. R. Covey, interview with Indra Nooyi, July 28, 2011.

P. 174 **"These parents have never gotten":** Ibid.

Chapter Seven: Smart Trust Action 4: Do What You Say You're Going to Do

P. 177 **Islam:** Qur'an 17:34.

P. 177 **Judaism:** The Holy Bible, Numbers 30:2.

P. 177 **Christianity:** The Holy Bible, Matthew 7:21.

P. 177 **Hinduism:** Basavanna, Vacana 440.

P. 177 **Buddhism:** Siddhartha Buddha.

P. 177 **Confucianism:** Confucius.

P. 177 **Humanism:** Paul Kurtz, *Toward a New Enlightenment* (Transaction Publishers, 1991), 17.

P. 177 **Greek Philosophy:** Epictetus.

P. 178 **"The best workplaces have differentiated":** Anita Borate and Joyoti Banerji, "Building a Great Place to Work," *India Times,* June 21, 2010.

P. 179 **"Buffett knew":** General Counsel Forum, "TGCF Panel Audio Transcription," November 19, 2010.

P. 179 **"As the co-founder and CEO":** Jeremy Hope, Peter Bunce, and Franz Röösli, *The Leader's Dilemma: How to Build an Empowered and Adaptive Organization Without Losing Control* (San Francisco: Jossey-Bass, 2011), 49.

P. 179 **"best funded start-up in history":** "A Network Built to Support the Silicon Economics Cycle," www1.level3.com/index.cfm?pageID=245.

P. 179 **"We had an obligation":** Laurence Haughton, *It's Not What You Say—It's What You Do: How Following Through at Every Level Can Make or Break Your Company* (New York: Currency, 2004), 236.

P. 180 **"Commitment means never asking":** Ibid.

P. 180 **"Though it was not my intent":** Lee Benson, "No-Sunday Stance Has Not Slowed Success of Costco Builder," *Deseret News,* November 1, 2010.

P. 181 **"Keeping my word":** Oprah Winfrey, "Keeping My Word," *O, The Oprah Magazine,* February 2010.

P. 182 **2011 Trust Index:** Mark Hofmans, "Trust in Charities and Judges Rising Internationally," June 17, 2011, www.gfk.com/group/press_information/press_releases/008190/index.en.html.

P. 183 **"Leaders can foster trust":** Kazuo Ichijo and Ikujiro Nonaka, *Knowledge Creation and Management: New Challenges for Managers* (New York: Oxford University Press, 2006), 247.

P. 183 **"The old cliché in business":** Rick Barrera, *Overpromise and Overdeliver: The Secrets of Unshakeable Customer Loyalty* (New York: Portfolio, 2005), jacket flap.

P. 184 **"to offer something outrageous":** Jack and Suzy Welch,"How to Bust into the Big Leagues: You Want A-List Clients? Begin with an Irresistible Proposition—Then Over-deliver," *BusinessWeek,* May 15, 2008.

P. 184 **"And one more thing . . .":** Carmine Gallo, "How to Wow 'Em like Steve Jobs," *BusinessWeek,* April 6, 2006.

P. 184 **"We are ladies and gentlemen":** "Gold Standards," http://corporate.ritzcarlton.com/en/about/goldstandards.htm.

P. 185 **most widely available:** "Visa Credit Cards," www.creditcards.com.

P. 187 **"concentrate on their separate responsibilities":** Rodd Wagner and Gale Muller, *Power of 2: How to Make the Most of Your Partnerships at Work and in Life* (New York: Gallup Press, 2009), 77.

P. 187 **"SayDoCo is the lifeblood":** Alan Fine, *You Already Know How to Be Great* (New York: Portfolio, 2010), 141.

P. 188 **"A brand for a company":** Robert D. Hof, "Jeff Bezos on Word-of-Mouth Power," *BusinessWeek,* August 2, 2004.

P. 188 **"[I]n a global network economy":** Tom Hayes, *Jump Point: How Network Culture Is Revolutionizing Business* (New York: McGraw-Hill, 2008), 141.

P. 189 **"We thought that we were selling":** John A. Byrne, *Fast Company: The Rules of Business: 55 Essential Ideas to Help Smart People Perform at Their Best* (New York: Currency, 2005), 25.

P. 189 **in the top ten:** "World's Most Admired Companies," March 21, 2011, http://money.cnn.com/magazines/fortune/mostadmired/2011/index.html.

P. 190　**"provide access"**: "Bridging the Gap Between Brand Promise and Expectation," September 16, 2009, www.designdamage.com/bridging-the-gap-between-brand-promise-and-expectation/.

P. 190　**world's biggest retailer:** Michiel Maandag, "Amazon.com: What Happened to the Promise of Earth's Biggest?," June 16, 2011, www.mondaytalk.com/2011/06/16/amazon-com-what-happened-to-the-promise-of-earths-biggest/.

P. 190　**"the brand promise has remained"**: "Happy Birthday, Coca-Cola!," May 7, 2010, www.thecoca-colacompany.com/presscenter/happy_birthday_coca-cola.html.

P. 190　**"In virtually every industry"**: Seth Godin, *Permission Marketing: Turning Strangers into Friends and Friends into Customers* (New York: Simon & Schuster, 1999), 91.

P. 190　**"A recent study"**: "Reputation Capital: Building and Maintaining Trust in the 21st Century," www.ketchum.com/Reputation_Capital.

P. 190　**a 2009 study:** "The New Social Economy & Currency of Trust," May 16, 2011, www.senseimarketing.com/Wisdom/Blog.aspx.

P. 191　**"If these reputation systems"**: Paul Resnick, Richard Zeckhauser, John Swanson, and Kate Lockwood, "The Value of Reputation on eBay: A Controlled Experiment," John F. Kennedy School of Government Harvard University Faculty Research working papers series, July 2002.

P. 191　**"The key to being trusted"**: Emma De Vita, "Trust and the Female Boss," *Management Today*, September 1, 2010.

P. 191　**"The trust that the general public"**: Kate Rogers, "Donors Pick St. Jude's, Komen as Most Respected," *Exempt Magazine*, March 2010.

P. 192　***Newsweek* compiled metrics:** Rana Foroohar, "How We Ranked the World," *Newsweek*, August 16, 2010.

P. 192　**"Anything good that's ever happened"**: Ibid.

P. 193　**"Be impeccable with your word"**: Don Miguel Ruiz, *The Four Agreements: A Practical Guide to Personal Freedom* (San Francisco: Amber Allen, 2001), 32.

P. 198　**"There's a reason I devote"**: Marshall Goldsmith, *What Got You Here Won't Get You There: How Successful People Become Even More Successful* (New York: Hyperion, 2007), 42.

P. 198　**"The culture at Continental"**: Gordon Bethune, *From Worst to First: Behind the Scenes of Continental's Remarkable Comeback* (New York: John Wiley & Sons, Inc., 1998), 14.

P. 199　**"Employees of a chronically broken"**: Ibid., 29–30.

P. 199　**number one in the two key:** "Company History 1991 to 2000," www.continental.com/web/en-US/content/company/history/1991-2000.aspx.

P. 200　**"I judge people"**: Hal Weitzman, "3M Chief Warns Obama over Business Regulation," February 27, 2011, www.ft.com/intl/cms/s/0/bd9b4100-429b-11e0-8b34-00144feabdc0.html#axzz1bBGEo1em.

P. 201　**"I've come to learn"**: *The New Gold Standard: 5 Leadership Principles for Creating a Legendary Customer Experience* (New York: McGraw-Hill, 2008), 111.

P. 201　**"For 113 years"**: "Coca-Cola 'Regrets' Contamination," June 17, 1999, http://news.bbc.co.uk/2/hi/europe/371300.stm.

Chapter Eight: Smart Trust Action 5:
Lead in Extending Trust to Others

P. 208 **a drop in recidivism:** Ward Clapham, " 'Positive Tickets' from the Police in Canada," FranklinCovey Center for Advanced Research, February 2011.

P. 209 **35 percent increase in productivity:** Daniel Schorn, "Working 24/7," February 11, 2009, www.cbsnews.com/stories/2006/03/31/60minutes/main1460 246.shtml.

P. 209 **"Results Oriented Work Environment":** Michelle Conlin, "Smashing the Clock," Bloomberg Businessweek, December 11, 2006, www.businessweek .com/magazine/content/06_50/b4013001.htm.

P. 209 **"No meetings.":** *BusinessWeek,* December 11, 2006, cover.

P. 209 **"If you trust people":** Video transcript of Dean W. Collinwood, interview with Al Carey, FranklinCovey, 2009.

P. 211 **"Leadership without mutual trust":** Warren Bennis, *On Becoming a Leader* (New York: Basic Books, 2009), 133.

P. 211 **"I can't answer that":** James M. Kouzes and Barry Z. Posner, *The Truth About Leadership* (San Francisco: Jossey-Bass, 2010), 80.

P. 212 **"The only one who earns trust":** Roy Ashworth, *Success: Utter Common Sense* (U.K.: Author House, 2011), 32.

P. 212 **"As our business grows":** Society for Human Resource Management, *Essentials of Strategy* (Boston: Harvard Business School Press, 2006), 116.

P. 213 **"As a company":** George Buckley, "To Our Shareholders," *Driven to Innovate,* February 16, 2011.

P. 213 **"Dr. Silbert's typical new hires":** Kerry Patterson, Joseph Grenny, David Maxfield, Ron McMillan, and Al Switzler, *Influencer: The Power to Change Anything* (New York: McGraw-Hill, 2008), 14.

P. 215 **"They had developed policies":** Greg Link, interview with Isabel Blanco and B. J. Walker, June 7, 2011.

P. 217 **"No, this is strategic":** Ibid.

P. 217 **"I was not suggesting":** Ibid.

P. 221 **"Why start out that relationship":** Chris Zane, *Reinventing the Wheel: The Science of Creating Lifetime Customers* (Dallas: Benbella Books, 2011), 163.

P. 221 **We choose to believe:** Jeanne Bliss, *"I Love You More than My Dog": Five Decisions That Drive Extreme Customer Loyalty in Good Times and Bad* (New York: Portfolio, 2011), 40.

P. 222 **The company also shows:** "Walk in Your Customer's Body Armor," March 1, 2010, www.baldrige.com/criteria_customerfocus/walk-in-your-customers-body -armor/.

P. 222 **USAA extends trust:** James M. Kouzes and Barry Z. Posner, *The Truth About Leadership* (San Francisco: Jossey-Bass, 2010), 81.

P. 223 **one Carglass employee shared:** Jan Vermeiren, public remarks made by a participant in a presentation in Belgium by Stephen M. R. Covey, The Networking Coach Blog.

P. 223 **by 54 percent:** Ju Young Kim, Martin Natter, and Martin Spann, "Kish: Where Customers Pay as They Wish,"*Review of Marketing Science,* vol. 8, no. 2, 2010.

P. 223 **"Basically, people are honest":** " 'Pay What You Want' Trend Hits Euro Eateries," *The Brunei Times,* February 17, 2008.

P. 224   **"This little store was started"**: Rose Anne Belmonte, "Honesty Café: Only in Batanes," January 25, 2009, www.philstar.com/Article.aspx?articleid=434387.

P. 225   **"I described the prospects"**: Jonathan M. Tisch, *The Power of We: Succeeding Through Partnerships* (New York: John Wiley, 2004), 56.

P. 225   **Best Hotels in the USA:** "U.S. News & World Report: Best Hotels in the USA!," June 14, 2011, www.loewshotels.com/blog/2011/06/u-s-news-world -report.

P. 225   **"To be honest, I viewed"**: Alison Maitland,"Managers Say: Suit Yourself," *Financial Times,* December 22, 2008.

P. 226   **"It's making people more responsible"**: Ibid.

P. 227   **Ritz-Carlton company research:** Joseph A. Michelli, *The New Gold Standard: 5 Leadership Principles for Creating a Legendary Customer Experience* (New York: McGraw-Hill, 2008), 115.

P. 227   **"No single set of rules"**: Letter from A. G. Lafley, President and CEO, P&G Values & Policy Manual.

P. 227   **A 2010 survey:** Caroline McCarthy, "Survey: Over Half of U.S. Workplaces Block Social Networks," October 6, 2009, http://news.cnet.com/8301 -13577_3-10368956-36.html.

P. 228   **"Employees are much more trustworthy"**: Martin Giles, "A World of Connections," *The Economist,* January 28, 2010.

P. 228   **Al Carey:** Video transcript of Dean W. Collinwood, interview with Al Carey, FranklinCovey, 2009.

P. 229   **"This is no longer"**: Thomas Friedman, *The World Is Flat 3.0: A Brief History of the Twenty-First Century* (New York: Macmillan, 2007), 175.

P. 229   **"The Texas machine parts guy"**: Ibid., 171.

P. 230   **"Most of these institutional collaborations"**: Ibid., 335.

P. 231   **"When we are happy"**: Shawn Achor, *The Happiness Factor* (New York: Crown Business, 2010), 176.

P. 232   **An interesting study:** Barbara Ortutay, "Report: Facebook Users More Trusting, Engaged," *USA Today,* June 16, 2011.

P. 232   **"If history is a trustworthy guide"**: Peter Guber, *Tell to Win: Connect, Persuade, and Triumph with the Hidden Power* (New York: Crown Business, 2011), 245.

P. 233   **"Very few hospitals are organized"**: Geoff Colvin, "Cleveland Clinic Chief on the Business of Health," *Fortune,* February 18, 2010.

P. 234   **with more than a million people:** Gabe Collins and Andrew Erickson, "The 10 Biggest Cities in China That You've Probably Never Heard Of," June 1, 2011, www.chinasignpost.com/2011/06/the-10-biggest-cities-in-china-that-you've -probably-never-heard-of/.

P. 234   **"The direction of the relationship"**: John Naisbitt and Doris Naisbitt, *China's Megatrends: The 8 Pillars of a New Society* (New York: HarperCollins, 2010), 66.

P. 235   **"released huge energy"**: Ibid.

P. 235   **"High trust societies produce more"**: Paul Zak and Stephen Knack, "Trust and Growth," *The Economic Journal* 111, no. 470 (April 2001), 296.

P. 235   **"A high level of trust"**: Friedman, *The World Is Flat 3.0,* 334.

P. 236   **"Culture eats strategy for breakfast."**: "In a Turnaround Put Culture First," *Harvard Business Review,* May 17, 2010.

P. 236   **"We want to make sure":** Tony Hsieh, *Delivering Happiness* (New York: Business Plus, 2010); also Greg Link, interview with Tony Hsieh, February 7, 2011.

P. 236   **20 to 100 percent increases:** Greg Link, interview with Tony Hsieh, February 7, 2011.

P. 237   **"Trust is optimized":** John Mackey, "Creating a High Trust Organization," March 14, 2010, www.huffingtonpost.com/john-mackey/creating-the-high -trust-o_b_497589.html.

P. 238   **"A boss's job":** Gordon Bethune, *From Worst to First: Behind the Scenes of Continental's Remarkable Comeback* (New York: John Wiley, 1999), 43.

P. 239   **83 percent of mergers fail:** Gene Gitelson, John W. Bing, and Lionel Laroche, "The Impact of Culture on Mergers & Acquisitions," ITAP International, www .itapintl.com/facultyandresources/articlelibrarymain/the-impact-of-culture-on -mergers-a-acquisitions.html. (This article originally appeared in *CMA Management,* March 2001.)

P. 240   **"the lowest ratio of corporate overhead":** "The Role of Trust in Governance," Stanford Business School, May 28, 2010.

P. 240   **"You have to understand":** General Counsel Forum, TGCF panel audio transcription, November 19, 2010.

P. 240   **"Everybody likes being appreciated":** "Charlie Munger responds in Q & A Session," Wesco Annual Meeting, 2005.

Chapter Nine: Creating Your Own Renaissance of Trust

P. 247   **"Increase the level of trust":** Thomas Friedman, *The World Is Flat 3.0: A Brief History of the Twenty-First Century* (New York: Macmillan, 2007), 424.

P. 247   **"Make a dent in the universe":** "The Magician," *The Economist* (October 8–14, 2011), 15; see also Jay Elliot, *The Steve Jobs Way* (New York: Vanguard, 2011), 5.

P. 247   **About a decade later:** "Yo Creo en Colombia [I Believe in Colombia]" foundation; US Ambassador in Colombia; Fondelibertad; The World Factbook; Embassy of Colombia.

P. 248   **"In Colombia, we are working":** Stephen M. R. Covey and Greg Link, interviews with Álvaro Uribe, May 26, 2011, and August 3, 2011; see also Álvaro Uribe, "Uribe: Colombia Investor-Friendly," *Latin Business Chronicle,* September 22, 2008.

P. 248   **"Our successfully hosting":** Covey and Link interview with Uribe; see also Camilla Pease-Watkin, "Uribe Closes 'Record-breaking' World Economic Forum," *Colombia Reports,* April 8, 2010, http://colombiareports.com/colombia -news/news/9059-uribe-closes-world-economic-forum.html.

P. 248   **Colombia's new tourism campaign:** "Campaign Colombia, the Only Risk Is Wanting to Stay," www.colombia.travel/en/international-tourist/colombia/ tourism-campaign.

P. 248   **"We were overwhelmed":** "Colombia's Uribe Gets Good Marks," United Press International, August 7, 2010, www.upi.com/Top_News/US/2010/08/07/ Colombias-Uribe-gets-good-marks/UPI-12401281200512/.

P. 248   **"When the crisis is over":** World Economic Forum on Latin America, April 14–16, 2009.

P. 249   **His name was Pedro Medina:** I Believe in Colombia Foundation, "Our History," *Foundation*, www.yocreoencolombia.com, accessed on July 2, 2011; also, Stephen M.R. Covey interviews with Pedro Medina on August 18, 2009, and August 11, 2011.

P. 250   **Yo Creo en Colombia:** Ibid.

P. 250   **Un Millón de Voces Contra Las FARC:** David Kirkpatrick, *The Facebook Effect: The Inside Story of the Company That Is Connecting the World* (New York: Simon & Schuster, 2011).

P. 252   **"persecuted, dispossessed, or even killed":** John Naisbitt and Doris Naisbitt, *China's Megatrends: The 8 Pillars of a New Society* (New York: HarperCollins, 2010), 45.

P. 253   **"Never doubt that a small group":** Geoffrey M. Bellman and Kathleen D. Ryan, *Extraordinary Groups: How Ordinary Teams Achieve Amazing Results* (San Francisco: Jossey-Bass, 2008), 14.

P. 253   **"The Colombia thing":** Kirkpatrick, *The Facebook Effect*, 6.

P. 254   **"Will the global Web":** Tom Hayes, *Jump Point: How Network Culture Is Revolutionizing Business* (New York: McGraw-Hill, 2008), 141.

P. 254   **"Historically there have been":** Kirkpatrick, *The Facebook Effect*, 298.

P. 255   **"Some years ago":** Dieter Uchtdorf, "Lift Where You Stand," *Ensign*, November 2008.

P. 255   **"Few will have the greatness":** Robert F. Kennedy, Day of Affirmation address, University of Capetown, South Africa, June 6, 1966.

P. 257   **"How wonderful it is":** Anne Frank, *Diary of a Young Girl*, 1952.

P. 258   **"The limbic system fires":** David Rock, *Your Brain at Work: Strategies for Overcoming Distraction, Regaining Focus* (New York: HarperCollins, 2009), 107.

P. 258   **"I am only one":** Katharyne Mitchell, *Practicing Public Scholarship: Experiences and Possibilities Beyond the Academy* (New York: Wiley-Blackstone, 2008), 46.

P. 258   **life was no "brief candle":** Tim Russert, "A Splendid Torch," June 16, 2008, http://ac360.blogs.cnn.com/2008/06/16/tim-russert-a-splendid-torch/.

Index